# Z88 MAGIC

**Gill Gerhardi, Vic Gerhardi and Andy Berry**

**Published by
Kuma Computers Ltd.**

First Published 1989
Kuma Computers Ltd
12 Horseshoe Park
Pangbourne
Berkshire. RG8 7JW
Tel 0734 844335. Fax 0734 844339

Printed in Great Britain

**ISBN 0-7457-0137-X**

# Acknowledgments

We would like to say a big Thank You to the following people:

Roger Osborn-King who planted the idea of writing this book at the beginning.

Richard Jones  who helped to pull it all to pieces and put it all back together again!

Anne from next door who put in loads of time taking out all the typing errors.

Dave Stewart who gave us his mailmerge routine.

## About The Authors

Vic and Andy have been business partners for nearly ten years and friends for much longer. They are now co-directors of Rakewell Limited. Rakewell is a computer consultancy which covers all aspects of computers from system design through to supplying hardware, which is how they got involved with the Z88. About a year ago (1988) they started running Z88 training courses.

Several highly successful courses later it was suggested that they turn the course notes into a book. They readily took the idea on board but soon discovered that that was not as easy as it sounded. Also finding the time to write was extremely difficult while managing a thriving company. So Gill was drafted in to help. When she started she was a plain everyday Z88 user. She had a Degree but in something that wasn't even remotely related to computers. She had spent twelve years of marriage to Vic bringing up their two sons and painting. She agreed to write the "easy bits" and ended up doing a great deal more!

# How This Book Was Produced

Most of this book was written on three Z88 computers.

Each of the three authors produced their original manuscripts on a Z88. While we were writing, we backed up files either on EPROM or zTAPE.

We then transferred the text to an Amstrad PCW 8512 for review and cor - rection. The text was then transferred back, via a Z88, to our 386 computer because the publisher needed it on IBM PC disks.

We're pleased to say that all this worked without a hitch, so any errors remain ours, not the Z88's fault.

# Contents

TIPS

# INTRODUCTION

Welcome to a magical mystery tour of the Z88. You are about to enter a world that is full of challenges and dangers. The ultimate prize that awaits you at the end of the quest is happiness in your relationship with your Z88 but you will have to travel far and wide to reach that utopia. You will encounter gremlins, witches cauldrons, magic languages and many-headed monsters, as well as helping hands and sympathetic shoulders to cry on when the going gets too rough.

The purpose of this book is to explain what the Z88 is, what it can do, and how YOU can make it do it. It will also show you the pitfalls and the delights of this fascinating little machine. All in a language that some - body who is new to computers can understand. At later stages however, it deals with more complex functions for the advanced user. In short, whether you are thinking about buying a Z88 or are an established en - thusiast, there is something in this book for you. We thought we were experts before we started writing but have learnt many new things along the way:- the major thing being never to underestimate the machine and never think you know it all! At times it feels as though the machine deliberately hides things from you so that you have more to learn next time. It is an infinitely accessible machine which encourages the user to explore without a guide. We cannot count the times one of us has said "I wonder if........will work?" When it does work the sense of satisfaction is enormous: when it doesn't you want to find another way of doing it either alone or with help. But because the hunches or intelligent guesses, whichever you prefer, work more times than they don't - unless you are barking totally up the wrong tree!- you are encouraged to do more. So you can use this book as a comprehensive guide to the Z88 if you want to, but you can also use it as polyfiller to fill the gaps in the knowledge you already have!

## About the machine

The Z88 was born at 00 hundred hours on the first of September 1987 after a nine month gestation period. It had an immaculate conception with Trinity Concepts as its mother and a knight for a father. It was sent forth into a hostile world after its coming had been much prophesied - some prophets getting the date far too early. After being schooled by the Cobra and others it was sorely tested. But at the end it was found not to be wanting. It quickly gained a small band of followers, many reduced to awe by its magnificence. Those who took the time to learn and work with it were rewarded. Membership to the secret society was sought after and those accepted were given the advantages that brotherhood and shared knowledge brings, together with bi-monthly copies of EPROM. Their numbers grew but slowly: what they lacked in numbers however they made up for in loyalty and enthusiasm. They sent forth missionaries to tell the world and they were scorned, mocked, and disbelieved. Yet they still continue undaunted, steadfast to this day believing the Z88 to be their salvation in many hours of need.

If you understood only a little of that fear not. You obviously have not yet gained full membership of this happy band. We are sure that by the end of this epistle you will understand the awe and loyalty that this un-pretentious little machine commands.

## The survival kit

Whether you fancy yourself as a gallant knight setting forth to overcome all the odds, or as the ardent disciple with bare feet and begging bowl, you will need to carry the survival kit at your side at all times. Wherever you go with your Z88 you must take the survival kit. The basic kit consists of:-

Spare batteries and mains adapter, Paper Clip, Eprom or other means of backing up your files.

You will no doubt add your own items to this list, but you use your Z88 without these items at your peril! With the kit by your side you can be secure in the knowledge that you have the means to cope with most situations that the world and the Z88 can throw at you.

And so we wish you well and send you on your journey. Mark well the contents of this book. Take particular note of the Tips. They will some-times guide you round the pitfalls and sometimes show you where the honey is! Keep your Z88 by your side at all times. Good luck.....

# Z88 AWARENESS

## Finding Your Way Round Your Z88

### Introduction.

This section is going to introduce you to the Z88, outlining its similarities and differences to other computers.

The main thing that physically sets the Z88 apart is its size. For those of you who haven't been introduced yet, IT'S SMALL, the size of an A4 piece of paper and the thickness of a folder. Add to this the fact that it runs on batteries and you have a machine that you can carry in your briefcase and use anywhere. Its limitations of size however do not inhibit its computing power or memory size. This book was written on it! At the time of going to print you could have 1 megabyte of RAM and 128k of EPROM memory in the machine at any one time.

O.K. let's start exploring........

## Where's The ON OFF Switch Gone?

Don't panic there isn't one! You press both SHIFT keys down together. Yes, it is a pain because you have to use both hands - unless you're a giant! But it has been done deliberately to stop you accidentally turning it on while you are carrying it around. To turn it off press the SHIFT keys again, although if you leave it alone for a short time it will automatically turn itself off anyway, to conserve power.

# THE KEYBOARD

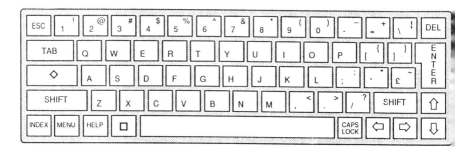

The keyboard is similar to that of a typewriter. All the letters and numbers are in their expected places. Where it differs from a typewriter is the extra keys which are arranged around the outside.

Starting from the top left hand corner and working round in an anti-clockwise direction -

ESC                              will put you back into the activity you were last in before you used a menu

TAB                              appears to work the same as a typewriter tab, but see the PIPEDEREAM section for more details.

    Whilst using tabs in columns -

SHIFT TAB                        will move you back one column

⇐                                will also act as a SHIFT TAB key when it reaches the left hand margin of any column, otherwise within a column it will work normally

◇ TAB                            will move the cursor back into the first column at the beginning of the line

◊
is a FUNCTION key which will release your normal typewriter keys so they can have a different job to do (see ◊TAB above)

Definition: Function = Command

SHIFT
The same as on a typewriter - use for upper case characters and the symbols at the top of individual keys. Occasionally it also acts as a FUNCTION key

INDEX
will put you back to the INDEX no matter where you are

MENU
allows you to access a range of FUNCTIONS from the application you are working in

Definition: MENU = A list of choices

Definition: Applications are the major programs you can use on the Z88

HELP
carries some useful information but is not for beginners

☐
this is the major FUNCTION key, It operates like the ◊key (above) but enables you to call up applications without going through the INDEX

CAPSLOCK
Has the same effect as shift lock on a typewriter. By pressing ☐ + CAPSLOCK together you can invert this mode so that you type in upper case and go into lower-case when shift is pressed. To reverse this back to the normal mode press ◊ + CAPSLOCK

⇐⇒⇑⇓
These are cursor keys which enable you to move about within a file or menu without disturbing your text

7

The cursor is the blue flashing square which indicates where you are in a file. The cursor keys alone will move the cursor one space in the direction the arrow is pointing

SHIFT + ⇐ ⇒                 will move the cursor one word in whichever
                            direction

SHIFT + ⇑ ⇓                 will move the cursor a screenfull - 5 or 6 lines
                            up or down and scroll the screen at the same
                            time

◊ ⇑ ⇓                       will move the cursor to the beginning or end
                            of the file

◊ ⇐ ⇒                       will take the cursor to either end of the typed
                            line (or column if you are using tabs)

ENTER                       This is a cross between a typewriter's carriage
                            return key and an execute key on a computer

                            It will put in a carriage return if you need one
                            before the end of the line. You don't need to
                            put one at the right hand margin in
                            Pipedream because the program will
                            automatically wrap the text round onto the
                            next line

                            As an execute key you use it to tell the Z88
                            what file, menu, or function in a menu you
                            want to be carried out after you have selected
                            it by moving the cursor to the correct location

DEL                         Deletes characters to the left of the cursor

## General Information on SHIFT and the function keys ◊□

When using the ◊ or □ keys in conjunction with other keys it is not
necessary to hold both down together. Just press the function key and
then the letter or sequence of letters. If however you are using the SHIFT
key as a function key you do have to press both SHIFT and the other key
down simultaneously like you would on a typewriter.

If you want to cancel a function command before it has been actioned just press the function key (☐ or ◇ ) a second time.

You will notice that when pressing either function key or the CAPSLOCK key a symbol will appear on the right hand side of the screen to show you that it has been pressed.

## Off The Keyboard - Switches, Sockets and Apertures

We will now move on to exploring the rest of the external areas of the computer.

### Display screen area

For those of you used to desktop monitors the screen is bound to seem small but because of the ingenious and economical way the system uses the available space, we are confident that within a couple of sorties into the system the space or lack of it, will not be noticeable.

Immediately below the display is a list of useful commands together with the control key and code needed to action them. These are useful for beginners but once we knew how the menu system worked we found that the internal menus were so much more comprehensive and better organised that we tended to use them all the time. So much so that we forgot to put this bit into the first draft of the book!

### Power supply socket

This is the larger of the two sockets, about two-thirds of the way up the left hand edge.

### Reset button

The Reset Button is adjacent to the Power Supply Socket. It looks like another socket because it has been set right into the machine to avoid it being activated accidentally. It can only be reached by inserting a blunt instrument into the hole. The manufacturers recommend using an opened out paperclip.

## Screen contrast level contol

This is the dial type switch lower down the left hand edge. It works like the contrast dial on a television set. We recommend you play with it until you find the right setting for you.

## Card slots

These are on the front edge of the machine, below and to the left of the space bar. This is where you insert either, extra memory (RAMS and EPROM) or, other programs. It opens from the front outwards.

Definition: CARD = Add on memory or application cartridge

## RS232 Port

This is the large rectangular socket on the right hand edge of the Z88, directly opposite the POWER SUPPLY SOCKET. This is used to connect your Z88 to other computers or computer accessories e.g. your printer.

## Stand

On the back of the Z88, opposite the screen on the front, is a large piece of plastic that hinges at the top to make a stand so your machine no longer has to lie flat on the table but can be tilted towards you. We find this makes the Z88 easier to use and the screen more visible.

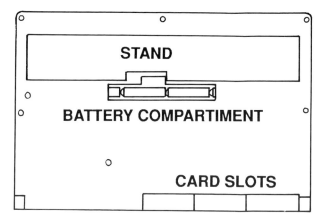

## Battery compartment

The opening for this is also on the back in the centre, just below the space
where the stand folds away when not in use.

# MEMORY

## Introduction

A computer's memory is where it stores all its information. Its capacity is already defined, but you can normally add more to it as and when you need it. This is certainly true of the Z88.

Memory is not, as we tend to think, simply a storage area like a filing cabinet. All tasks or programs need space in the memory to enable the computer to do them.

We think that a very good analogy is to compare the memory to our working area, say like an office. There some space is taken up by the filing system, but you also have a desk which not only provides you with space for you to do your work, but also space for in/out trays, and piles of work that you have started but not yet finished. Well our desks are like that anyway! There's also space for you: the job wouldn't be done if you weren't there. That is the same with the computer: it wouldn't be able to do anything without its various programs and its operating system. They all take up space in the memory as well as the text and data that you are inputting and storing.

**Memory is fragile** - not fragile in the sense of easy to break, but very easily lost.

This is the most important thing to remember about your computer's memory. In your office if you do some work its there somewhere even if you mislay it or file it wrongly. **In the computer's memory something can be there one minute and gone the next**: areas of memory can be erased much quicker than you can type one sentence in. Your computer is not smart enough to understand the importance, or lack of it, of any of your work. In its memory everything is broken down into minute pieces of digital information so if something does go awry it will erase whatever is there however important it was to you. WHICH IS WHY BACKING UP IS SO IMPORTANT.

## BACK UPS

When you back up your files, you put them into a 'safer' form of memory or data storage system. There are several different methods both internal and external that you can use.

TIP:
**Backing up is very necessary but it tends to be a bit of a chore. Consequently nobody bothers until the inevitable happens and we either make a mistake or the machine goes wrong, normally the former, and we lose some if not all of our files. After that we all get on with the backing up, chore or no chore!**

In any other type of computer, back ups would normally involve copying everything you were currently working with onto a second disk. Then if you lose your working copy you have got another one to fall back on. This is normally a very inadequate way of doing it because using floppy disks is quite time consuming and unless you do back ups every hour, your back up copy is never as up to date as it could be. If you have an IBM PC compatible desktop computer plus a Z88 you can link the two together and do your backups this way if you want. The Z88 has several different types of memory cartridges (or Cards) which are very easy to work with and not as physically vulnerable as floppy disk. Here is a brief description of these.

# Different Types of Memory

## RAMS

RAMS are similar to the internal memory in the Z88. You can write to it and read it back. providing the power is left on. You can also erase data and fill that memory again with new information.

---

**TIP:**
**Your Z88 is continually on duty even when it is turned off. It has to be to keep its internal and external memory continually serviced. It also needs power to keep the clock and calendar running. Therefore you must never let your batteries run down. Always have a spare set with you or a mains adapter so that you can change them as soon as your 'battery low' symbol comes up on the right hand side of the screen. If you lose your power you will loose everything held in RAM.**

---

## ROMS

ROM is short for Read Only Memory. Which means that you cannot write to it. Many of the additional programs you can buy come on a Rom cartridge. Roms do not need continual power so you can take them out of the Z88 without fear of losing what is there.

---

**TIP:**
**While you are using a program on a rom card you SHOULD NOT remove the cartridge from the Z88. If you do try the Z88 will bleep at you and flash 'card' in the top right hand corner. You must put the card back and ◇KILL - see INDEX - the suspended activity that was using that program before taking it out again otherwise the Z88 may take umbridge and force you to do a reset.**

---

## EPROM

EPROMS are similar to RAMS in that you can both read from and write to them. There are two major differences however. Firstly, you cannot erase individual files. You can only erase the whole thing by putting it under the ultra violet light in an Eprom Eraser. This will erase everything and you can then fill it all over again. Secondly, you can take them out of the Z88 without fear of losing the data. This facility makes them the ideal backup medium for any files but in particular the really important ones.

# POWERING UP

This section is only relevant if you have only just got your Z88 and are powering it up for the first time.

For information on battery installation see Appendix 2.

## Hard reset

A hard reset clears everything that was on the system ready for you to start with a new slate. It is therefore essential to do this before you do anything else.

First open the card slots on the bottom edge of the Z88. It will bleep once to alert you to the fact that it is open. Then with an unbent paper clip press the reset button (see above for position) twice and then close the card slots. Your Z88 is now ready for work or play!

After an initial or hard reset everything has to be set up.

## Setting up the clock

The clock is one of the applications that you can access with the ☐ function key.

To call the Clock up on the screen press ☐ and then T. This will bring the rectangular clock display into view. Apart from the title, one of the words at the bottom will be highlighted. Both these, EXIT and SET are functions. You can move between them with the ⇐ or ⇒ arrows. When the one that you want is highlighted you press the ENTER key. In this case you want the SET function. When you press ENTER the display will change so that just the date and time will be shown. The cursor will be flashing over the first number under the NEW DATE heading. You type in today's date in the same format as it was before. You must make sure you put the '/'s back in the right place. If you don't need to change the whole thing move the cursor with the right arrow until it is over the number that needs changing. When the date is right press DOWN ARROW. The cursor will then move down to the 'NEW TIME' line. You can change this to the correct setting in exactly the same way. When they are both right press ENTER. You should now see the original clock display showing the correct date and time.

## Setting Up The PANEL

You only need worry about this if you have an external memory pack inserted into one of the slots.

The Control PANEL can be reached by pressing ☐ S. When you enter it you will see many options that you can change. The only one you need to worry about at the moment is the DEFAULT DEVICE. This tells the system which memory you want it to use. When you enter the PANEL the default device should read :RAM.0 because the system assumes there is no external memory. In order to allow it to use the new memory the DEFAULT DEVICE should be changed to which ever slot number your RAM is in. If you are using slot 1 then the default device should be :RAM.1. To change it, move the cursor down and to the right until it is over the 0 of :RAM.0. Then press ◇ G which will erase the 0 and you can then type 1 in its place. To ensure the system has registered the changes you've made and updated itself, you must press ENTER to update. If you leave the PANEL by pressing ESC, any changes will be disregarded.

## The Display Screen

Each application has its own display layout which has been tailored to that application's needs. We will explain those in more detail later but for now these general rules apply.

The screen is divided into three main areas. The left hand side tells you which application you are in with that application's menus. The main section in the middle is your working area. The right hand side of the screen is where the Z88 tells you major functions that you have selected and alerts you when its power or memory is low. The operating system displays OZ in the top right hand corner when it is ready to work.

Along the very top of the screen is the system's comment line. This is where it asks you questions or sends you information. The messages range from 'no room' which means there is not enough room in the RAM or EPROM to save your file, to the number of words in the file when you have asked it to do a word count. It is here also that the system tells you what it is doing i.e. saving, loading. calculating etc. While you have one of those flashing on the top of the screen the cursor disappears because the system is busy. You will not be able to do anything else until the cur - sor returns.

## WHAT THIS LITTLE BEASTY WILL DO FOR YOU WHEN YOU KNOW HOW

### What Computers In General  Can Do

Computers have been put to many uses but the most common ones are word/figure manipulation and information organisation. There are many different word processor, accountancy and database program packages on the market and generally you go and buy what you want off-the-shelf, either at the same time as you buy your computer, or later when the need arises.

# How the Z88 Is Different

With this little machine however, you get most of these facilities when you buy it. The major programs you are likely to need are actually incor-porated into the system. Although of course you can always buy more! You get an integrated wordprocessor and spreadsheet program, which means that you can use both these facilities together. There is also a limited database facility within the wordprocessor. As well as these you get a diary, calendar, clock, alarm, calculator, filing system, BBC BASIC language interpreter and an in-built transfer program to get your data from the Z88 to another computer.

Another major difference is that the Z88 never turns itself off so you don't have to boot the system up everytime you turn it on. Normally you first have to load the program you want to use, then the file you want to work on. You then have to wait while it sorts itself out. With the Z88 however, you just turn it on and it puts you where you left off. This means that you can leave unfinished work on the computer ready to get on with whenever you have got a minute. The Z88 puts everything you do into a suspended activity even after that particular piece of work has been filed, and hope-fully backed up, until you ◊KILL - see INDEX that activity. If you want to work on it after that you can load it back into PIPEDREAM from your saved copy and it will then become a suspended activity again.

DEFINITION:- a suspended activity is a copy of one ap-plication together with its unsaved file. When you save the file, the copy you create is dependent on the activity.

## MENUS

All the applications have commands or functions which allow you to per-form a range of tasks within that application. These are grouped together on different menu pages. A list of the pages relevant to that application appears on the extreme left hand side of the display in a slightly fainter typeface than your text. You can select a function from the menu page with the cursor and ENTER keys. Repeat pressings of the MENU Key will reveal other Menu pages and ESC will put you back into the applica-tion you were working in before entering the MENU.

Certain applications have a secondary Menu which appears alongside the ordinary one. In the INDEX this is the Application Menu, which is one of your points of entry into the Applications available on your Z88. The FILER also has a secondary menu which is a shortened version of the FILER's Commands Menu page. This makes access to the major FILER functions even easier.

## PIPEDREAM - WORD AND FIGURE MANIPULATION

PIPEDREAM allows you to do things a typewriter never did. With a typewriter you could type text in and that was about it. When you made a mistake you could only alter it with the help of a whiting-out agent so you could then type over it. This inevitably made typing a skill in manual dexterity. You could either type or you couldn't and there was no room for those of us who could type with one finger to call ourselves typists! Now it no longer matters because whatever mistakes are made on a wordprocessor can be corrected before they ever reach the paper they are going to appear on. But as well as correcting the odd one or two - or in our case hundreds of - typing errors you can change anything. Nothing is too big for this little machine. You can centre text, reformat paragraphs, in fact change the whole thing so much that the first draft wouldn't be recognised as having any connection at all to the final draft. All of which can be achieved with only typing the main body of the text once plus the changes. This is a tremendous boon whether you are writing a parts list, a poem, or a book on the Z88!!

PIPEDREAM can also manipulate figures in much the same way. They can be put into columns, altered, moved around, and updated whether they are part of a page full of figures or embedded in text. An added bonus is that as a spreadsheet program Pipedream can calculate. So whether you need a column of figures totalled, or complicated relationships between figures involving formulas, the Z88 can handle it.

One of the major advantages of this facility other than book keeping becomes apparent when you use the Z88 as a financial forecasting aid. Once the information has been typed in, if you change one figure the machine will change all the others automatically, providing you have told the system what you want it to do. This makes the forecaster's job so much easier. It also makes the figures much easier to read when you don't see all the crossings out that would have been visible normally.

## FILING SYSTEM

Your Z88 organises its memory by putting each individual piece of work that you want stored into a file which you have to identify by a distinct name. So unlike a cardboard file which can hold different documents on the same subject, a file on your Z88 only contains one piece of work. This makes identification and retrieval simple and indeed makes the management of the 160,000 memory locations - internal memory plus one external 128k RAM - possible!

The filing system is like your filing cabinet. When you want either to back up a file that you are working on, or have finished with it and want to add it to your archive, you have to Save it. The first place you save it to would be your FILER but then, if you want a more permanent record, you can get the FILER to save it to EPROM.

Once you have saved a file, with ◊FS the name appears in the directory when you press ☐ F - which is always reassuring! The file remains in the FILER, even if you are still using it. So in fact the FILER gives you a copy to work with and keeps a copy for itself. Then when you resave it again with any updates (providing you save it under the same name) it will update its copy too. You could of course file the update under a different name if you wanted to keep both versions in the archive.

## NAMING AN ACTIVITY

We recommend that as soon as you open a new activity you name it by doing the following, depending on which application you are working with:

### DIARY
Typing ◊FS or ◊FL, Z88 will ask you either for "name of file to save or, load". It doesn't matter that there is nothing in the file yet. It just means that the suspended activity will be easily identifiable.

### BASIC
In BASIC, the command is        *NAME

**PIPEDREAM, PANEL and PRINTER EDITOR**

To name your suspended activity you can use ◊FC. Z88 will ask you for "the new name of file". It is the command for changing a file's name but you can also use it to name your new file. You can also name a file with the ◊FL and ◊FS commands.

File names can be up to twelve characters long plus a full stop and an extension of up to three characters which you can use to denote what sort of file it is. For example ".BAS" would tell you instantly that that was a Basic file.

The name you choose can include both numbers and letters. They must not however, have any spaces or punctuation marks in them - except the ". " before extensions. We recommend you keep your names simple and easy to remember. There's nothing worse than looking in your directory and thinking 'what on earth is in that file'! The name you pick should make it easy for you to relate it quickly to what that file contains.

## Filing options

You can split a file up into smaller files by marking the part you want to save separately - see 'marking blocks' in the PIPEDREAM section, and saving it under a different file name. You can also join files together by loading one in, putting the cursor where you want the other file to go, and asking the filer to 'load' the other file by pressing ◊FL. You type in the name of the other file and change the "Insert at slot" command to Yes. But be very very careful when you get the "overwrite? Yes, No" prompt on the very top of your screen. If you press y for yes it will erase everything previously in the file and put your new file under the old file name. If that does happen and you have backed your files up adequately there won't be a problem but if you have not got an adequate back up you will have lost that file for good.

You can also create directories and sub directories of your own if you wish. We will tell you how later on.

## The Database Facility

The database is actually a PIPEDREAM facility. It allows you to input, store, reorganise, and search for specific information in much the same way as you can do with figures in a spreadsheet.

## A BRIEF INTRODUCTION TO THE OTHER FEATURES OF THE Z88

### The INDEX

The INDEX is your first port of call when you use the Z88 at least until you get to know what there is available. As well as giving you access to all the major applications it also lists, and gives you the way into, all your suspended activities.

### The PANEL

The PANEL is the way you control physical aspects of your Z88. You can alter things like the auto repeat rate of the keys (how many times a key repeats itself when you hold it down), the DEFAULT DEVICE (which RAM you want the filer to store files), and the TIMEOUT (how long you want the system to give you in thinking time before it turns itself off to conserve power).

### The CALCULATOR

The CALCULATOR has the same facilities as a normal desktop or pocket model. You have a choice of how you input figures and functions, i.e. you can either highlight the figure or function you want with the cursor and press the ENTER key or, you can use the number and letter keys. You also have ten different memories to help with calculations.

### The DIARY

The DIARY allows you to note your appointments and lists of jobs you have got to do. It allows you to choose the format that you want to use.

For example, you might want to note where an appointment is, or give each entry a priority rating.

The secret, when using the diary, is to use keywords because this allows you to search for, and find quickly, any appointment or job.

It can work in conjunction with the CALENDAR and the ALARM to give you a very effective time management tool.

## The CALENDAR

The CALENDAR allows you to look up dates easily from wherever you are working within the Z88. When you enter the CALENDAR it will display the current month - if it has been set up right!

It starts as far back as 1753 - would you believe - and goes forward to well after 2020 which is where we gave up! So whether you are an eighteenth century historian or a long term planner this should be useful.

## The ALARM

The ALARM can be used like an alarm clock but it can also be used in a much more sophisticated way. You can set up as many alarms as you like and for each one you can specify the date, time, and reason. The reason may also include a sequence of Commands that can be started by the ALARM.

This page intentionally left blank

# THE CAULDRON - APPLICATIONS IN DEPTH

## Introduction  "If in doubt try it out"

The Cauldron is where we will look at the applications and programs on your Z88 in detail, going through each one to give you a fair idea of what they can do for you and what they don't do very well. All with a sprinkling of tips to help you along the way. Keep your Z88 at your side at all times and try things out as we are telling you about them. IF IN DOUBT TRY IT OUT has been our trusty motto while writing this and we don't see why it won't work just as well for you too!

## Types of Program

There are two distinct types of program used in the Z88. We will call them applications and popdowns throughout this book. The major difference is that popdowns cannot be shown as suspended activities in the index whilst applications can. The applications are generally involved in lengthier operations like wordprocessing or time management. As suspended activities the applications can be worked on, left and then picked up again. Generally, popdowns are used either as quick reference tools like the CLOCK and CALCULATOR, or they are used as control centres like the INDEX, PANEL, ALARM.

## Applications

The application programs in the Z88 are:-

PIPEDREAM                        DIARY
BASIC                            TERMINAL
PRINTER EDITOR

## Popdowns

The popdown programs are:-

INDEX                            PANEL
CLOCK                            IMPORT/EXPORT
ALARM                            CALENDAR
CALCULATOR                       FILER

# USING MENUS

## How They Work

Menus are the lists of functions that appear on the left hand side of your display. They can be accessed by the MENU key. When MENU is selected, normally the top menu option will be displayed in bold characters and the display screen will then be taken over by the choice of functions that that menu has available. You can move from menu to menu in a downward direction via repeated pressings of the MENU key. When you reach the bottom of the menu list and press MENU again it will put you back at the top. Therefore if you miss the one you want the first time, you can go round and round until you get it. Once you have got to the one you want the usual combination of CURSOR (arrows) and ENTER keys will allow you to choose the function you want. Once you have selected one of the menu functions the system will put you back into your working activity and carry out what you asked it to do. The cursor will only reappear on the display when it has completed the task. When you press the menu key again the system may place the cursor back on the last function you used in case you want to repeat that function by pressing the ENTER key again. If you press MENU by mistake or you change your mind after pressing it you can return to your activity by pressing ESC.

All the functions in the various menus have a code. These consist of a function key plus a series of other key strokes. You can use these codes as a quick way of carrying out functions without going through the menus. The codes will appear on the extreme right hand side of the display after, and/or below, the function key ( ◇ or ▢ ) symbol. If you make a mistake (unless you have typed the commands code for another function) the symbol and letters will disappear and you will have to type them in again. You will quickly learn the codes for the ones you use most frequently and it is sometimes quicker to type these straight in.

The only time you cannot use Menus is when the 'memory low' indicator shows on the right hand side of the screen. Then OZ (the operating system) switches off the menus to conserve memory. You can then only access the functions via the codes until some more memory has been released.

When you have selected a command from any of the menus some of the commands have other options available with them. Any of these options (which allow you to type in what you want, or where you want them done - like file names ) can be edited and the cursor moved around them with the simple PIPEDREAM Cursor and Edit commands. The Cursor commands have already been listed in the keyboard layout section in Part One. The main Edit ones are:

◇DEL                    deletes one or more characters or spaces to the left of the cursor position

◇ G                      Deletes the character or space under the cursor position

◇ T                      Deletes the characters from the cursor position, right, to the next space

◇ D                            deletes everything from the cursor to the right
                               hand end of the line.

# THE INDEX - GETTING WHERE YOU WANT TO GO

| INDEX COMMANDS | APPLICATIONS | SUSPENDED ACTIVITIES |
|---|---|---|
|  |  |  |

The INDEX is normally your way into your Z88. It is the access point to all the applications that you can get your Z88 to do. You therefore have to go through the INDEX to get a new copy of PIPEDREAM or BBC Basic. It is also the way into all the suspended activities on your Z88. You need not go through the INDEX when you start work if you are carrying on in the suspended activity that you were when you turned the Z88 off.

## Index Display

The INDEX display consists of three menus:

The first one on the left hand side is the index's own FUNCTION menu which has one page of commands listed. Moving to the right of this is the APPLICATIONS menu which lists all the different programs available. This menu also gives the function key - in this case ☐ - and code that allows your entry into an application without selecting it via the CURSOR and ENTER keys. If you want a new copy of PIPEDREAM or BBC BASIC you do have to go through the INDEX. This is because ☐ P will put you into the next PIPEDREAM suspended activity in the suspended activity index and likewise for BBC BASIC.

The third menu is a catalogue of your suspended activities. You can gain access to any of them from the INDEX. This menu also tells you your name for that activity, what application it is working with, the time you last looked at it - if it was "Today" - otherwise it will either show "Yesterday" or the date.

This menu allows you to see at a glance whether any of your suspended activities are using an external program by showing the card slot number that the application is using. This is very useful if you want to change the cards because you must ◇Kill any suspended activity which is using the external application cartridge that you want to remove, before removing that cartridge from the Z88. If you try to remove an application cartridge which is still being used by a suspended activity the Z88 will give you a continuous warning tone and flash 'CARD' on the top right hand side of the display. You must put the cartridge back, find the activity that is using it, and ◇Kill it. Then you can take it out of the slot again.

# Suspended activities

Suspended activities are unsaved files which are using copies of the applications and whatever you want to do with them. They will remain suspended activities even after you have saved them to the Filer. You can have as many different copies of PIPEDREAM and BBC Basic as you wish. Every time you select PIPEDREAM or BBC Basic via the Index directly, the machine will give you a new copy to work with. With the other applications e.g. TERMINAL PRINTERED and DIARY you can only suspend one each of these at any one time.

The ways you can lose your suspended activities are: -

a)                          Deliberately, by either ◇KILLing them individually or doing a global ◇PURGE - see below.

b)                          Accidentally, if you are forced to do a soft or hard reset.

## INDEX Functions

The INDEX has two functions. Firstly it is used to select and erase suspended activities. Secondly it is the place where you should be when you are putting in or taking out any memory or program cards.

The following appear on the INDEX Commands menu -

## ◇CARD

◇CARD allows you to see at a glance what external cards you have got in your system. It is particularly useful when you have just inserted a new card because you can check that the Z88 has recognised the new card.

## ◇KILL

This is the command for erasing your suspended activities. Although this command appears on the INDEX commands menu it is one of the few that you cannot action in the menu. Normally you have a choice of how you action a function but for this one you have to press INDEX, position the cursor over the application you want to erase and type in ◇K.I.L.L. This has been done to eliminate as far as possible you making a mistake and erasing a suspended application before you are ready to. Once you have killed an activity there is no way of getting it back unless you have saved it in the FILER and backed it up elsewhere.

## ◇PURGE

◇PURGE is the same as ◇KILL but more so because it erases all your suspended activities at the same time. It works the same as a soft reset. To action this function, as with ◇KILL although the command appears in the INDEX commands menu it can only be actioned by typing in ◇P.U.R.G.E. This should only be done if you have saved all your suspended activities with the ◇FS and the relevant named files appear in your directory when you press ☐ F .

---

**TIP. Using purge when you are running out of memory.**
**◇PURGE is useful when you are short of memory. If you have backed up your suspended activities adequately, by keeping them as suspended activities as well, you have in fact got two copies of each one. It should therefore be possible to keep just one activity (the one you want to work on) suspended and free the rest of the memory. You can load the one you want back into the relevant application as a suspended activity after you have purged the system.**

---

# THE PANEL

## Introduction

The PANEL is the main Set-up program and has direct links with all the other programs used in the Z88. Any changes you make to the PANEL may affect all the programs you are using. The first thing that the machine does when you start a new activity is to go to the panel and copy the settings. These are then used in the activity you have started.

When you change a setting in the PANEL this has immediate effect on all activities.

The only exception to this is changing the insert/overtype, default device, and default directory. These will only be actioned on new applications, i.e. applications created after the changes to the panel have been made.

---

**TIP: Leaving the PANEL**
**After each change made to the PANEL you must press ENTER to leave it otherwise the changes you have made won't be implemented. If you leave it any other way it will revert to what it was before you changed it.**

---

**TIP: Saving the PANEL settings**
**You can Save the FILES settings in a Panel file by either going into the PANEL MENU and selecting 'file save' or by typing ◇FS. This can be useful if you have to do a soft reset because that will put all the options back to the original default settings. So if you haven't saved your panel options in a file you would then have to type them in all over again.**

---

When you no longer want the settings that you have saved you can instruct the Z88 to return the settings to their old default values by using the 'new' command from the panel files menu page.

# PANEL OPTIONS

## Auto Repeat

The auto repeat rate is normally set at 6. Your choice ranges from 1, which is extremely fast, right the way through to 9. It then goes to 0 where the keys don't repeat themselves at all. There are advantages both ways. If you set it to 0 then and you accidentally hit a key for longer than you meant to you don't get loads of unwanted characters. But such a change will slow the cursor right down and therefore give your hand cramp much quicker! If you alter it to 1 however the reverse is true. The cursor then flies around like a mad thing and the slightest pressure on any key gives you twenty characters you didn't want. We reckon 6 is about right for us but we suggest you experiment to find what is best for you.

## Key-click

You have a yes/no option with this and it is entirely up to your own preference whether you want the reassurance of a sound to tell you when you have pressed a key or not. We like ours on because with touch-sensitive keys it is not always easy to know when you have actually pressed a key and when you haven't.

---

**TIP : Changing the options on commands**
With all 'yes/no' options on the Z88 you don't have to delete one and insert the other. If the option is set to yes and you want to change it to no all you have to do is position the cursor over the Y and type N. The system will do the rest for you. The same rule applies for changing insert to overtype and visa versa.

If you are unsure of what options you can choose from, put the cursor over the option and use ◇J which will show you what the next option is. So you may have to press ◇ J more than once to get the full range of options that are available.

---

## Insert/overtype

When you are in insert mode the system will allow you to add a new
character, word, or sentence in the middle of existing text by moving the
rest of the text along to the right.

In overtype mode you can type over old words without deleting them. If
you need to insert anything you have to use the INSERT CHARACTER
Command to create space, this is on the Edit MENU page of any Application that has one. ◇U is the shortcut command.

## Default Device

We touched briefly on this in Part One when we told you how to set the
Z88 up before starting work. It is important to understand here that this
setting in the Panel is only consulted once when you open a new application. So if you change the default device from RAM.1 to RAM.2 the
application that you are working in will have already been to the Panel
for its settings so the change will have no effect. Changing the default
device will only affect applications that you start after you have changed
the setting.

It is useful to be able to change the device because a file cannot be spread
over two devices and in theory it allows you to anticipate when you are
running short of space in one device and direct your files to where there
is more space. In practice you can really only use guess work to judge
when to change because there is little accurate information to tell you how
much memory you are using and where it is. You can use different devices
to separate different types of files, but this is only one way amongst many
to organise your files effectively. Other ways will be talked about in
greater detail in the FILER section later. If you have changed the device
and later want to get to files that were filed elsewhere, you can get to them
by selecting the appropriate device with the select device command on
the FILER menu. So if you select RAM.2 in the FILER, the FILER will
then display all the files and directories that you have stored in that RAM.

If you don't want to change the default device globally with the PANEL
you can in fact instruct the FILER to send individual files to different
memory devices by incorporating the device name, device number and
then a slash into the front of your file name when saving or loading a file,
e.g. you would put :RAM.1/filename - not forgetting the colon at the front.

## Timeout

This option allows you to set the amount of time you want your Z88 to remain turned on when you are not doing anything with it. This is here primarily to conserve power. It is normally set at 5 but if you are running your Z88 on batteries you can prolong their life quite considerably by cutting the timeout to two minutes. If you normally run your Z88 on mains power however, you will not be so concerned about power levels and may therefore prefer a longer thinking period before the timeout cuts in. If you set your timeout option to 0 it will not work at all. We suspect however, that if you have got used to the machine turning itself off and then it doesn't do it any more you just might not remember to do it manually. We know we wouldn't!

This option is not allowed to work if you have the Clock display on the screen. You might be using it to time something. You may not be doing anything with the Z88 to keep it from turning itself off. The authors of the programs decided it would be better to disable the timeout option while the Clock is in use. This is great as long as you don't leave the Clock on by mistake and then lose everything in RAM because you ran out of power!

## Sound

This allows you to turn the internal sound system on or off  But since it doesn't effect the keyclick or any of the warning tones that the Z88 can give you, the only thing this option affects is the Alarm.

## Map

In PIPEDREAM there is normally a page map on the right hand side of your text which allows you to see what your whole page looks like. If you turn it off at the panel, it is possible to make typing and editing faster. You can also use the area where the page map was to view more of your working area if you are using wider than average margins or multi column spreadsheets.

## Map Size

This allows you to alter the page map width. The normal setting is 80 characters because normal printers print 80 characters per line, but you can increase it to 92. This can be increased still further, to a massive 255 characters if you have a 128K RAM cartridge in slot 1 - it obviously eats memory!

## Date Format

You have a choice between European and American date format. In the U.K. when we write the date we put the day, then the month, and then the year. In America however, they change the month and the day round so they put the month first, then the day, and finally the year.

## The Final Column

The final column contains options which relate specifically to your Z88 communicating with other machines. These could include printers, modems or other computers and we propose to leave explanation of these until later when we cover the subject in some depth.

# PIPEDREAM

## Introduction

This section is one of the longest in the book because PIPEDREAM is so versatile that there is a great deal for us to talk about! There are also several exercises in the TUTORIAL Appendix which will encourage you to try out what you have learnt here.

## Terminology

PIPEDREAM uses a small number of words slightly differently to the Z88. The glaringly obvious one is slot. The Z88 calls its memory com-

partments slots whilst PIPEDREAM gives the same name to screen locations or what the Z88 calls cells. We know that while you are struggling
to learn a new language, especially one that is full of gobbledegook, it is
better to call a spade a spade and not start calling it a topsoil-turning-in-
strument or worse still, a fork, half way through! So we intended to stick
to the original cells. The only problem with doing that however is that the
PIPEDREAM commands use the PIPEDREAM terminology so all the
commands to do with cells call them slots. For instance the 'Go to slot'
command which is abbreviated to ◇CGS. To try and avoid as much confusion as possible we will use the names that we think are right for the Z88
but put the PIPEDREAM name for it in brackets alongside for easy
reference. So a location on your page will be referred to as a cell[slot].

# PIPEDREAM AS A WORDPROCESSOR

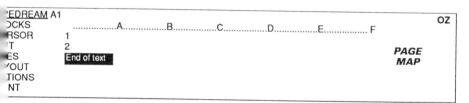

## HOW YOUR WORKING AREA IS MADE UP

After selecting a new copy of PIPEDREAM via the INDEX - see Index
section if you haven't read it yet! - you will have a virtually clear screen
with a full compliment of menu pages on the left hand side. Apart from
that you will have a border made up of dots and letters, a small downward
arrow, a number one with the flashing cursor next to it, an "end of text"
printed in a reverse colour block, and an A1 next to the application name
PIPEDREAM.

## The Top Border

The top border serves two purposes. Firstly it acts as a border between
your working area and the Z88 comment line where it tells you what it is
doing or asks you questions. Secondly the spacing of the letters gives you

the preset TAB settings. Each of the six columns are twelve characters apart and take the name of the letter to the right of its space. The F column is therefore the space between the E and F. The system tells you which column you are in by filling the top margin of that one with a continual dotted line. You should be in the A column now.

It is perhaps worth noting here that until you press the TAB key you will stay in column A even when the cursor is actually under another column. So if you are doing a straight forward page filled with text you should stay in column A all the time. If however, you want to have an indented passage you can press the TAB key which will then put the cursor into the first character space of the B column.

---

**TIP: Changing Column widths**
It is possible to alter the gaps between columns with ◇W, but be very careful when altering the width of columns that you have already put text into because if Wrap is turned on in the OPTION PAGE (to check press O) the system may not do what you think! DO NOT set the width to 0 as this will delete the column altogether although you can retrieve text or figures that were in it by widening it again.

---

## Right Hand Margin

The small downward pointing arrow is your right hand margin indicator. It is preset at 72 characters. You can change this either by pressing ☐ and LEFT or RIGHT arrow, which will move your margin one space in whichever direction, or if you want to alter it more radically than that you can press ◇H and type in the number of characters you want on a line. If you change the right margin and the downward arrow goes behind a column label (A to F) that label will be shown in bold and you won't see the little arrow.

## Row Numbers

The number one to the left and slightly below the top border is the row or line number. PIPEDREAM has given you one line to work with! Do we hear you saying "you can't do a lot of word manipulation in one line!" Well you're right, but as soon as you have filled that one line up with text, or pressed ENTER to tell the system you want a new line, a "2" will ap-

pear under the 1 and the "end of text" marker will move down a line.
PIPEDREAM will give you as many lines as you need.

## Cell[Slot] Number

The Cell[slot] number is the little "A1" on the top comment line next to
the application name PIPEDREAM. If you move down a line this will
change to "A2" and if you then press TAB it will change to "B2". This is
telling you the co-ordinates of where you are in your activity, the column
code letter first followed by the row or line number.

## Page Map

As you start typing text in you will find a series of dots appearing in between the end of your ruler line and OZ. Each dot corresponds to a
character you have typed in. This will build up into a representation of
your page. Although you can only see six lines at a time on the display
the page map gives you an idea of what the whole page looks like.

## End of Text Marker

This tells you the bottom edge of your present activity. The cursor will
not move onto or below the line that the marker occupies. It will move
down with you as you type more text in or if you add more lines in by either
pressing the ENTER key or ◊N for inserting a new line.

# MOVING AROUND - THE CURSOR

Once you have typed in some text you can move round it with the cursor.
All the various cursor keys are detailed earlier, but they can also be found
on the PIPEDREAM cursor MENU page.

Moving the cursor around your text allows you to go back and look at the
earlier bits of your activity which are no longer on the screen. It also allows you to tell the computer where you want a particular command
carried out.

## Using Tabs

The tab key moves the cursor between columns. "Oh heck, we haven't told you about columns yet have we?" Well, we had better do that before we go any further because like many things when you enter the realms of magic, columns are not what they seem!!

On a typewriter the tab key physically moves the carriage over the required number of spaces. When you first use tabs on the Z88 it appears to do the same thing. There appear to be six preset tab settings which help facilitate the cursor movement across the page. But BEWARE, what looks like an inert everyday object is really a double headed serpent waiting to spring onto your activity and turn it into something beyond recognition!

Although it looks as though you have got six columns, A to F, all twelve characters wide, this is not true because five of the columns are partially hidden. PIPEDREAM overlays B on top of A and C on top of B and so on. So it is only F which is totally visible - unless of course you add more columns! You will only see what is in any one column's row in its entirety if there is nothing in any other column on that row. If there is something in column B you can still edit whatever is hidden in column A by moving the cursor and editing in the normal way. However, what you cannot see on the screen normally will not be printed.

Until you change the margin of any column from its default setting, all columns will end at the right hand margin - so A will be 72 characters wide, B will be 60 and so on until F which will be only 12 characters wide. The right hand margin also determines the wrap point of any row.

PIPEDREAM stores each column as though it were a separate page, one below the other in memory, which is totally different to how you see it on the screen.

This can cause problems if you try to move a block of text from one column to another because you are never quite sure where the system is going to move the rest of the text to while it makes room for the new bit.

---

**TIP: Antidote to Tabs**
**If you press the tab key accidentally, without knowing it until you suddenly realise that you are typing text into the wrong column and covering**

up text you have already done. You will end up with a bewildering mess which makes you want to tear your hair out.

It is quite simple to get out of however: all you have to do is mark the block that you have put into the wrong column - remembering to clear any previous marked areas with ◇Q - then, after moving the cursor to a clear line in the column you should have been in, you press ◇BM. The system will then move it to where you want it.

This can be used normally to move text between columns but it may well save your life the first time you meet the double headed monster so mark it well!

# TEXT MANIPULATION IN DETAIL

Once you have typed in your piece of text there is no limit to what you can do with it. We would need a much bigger book to cover everything but we will try and give you the information you will need to find out more.

# PIPEDREAM MENUS

PIPEDREAM has a comprehensive set of menus. If you want to do anything there is normally a command or function in one of them that will help you. We suggest that you spend some time learning what functions are stored in what menus. We hope the sections below will help you do this.

## Blocks

The blocks menu as the name suggests will help you deal with lumps of text. You can move, copy, replicate, and delete whole areas of text. A block of text can be any length you like. You cannot however do it easily with anything smaller than a line because the command which marks the area you want to deal with, ◇Z, marks the whole line that the cursor is occupying.

## Marking, Moving, Copying, and Deleting

Before you can do any of that however you have to mark the block to identify the area you want the computer to work with. All you have to do is
place the cursor over the top line and mark it with ◊Z. Move the cursor
to the bottom line of the block and mark that. The marked area will appear on your screen as white print on a blue background - the colour
reversed to normal. The system will only deal with one marked block at
a time however, so if you make a mistake and mark another line when
there is already a marked block in the document it will assume that it is
the last one that you really want marked and clear the previous two
markers: you will then have to start again. Of course if you have only put
in one marker earlier by mistake and you then try and mark a new block
it will mark totally the wrong area for you.

TIP: Marking a block in a multi-column activity.

**If you want to work with a block that extends across more than one
column all you have to do is mark the top of the left hand column and
the bottom of the right hand column of the total area that you want
marked.**

**If the area you want to mark extends across the whole activity then you
can use ◊CFC and ◊ CLC for speed. They will move the cursor straight
to the beginning of the first and last column respectively.**

TIP: Clear any marked blocks before marking a new one.

**It is always a good idea to clear any previously marked lines before you
start marking a new block. You do this with ◊Q. Otherwise if you have
got a marked line somewhere else that you don't know about you could
mark more than you had bargained for.**

TIP: Marking a block that is embedded in a larger paragraph.

**If the block you want to deal with is embedded into a larger paragraph
and includes a half line at the beginning or end that you want to move
with the rest of the block, you can do this by splitting the bit you want
from the bit you don't. Position the cursor over the first letter of the bit
you want to split and press ◊ESL. That line will be split in two on two
different lines. You now need to put in a blank line between the bit you
want and the bit you don't by putting the cursor on the lower half of the
line and pressing ◊N. Repeat the splitting procedure at the other end**

of the block if you need to and put a blank line there as well.  Then, posi -
tion the cursor over the top left hand character in your block and press
◇R.  Your block will now be formatted into a proper-looking paragraph.
You can then move it where ever you want it to go by putting the cursor
on the line where you want the top of the block to go and pressing  ◇BM.

There is one other limitation on ◇BM, the block move command.  That
is, if you try to move your block to an area where part of the block
originated from you may get an 'overlap' error message come up on the
comment line.  We say 'may' because in some cases the system does allow
you to do it.  For example, if you want to move a block of ten lines down
three lines even though you will have to place the cursor in the middle of
the marked area, the system will move the block down.  The only time we
could make it come up with the 'overlap' error message was when we
placed the cursor in column C within the marked block.  If you need to
do that sort of procedure you can use Replicate.

The same procedures apply for deleting and copying.

## Replicating

Replicate ◇BRE is a more elaborate copy function.  It allows you to copy
one cell[slot], a vertical or horizontal line of cell[slot]s, or a whole area of
cell[slot]s in another part of the document.  You can also select how many
times you want it copied.  For example if you want one cell[slot] - lets say
A1 - copied across the whole line, 'the range to copy from' will be A1 and
the 'range to copy to' will be B1 F1.

---

**TIP: Putting a space between the ranges.**
**If you use more than one cell[slot] number range there must be a space
between the two co-ordinates otherwise the Z88 will come up with 'bad
range' on the comment line.**

---

If you want to copy A1 in a vertical line for ten lines the range to copy to
would be A2 A10.  To copy A1 to more than a block of lines and columns
all you need to do is put the top left-hand cell[slot] co- ordinates and the
bottom right-hand cell[slot] co-ordinates of the range to copy to and the
machine will do the rest.  So if you wanted to fill the screen with what is
in cell[slot] A1 the range to copy to will be A1 F6 .

To copy a multi-column block to a new location you need to put in the cell[slot] co-ordinates of the range to copy from, e.g. A1 F6  But for the range to copy to you only need to put the top left- hand co-ordinate of the new position of the block.

With this function you can also copy a vertical line of columns to a horizontal position and visa versa.

## SORT  ◇BSO

◇BSO is the sort command.  It will sort texts into alphabetical order, numbers which have been turned into expressions will be sorted into numeric order.  Dates which are in expression cell[slot]s will be sorted into date order.

To carry out a sorting operation you must first mark the block that you want sorted.  This could be two lines or the entire activity.  You then call up ◇BSO and it will ask you which column you want the sort done on. This enables you to state which column is the most important one for you, for example if you had a name and address file with first names in column A, surnames in B, company names in C and the address in D, you could specify any of them for the Sort to be carried out on. If it was your private address book you would most likely want the surnames to be sorted - in which case you would ask for the Sort to be done on B. If it was your business address list you would probably consider the company name the most important element, in which case you would ask it to sort on D.

Asking for the sort to be done in reverse order is straightforward.

Updating references is useful if you need to do it but it is very time con - suming because for every Cell[slot] it moves, PIPEDREAM checks all the other Cell[slot]s in case you have used the first cell[slot] in the calcula- tions. If you have it will take out the old reference and put in the new one. If you know you have not used any such references, especially if you are doing an alphabetical sort on a text activity in any case, you will save a great deal of time if you put Yes in the 'don't update reference'.

---

**TIP: YES/NO Options.**
**If you are like us and get confused by whether the options should be put to yes or no remember the double negative rule in English - i.e. a double negative always makes a positive.  So when the option is worded in the**

negative and it is set to No it means that it will carry out what it is saying not to do! If you don't want it to do it, in this case 'don't update reference' you have to change the option to Yes. We hope this is clear! If not don't blame us, blame whoever wrote the software!

The only other thing you ought to know is that if you are doing a sort on numbers into numeric order, the numbers you are sorting must be put into what PIPEDREAM calls expression slots. You do this either by pressing ◇X and typing the figure or formula into the Expression Edit area in the comment line, or you can type the number in normally, place the cursor over the left-hand figure and then press ◇X. That will then pick up the number and put it into the expression edit area for you. Then all you have to do is press enter. If you do not put the numbers into this form you will have some very weird effects on your sorted list, for example it will put 223 in between 22 and 23. The reason for this is that when there are no expression slots in the marked block it will sort alphabetically, starting with the letter on the left and working towards the right. Whereas if it is sorting numbers in expression cel[slot]s it will sort numerically, starting on the right with the units and working leftwards.

## SEARCH & REPLACE

With these functions you can search for and/or search for and replace, a string of characters. It will scour either your current activity or, if you have joined several activities together in a list file (we will deal with that later) it will carry out the command throughout all the files linked in the list.

As the name suggests Search ◇BSE can be used to find a particular word in the activity. If the first one it finds is not the one you want you can press ◇BNM for Next Match. This can be useful if you want to scan the file and carry out more than the one operation that the Search command will allow you to do at any one time.

The search command has a number of options for you to choose from. You can ask it to search a specific column or number of columns: which is very useful if you are working with a multi column activity, like a spreadsheet or database. The "equate cases" option, if left at 'yes', will find you the character or string of characters that you have asked for regardless of whether it is in upper or lower case. If you only want to find it in the case you have typed it into the 'search for' space, then you must turn this option to 'no'. You can also 'search only within a marked block'.

The last two options are only relevant if you are working in a list file. You can choose whether you want to search all the files that you have linked, or just from the file you are working on.

'Search' can also be used to move you to the exact spot you want anywhere in the document much faster and more accurately than you can get there via the cursor commands.

'Replace' is really a quick edit function. It allows you to change one word, or a string of words or numbers up to 240 characters for any other characters, with ease. So if you have a bad spelling habit and often mis-spell a particular word, then you can change all the baddies in one fell swoop.

**TIP: Spell it the same as you did in the text otherwise PIPEDREAM won't find it!**

**When using the search or replace command make sure that the spelling is the same as you used in the main body of the activity otherwise it will not find it.**

**The thing to remember with these two functions is that they will only do what you tell them to do. So if you have typed Jane and the correct spelling is Jayne, you would search for Jane and replace with Jayne. It will however only replace the ones you have spelt like that. It will not recognise anything that you have spelt differently even if you didn't mean to. It is therefore a good idea, unless you are an immaculate typist, to only use this command globally after you have proof-read your activity.**

Unless you tell it otherwise the system will look for the string everywhere including inside other words so, for example, if you asked it to replace 'every' with 'all' automatically, it would do it and you would end up with allwhere and allthing! You can get round this by putting a space before and after the 'search for and replace with' options. But this is not as simple as it sounds.

Once you have used these commands a few times and are happy using them in a straightforward way, you will find that there are certain things like spaces that you cannot search for, either on their own or at the beginning or end of a string. One of our "favourite" - perhaps that should be "unfavourite" - typing errors is to hold down the space key too long. This means that we frequently end up with three spaces in between sentences when we should only have two. When we first acquired the Z88 we thought we could correct these with the search and replace commands.

So we gaily typed in three spaces in the 'string to search for' and two spaces in the 'replace with' location on the replace command list. We then pressed ENTER and waited, only to find much to our annoyance that nothing happened! We realise now that as far as the machine was aware we hadn't put anything in! It was only then that we discovered wildcards......

# WILDCARDS

"What the heck are 'Wildcards' do we hear you ask?" Well, before you let your imagination run wild - pun not intended - they are like magic words in a spell. They act like codes and can be used either to instruct the Z88 to carry out a number of functions or they can be used as a means of constructing rules. PIPEDREAM uses ^ as a function key in the search and replace commands. When you use it with the correct codes, it enables you to have a very powerful tool. It allows you to search for things like spaces which do not appear on the screen. As we have found out, a space cannot be shown on the screen on its own because it is the characters on either side that define it. ' ^ s' is the code for space.

But Wildcards have a much more important role than that because they allow you to specify a small part of what you want it to do, in this case 'search for and replace with', and it will do the rest for you. They were called Wildcards after the Joker in some card games where it could become any card the player wished. Sorry we are not gamblers ourselves, but those of you who are will probably, at the very least, be able to fill in some more detail on this. But in any case we think that the Joker concept is very useful in illuminating wildcards because that is just what a wildcard is. For example if you are using the wildcard for a word (which is ⌃#), it can be any word in that activity until you define which word you want it to be.

Using Wildcards in the search and replace mode enables you not only to search for three spaces and replace it with two, which is a standard search and replace operation, but once you know the codes you can change and/or interchange characters - either letters or numbers, strings of letters - words, and strings of words - sentences. If you are working with a string of words the spaces in between can be entered with the space key. It is only where you are not working with characters on either side of the space that you have to use ⌃s.

While you are using the search command there are other codes like ⌃s which work in exactly the same way.

You can use ⌃ followed by a number to tell PIPEDREAM to search for a print Highlight Code.

---

**Tip. Highlight Codes**
These are the commands that you use on either side of a word or heading to tell PIPEDREAM that you want it in a different form. They are only displayed on the screen while the cursor is on that line, as a numeric code in an inverted colour block, otherwise it will be shown on the display as it will be printed. The codes are set up to be the following;-

1 - underline
2 - bold
3 - extended sequence
4 - italic
5 - subscript
6 - superscript
7 - alternative font
8 - user defined font

**We will describe what they all are, how you call them up and what you could change them to in the Print section.**

So if you ask the system to search for $\wedge 2$ it will find you the first word that you have asked to be put into bold. If you use these codes in replace mode you can either use them to change the code or you could ask it to change one or all of the words or characters that you have bracketed with the number code.

The code for a character in a predetermined position is $\wedge$ ? in search mode. You have to define the position of the unknown character you want it to look for.

An example materialised while we were writing this book. We had always intended to put all references to PIPEDREAM in upper case. But with our fingers going slower than our thoughts the top priority very quickly became getting it down on paper - or rather in RAM! - any old how and sorting out the errors later. But that meant we had three different ver-sions of PIPEDREAM. About a third were what we wanted, a third were all in lower case and the final third had the first P in upper case. To change them all with the straightforward replace mode would have taken two goes. While we were struggling with the concept of Wildcards and how to put them into practice however, an idea suddenly hit us like a flash of lightning! Now those of you who are prone to being hit by ideas like that will know that they don't always work! And one thing we have learnt while writing this book is that you have to try everything out before believing anything because the Z88 is the final arbiter on such matters! So we put our lightning- strike into practice: we bravely went where we hadn't been before. We typed ' $\wedge$ ?ipedream' into the 'string to search for', replaced with PIPEDREAM and asked it not to equate upper and lower cases. We then sat back and waited to see what it would do, half expecting '0 found' to appear on the comment line that had greeted previous efforts. But no, there was the cursor flashing over pipedream: then it found Pipedream. It worked, it actually worked!

" $\wedge$ # " is the code for a string of characters without a space e.g. a word or number. You must specify which one you want to work with by defin-ing where these characters or strings of characters are. As with $\wedge$ ? you do this by typing in what is before and after the string of characters that you are interested in. If you don't specify this it will match what it is sear-ching for with every string of characters or numbers in the activity!

If you have used more than one ⌃ # or ⌃ ? in the string to search for, the machine will number them internally so that if you want to use one or more of them in the 'replace with' string you can specify which of them you want the machine to use. The first ⌃ # in the 'search for' string would therefore be ⌃ #1 if you wanted to put it into the 'replace with' string . You can of course put them in any order you like and do not have to use all of them. You may have used three ⌃ #s in the 'string to search for' and only need to use one of them in the 'replace with string'. A string may contain up to nine ⌃ ?s and nine ⌃ #s.

⌃ B directs the search and/or replace function to start at the beginning of the line and can be used in conjunction with other ⌃ codes as long as there is a space between the ⌃ codes.

This has been a particularly difficult section to write because Wildcards do not lend themselves to simple explanations. But we hope that by in-troducing them gently now, they will cause all of us less pain when we get to the more complicated procedures, where they really come into their own. Then they really will give all of us twisted brains at the very least!

To get back into the main blocks MENU! The description of the next three commands are going to be deliberately brief because they are fair-ly self- explanatory

## ◇BWC

◇BWC counts the number of words in the current activity. The number of words will appear on the left hand side of the comment line. A word is taken to be a character or string of characters which has a space on either side. This means that the system will also count a number as a word.

Who will lay me odds that they used wildcards to get PIPEDREAM to do this one!!

## ◇A

◇A is a spreadsheet command which tells the system to recalculate. It will recalculate all the figures in the activity and is useful if you have made lots of changes. If you put the calculate option on the Options Page shown as 'Calc: auto/man' to Automatic, you will not need ◇A because it will normally recalculate everything. You might use this to bring a spreadsheet completely up to date.

## ◇BNEW

◇BNEW clears the activity you are in so you can start again. After selcecting it the machine will ask you if you want to overwrite the text that is already there. If you do not want to lose what you have got in that activity you must press N. If you press Y the system will erase the  activity that was there, reset all the options on the options page and give you what looks like a clean copy of PIPEDREAM to work with. It is not a new one but just the old one erased clean and ready for you to use again.

It is a quick way of getting rid of an activity that you don't want. We felt like pressing it many a time in the preceding section on wildcards!! It is also a quick way of getting a new copy of PIPEDREAM if you have saved the activity first and no longer need it to stay as a suspended activity. You then do not have to collect a new copy of PIPEDREAM by going into INDEX and selecting PIPEDREAM with the cursor as you would normally.

---

**TIP: Change the file name after using ◇BNEW.**

**If you use ◇BNEW as a shortcut to getting a clear copy of PIPEDREAM do not forget to change the activity's name with ◇ FC. Otherwise you could end up saving the new activity under the old name and wipe out the old file altogether.**

---

This page left intentionally blank

# Cursor

The Cursor menu contains all the commands that you can use to help you move quickly and easily around the current activity in PIPEDREAM. Many of them are common to all the applications on the Z88. All the simple ones using arrow keys or a combination of arrow and function keys have already been dealt with in the keyboard layout section in Part One. We will therefore just look here at the ones we have not yet told you about.

## ◇CGS

◇CGS is the Go to Cell[slot] command which allows you to move direct-ly to the Cell[slot] that you want to move to (which could be in the middle of the activity 4 pages away) by typing in its co ordinates. This can be very useful if you are working in a large activity, providing you know where you want to go! If you are like us and have a memory like a sieve that is not always easy. Of course if you are working with text and are just in column A it is a bit better because then you only have to worry about remembering row numbers. But even then, if you are working with a large text it is difficult to keep a large map of it in your head. We have however found it useful as an approximate tool rather than a deadly accurate one.

This command probably comes into its own however, when you are work-ing with figures spread over a large number of columns in a spreadsheet. Then you would be more likely to be able to see the cell[slot] you want to go to and therefore use the command more accurately.

Whether you use it as an approximate or accurate tool it will cut down the amount of time you use moving from one place to another, especial-ly if you are moving to a cell[slot] a long way away from the previous cursor position.

## ◇CFC

◇CFC will move the cursor to the first column, i.e. column A. It has the same effect as ◇TAB.

## ◊CLC

◊CLC will move the cursor to the beginning of the last column on that row.

## ◊CSP

◊CSP allows you to save the present cursor position. You can save up to five of these positions. If you forget how many positions you have already saved and try to save a sixth position the Z88 will bleep a warning at you.

## ◊CRP

◊CRP will move the cursor back to the last saved cursor position. Therefore if you have got five saved positions and want to get back to the first one you saved you will have to press the command five times. In a case like this it may be quicker to go into the menu, position the cursor over the command and press enter. When you go back into the menu a second time the cursor will already be over the command you want, you just press ENTER to select the command again.

Both these two commands, ◊CSP and ◊CRP, work together as further means of moving around the activity quickly and accurately. Say for example you were writing a letter of complaint which itemised all your previous correspondence at the top and you needed to remind yourself which letters were sent, you could save the cursor's position when it was at the top of the list and then go back to the list with a ◊CRP command.

Having said all that however, we found the use of these commands limited by three factors. Firstly, when you restore the cursor position it will only put you at the beginning of the cell[slot] which in a text file would be at the beginning of the row - not necessarily where the cursor was when its position was saved. Secondly, once you have restored the cursor to the line of the saved position you cannot go back to it again because PIPEDREAM forgets it. Thirdly, when you save a position no indicator is put on the screen so you have no sure way of knowing that you have been restored to the correct place.

It may be better, to make a mental note of the row number yourself, then you can go back to the same place again and again using the ◊CGS command. Otherwise you would have to re-save the position every time you restore the cursor to it.

The commands could be useful with some of the block functions because you could save the position where you want the block either to move to or be copied to before going back to mark the block.

# EDIT

## Introduction

The Edit menu has the greatest number of functions of all the menus. It is filled with the commands that you use most often while using the Z88 as a wordprocessor. They enable you to add in and take out everything from single characters to whole lines and whole columns.

Most of them are very straight-forward and a large number of them are on the hard menu just below the screen, so you don't even have to look them up in the Edit menu at all. We intend to describe these very briefly.

## DELETING

### ◊G

To delete the character that the cursor is on press ◊G. To delete the character to the left of the cursor press the delete key. You can delete more than one character at a time with the delete key by holding the key down, but be careful because it tends to go faster than you realise and you may end up deleting more than you bargained for. You cannot delete single characters to the right of the cursor.

### ◊D

◊D will delete all the characters between the cursor and the right-hand margin of the column that you are working in. If you put the cursor at the beginning of the row or line and press ◇D, you will delete whatever text is there without getting rid of the line. This saves you having to insert another line, as you would if you used ◇Y.

## ◇T

◇T will delete all the characters from the cursor position, right, to the next space. So you can use it to delete either a whole word or part of a word.

## ◇Y

◇Y or ◇ DEL will delete the whole line that the cursor is positioned on, across all the columns.

## ◇EDRC

◇EDRC will delete the row that the cursor is on, but only in that one column.

## ◇EDC

◇EDC will delete the whole column. therefore you will lose everything that was in it. BE CAREFUL. You can achieve nearly the same effect by changing the column's width to zero with ◇W. The major difference is, however, that if you collapse a column with ◇W you can recover what was in it later by changing the width back.

## INSERTING

Inserting characters, words, lines of text and even whole paragraphs is generally very easy. The machine will move everything else forward one character for every character you add. So all you have to do is type away and leave the machine to worry about the rest of the text.

---

TIP: Accidentally putting the machine into overtype mode
The only time it won't work like that is if you accidentally put the machine into overtype mode. You can do this two ways. Firstly by selecting

'overtype' on the insert/overtype option in the PANEL and secondly by pressing ◊V.

Changing the PANEL setting will not change the mode on the present ac-tivity because it will only be actioned on new activities. This is very bewildering when it happens because there you are with a brand new ac-tivity which is behaving very strangely and it doesn't appear to relate to anything that you could have done. The fact that two days ago you did something to the PANEL won't even enter your head!

Changing the mode to overtype in PIPEDREAM by pressing ◊V is easier to do but slightly - only slightly mind you! - less puzzling because it relates to something you have just done even if you did not mean to.

**TIP: Toggles - ◊V is a toggle:**
It changes insert to overtype and overtype to insert. If you press ◊V by mistake the mode will be changed and you will either be knocking one character out for every new one you insert, or inserting characters when you actually wanted to overtype. Of course if you are just typing text in when you press ◊V you won't notice anything different until you try to alter it or add something into the text that is already there.

DEF. A TOGGLE IS A SWITCH WHICH HAS TWO POSSIBLE SET-TINGS.

**TIP: How to check which mode you are in.**
Your first port of call is the Options page which you can get to either via the options menu or by pressing ◊O. There, on the extreme right hand column on the second row down it will tell you whether you are in insert or overtype. If you are in the wrong one pressing ◊V will change the mode regardless of what the panel is set to. It might however be a good idea to check the panel settings too, either via the INDEX or with ☐S, because if that is the culprit and you don't change it you will have the same problem every time you start a new activity.

## ◊N

◊N will insert a clear line at the line where the cursor is across however many columns you are using. This in effect pushes the rest of the text down one line. ENTER will give you the same effect but only at the bottom of the activity. If you press ENTER in any other place in the activity it will behave like a cursor key and move the cursor to the beginning of the next line.

So if you wanted to insert a new paragraph into some existing text all you would have to do is to use ◇N put in a couple of extra blank lines and type the new text into them.

## ◇U

◇U is the insert command which will insert a space at the cursor position you only need to use it if you have put the machine into overtype mode.

## ◇EIP

◇EIP will insert a new page.

The normal page length is set at sixty six lines which is determined by the page length option on the option page. You can change it by typing another number into that option.

If the piece of work needs the next part to be printed on a separate page then ◇EIP will insert a page break for you.

A normal page break is shown by a zigzagged line which extends across the screen and cuts through the left hand margin where the row numbers are. A page break that you have inserted will be shown on the screen in the same way but it will stop at the left hand margin and will not cut through it.

You can also ask the machine for a conditional page break. You can, via the 'specify no. of unbroken lines' option that comes up when you call up ◇EIP, tell the system that you want the rest of the text put onto a new page if there is less than the specified number of lines left on the present page. If PIPEDREAM decides you do not need a new page because it has more than the specified number of lines left, it will put a ~ and the number of lines you specified at the beginning of column A. Although the symbol and number appear on the screen they do not appear on the page map and will not be printed as part of the activity. They will however, stay with the activity even after you have filed it. If later on, you added some more text above the conditional page break and there was no longer the specified number of clear lines PIPEDREAM would automatically put in a page break for you.

## ◇EIC

◇EIC will insert a new column to the left of the column containing the cursor. Once the new column has been created the cursor will move into it. It will be the normal twelve characters wide until you alter the width with ◇W and ◇H.

## ◇EIRC

◇EIRC will insert a new row just into the column where the cursor is situated.

## ◇EAC

◇EAC will add a new column to the right of your working area. The system initially give you six columns to work with but it can handle up to forty columns altogether so you should have plenty of scope! Unless you need each column to be two characters wide however, you may have difficulty getting your printer to print it in one go because it would be more than eighty characters a line! There is a way of printing an activity file in sections a bit at a time. If you want to know more, turn to the Print section.

# Manoeuvring Text

The next four commands are used to change the text and sometimes numbers into a different format to the one they were put into the machine. They are very much used by us.

## ◇S

◇S tells the machine to swap the case of the character that the cursor is positioned over. Compared with other word processor packages we have used this is very easy to use. Mind you, it probably has to be because with the CAPSLOCK key so close to the cursor keys everyone gets more uppercase characters than they really want! Nonetheless it is nice to be able to action the change in case so easily.

## ◇ESL

◇ESL splits a line of text into two. The line will be split from the cursor position and everything from there to the right hand margin will be moved down to the left hand margin of the line below

## ◇EJL

◇EJL will join two lines together. The cursor has to be placed on the first line. PIPEDREAM will move the line from below up to that line. If the new line is longer than a normal line and disappears underneath the page map don't worry, it is still there and you can get to it with the cursor. You will find that if you edit that line further, or the lines above that, it will sort itself out automatically. If, by the end of the paragraph you have still got half a line hidden from view, you can use ◇R to prompt PIPEDREAM to get on with it!

## ◇R

◇R Is the command which will reformat your current activity from the cursor position to the end of the paragraph. It will reformat a paragraph at a time. Normally PIPEDREAM formats your work as you are typing text in, and even when you add text into the paragraph it normally does it all for you. But if you have deleted something like three quarters of a line you could be left with a gaping hole in your nice neat text. This can also happen on a smaller scale if you have typed in two words without a space between them at the end of the line, the wrapping system will decide that it is too big and move both words down to the next line even if there really is room for one of the words. When you have corrected it, if you return the cursor to the beginning of the paragraph and press ◇R PIPEDREAM will re-look at all the wrapping points and sort it all out.

---

TIP: Separating Paragraphs - You must allow one clear line between paragraphs to show PIPEDREAM where one finishes and the next one starts. PIPEDREAM considers that any of the following will show it where the end of a paragraph is.

> A space at the beginning of the line,
> An expression cell[slot],

> A place where you have requested any form of alignment e.g. right-alignment or a centred heading - details in Layout section -

◇R will stop if it hits any of these.

But if you don't use one of these to show where one paragraph ends and another one begins ◇R will join them all together into one great long scroll of text.

---

**TIP : Using ◇R Instead of ◇EJL**
You can however, sometimes turn this feature to your advantage because as long as there aren't any of the things listed above in the way, you can use this command instead of ◇EJL to join broken lines together. Especially where you have done a list of things and then decide you want them in normal prose format because ◇ R will do the whole lot in one go whereas ◇ EJL will only deal with joining two lines at a time.

---

DON'T USE ◇R IF YOU ARE WORKING IN A MULTI COLUMN ACTIVITY - it sends the layout haywire!

When using ◇R, you may compress the text, leaving spare lines at the end of the paragraph. These can be deleted in the normal way with ◇Y.

## ◇ENT

◇ENT will change a text cell[slot] into an expression cell[slot] and vice versa. This has several uses as well as enabling you to correct potential disasters when you have put something into the machine in the wrong sort of cell[slot]!

If you have got formulae in expression cell[slot]s they are normally hidden from view. You only actually see the answers in the spreadsheet not the calculations, so if you want them displayed either on the screen or on a printout you have to use ◇ENT to change either selected ones or all of them to text cell[slot]s. Before typing in the command however you must save the activity because it will never be the same again! Mark what you want to look at, because if you don't the command will only take effect on the one cell[slot] that the cursor is situated on. Then you type ◇ ENT. Any text will be displayed as typing errors but all the formulae should be clearly visible on the screen. You may have to widen the column widths with ◇W so that you can see the complete formulae.

## ◇K and ◇X

Although these both appear on the edit menu we are not going to cover them here because they are spreadsheet commands and they will be covered elsewhere.

## ◇J

◇J is the next option command. It seems to be the odd one out in this menu because it has nothing to do with editing text at all!! It acts like a toggle on any command or option within a command.

◇J therefore enables you to check what options - if any - are available on any one command. You can do this by going into the menu, putting the cursor over the command you are unsure of and pressing ◇J. The next available option will then be put against the command. For example if the default setting to a command was y for yes ◇J would tell you that the next option was n for no - that one is fairly obvious but there are some more obtuse ones!

# FILES

The Files menu contains a list of file commands that you can use from within PIPEDREAM

## ◇FL

◇FL enables you to load a file from the FILER, into a new PIPEDREAM activity. If you ask it to 'load at slot' by typing 'Y' followed by the slot co-ordinates it will load the file into the existing activity at that point. If you

give it the cell[slot] co-ordinates of where you want the new file to go, or
if you don't give it any co-ordinates, it will load the file at the current cursor position.

You can load a file without typing in the full name by pulling the name
out of the FILER. To do this type in ◇FL and then go into the FILER
with ☐F, position the cursor over the file you want and press ENTER
which will mark it. If you then press 'ESC' PIPEDREAM will pick up
the file name for you automatically and put it into the 'name of file to load'
space.

If you are already in an activity - not a clear copy of PIPEDREAM - and
you ask it to load in a file without asking it to insert it at a particular
cell[slot] PIPEDREAM will ask you whether you want to over-write the
text that is already there. Approach with caution. If you type "Y" it will
erase whatever you had in the activity and put in the new file - which would
leave you in the same situation as with the ◇BNEW.

If you are short of memory and the file is too big to fit in, the system will
only load in part of the file if it loads anything at all! It will then put a
'memory full' message on the comment line.

---

**TIP: Managing Your Memory**
**If you run short of memory in whatever it is you are doing, to carry on
you will have to find the machine some more memory to work with. You
will either have to put in some additional memory in Ram - in other words
spend lots of pennies! - or release some of the existing memory.**

**To reclaim memory, your first port of call will be the INDEX because,
providing you have been good little people, you should have a copy of all
your suspended activities in the Filer as well as backed up elsewhere. So
you can ◇KILL all activities apart from the one you are working in.**

**If PIPEDREAM still says it hasn't got enough memory things get a lit-
tle more drastic! You will then have to go into the Filer and start pruning
your files. Any of the unimportant files you should erase. If you are like
us, you collect files like magpies. We know that we keep everything just
in case! "Think of all the work you would have to do typing all that stuff
back in again if we erased it" is always the argument for not erasing anything. But if you are honest with yourself there are files that you have
started and never finished, or did in note form, or routine letters that
you wrote because you had to but which nobody ever keeps even if they**

read them. You can take it from us, you can get ruthless with these and erase them quite safely without ever missing them again.

Of course there will be the ones that you cannot afford to lose like the company accounts or the diary with the next total eclipse of the sun! But provided you have got them backed up in a retrievable form, e.g., on EPROM or tape and not just a hard copy on paper which you would have to type in again to work with, there is no real problem.

The system we have worked out for ourselves, but don't always keep to, is this! Only keep activities suspended while you are actually working with them or are going to have to work with them very shortly. Keep back ups of those in the FILER, together with files that are no longer suspended but you might need to work with again. Keep copies of all the files in the FILER on whatever backup medium you use, together with an archive of all the files that you have finished with.

If you do this you are covered even if you have to do a soft or a hard reset, provided you have done a back up a comparatively short time beforehand. Since you have no prior warning of a problem which may force a reset on you, it pays you to do your back ups regularly.

To get back to the file load command!

If you know you are short of memory before you try to load a file, you can save yourself time in the short term by telling PIPEDREAM to only load a specific section of the file. You can do this with the 'limit range to load' option. You type in the two cell[slot] co- ordinates of the beginning and end of the section you want to work with.

We have never used this option ourselves and question its usefulness be - cause unless you have a phenomenal memory or are the sort of person who writes these things down, if you cannot see the file it would be very difficult to guess the co-ordinates of the part you want.

## Loading as Plain Text

DEF.: PLAIN TEXT IS A FILE STRIPPED OF ALL WORDPROCESSOR AND SPREADSHEET FUNC- TIONS LEAVING JUST BARE TEXT

There are very few occasions where you would load a file into an activity as plain text. You would use it if you had written a file in PIPEDREAM which is actually a list of instructions to tell the Z88 what to do, for example, if you have created a list file which links several PIPEDREAM files together (see list files later in this section). You would also use it if you wanted to transfer the file to another computer which perhaps uses another wordprocessing package and doesn't need PIPEDREAM's special characters.

## ◊FS

◊FS is the file save command, which is the way you copy your whole activity to the FILER. If you have already given the activity a name when you first started working with the new copy of PIPEDREAM with ◊FC then that name will automatically appear in the 'name of file to save' space. You can of course change that name to something different if you want to, especially if you have already saved a previous copy and want to keep the two versions separate.

You do not however have to save the whole activity because there are several different ways you can define which part of the file you want to save.

You can save a range of columns by changing the relevant No to Yes and typing in the letter of the first and last columns that you want saved.

You can also save a selection of rows by giving PIPEDREAM a conditional statement to work with. A condition statement is where you tell PIPEDREAM that you want it to carry out the command only if it finds what you have told it to look for. In this case you can say what you want it to look for and to only save that row if it finds it. It is a very powerful tool because it is so versatile. You can ask it to only save names beginning with S or all people living in Canada out of your address list. But because you type the instructions in in expression format it can also deal with figures. So you could ask it to save those people who brought items worth more than £50 from your herbal remedies catalogue and haven't paid you yet! You can even ask it to look for a combination of things. It can therefore help you if you wanted to have a credit clampdown in Canada and it was the S's turn to have pins stuck into them!!! You could even ask it to save only those people on your address list whose name begins with S, lived in Canada and who owe you £50 or more. It can also cope with saving the row if it has got someone EITHER whose name begins with S OR living in Canada OR owing you money.

If it doesn't find what it is looking for that row won't be saved and it will move down to the next row and start again. Such a procedure would normally be carried out on a table, list or spreadsheet where you can easily pinpoint the information you want to extract via Cell[slot] co ordinates.

To give you a taste of what you need to put here - supposing we have got these things in our database:

Name            - in Column A
Country         - in Column B
Money           - in Column C

To save people beginning with S, living in Canada and owing more than £50, type -

A1 = S ^ # & B1 = "Canada" & C1 > 50

What you are telling PIPEDREAM to do is save any row which has, anything in column A which begins with an S (wildcards again!) - Canada in B (text in expression cell[slots] has to be in inverted commas) - and a figure greater than £50 in C.

We will be coming across conditionals again and again throughout this book so you will have plenty of time to get acquainted with them.

You can also save just a marked block providing you have marked it with ◊Z at the top and bottom first!

If you do take any of these options don't forget to change the file name if you already have a copy filed. For those of you who haven't read all the book - naughty, naughty, - if you don't call it another name it will save it under the original name and overwrite the whole file that was already in the FILER.

## ◊FC

◊FC has already been talked about as the way to name all your activities. It is worth noting here, however, that the name you give an activity, either by ◊FC or with ◊FL, will be put onto the "file" space at the top right hand corner of the options page of that activity. The file name does not however have to be the same (although it can be) as the title of the document which also had a space on the options page: you can use that in the header/footer of every page. The file name will also be shown on the INDEX alongside that activity.

The other commands on the Files Menu facilitate fast movement between files which are joined together in a list file. So, before we can tell you about those we'd better explain what a list file is.

---

**TIP: List Files**
**A list file is a file which contains a list of other files that are linked together so that you can move between files on the list without going through the normal file load and save procedures.**

---

There are two main reasons for creating a list file apart from convenience. Firstly you can save computing time and secondly you can save memory space by linking files together in this way. If you are working in an activity that is large and likely to grow larger the Z88 begins to slow down. Even if you turn the page map off on the PANEL and the automatic calculate option off on the Options Page - which will help - it will still slow down proportionately to the size of the activity. So if you break your large activity into several smaller ones you can avoid this because the machine will not be handling all the data all the time.

However, if you were just breaking the activity down into smaller chunks, but were still working with a lot of them all the time, you would need to keep them all as suspended activities. You should also have back up copies in the FILER - that would mean that you are using two lots of memory which is often in short supply. A list file enables you to cut down the amount of memory you are using by only loading one file into the suspended activity at a time, but allowing you to have access to any of the other files in the list, as easily as you would if they were suspended activities in their own right. If you are working on one file in the list and you wanted to move to another, PIPEDREAM will automatically save the one you are working on and load the next one into the suspended activity -so you are only using one suspended activity for however many files you have in the list

To put files into a list file

1 Create the files you want to go into the list if you haven't already got them. If there isn't anything in them yet it doesn't matter as long as the files exist in the FILER. Just pull out as many copies of PIPEDREAM as you want and save each one under a different name. Remember to ◇KILL the copies of PIPEDREAM once each file has been saved.

2 Get another copy of PIPEDREAM for the list file - you could use ◇BNEW. Type in the names of the files you want in a list form, i.e. one after the other with each one on a separate line. Make sure they are in the order that you want the files to follow each other. DO NOT LEAVE ANY BLANK LINES ANYWHERE and especially not at the end of the list. They are:

    a) not needed and
    b) WILL MAKE PIPEDREAM GO WRONG!

3 Save that file as PLAIN TEXT with .L on the end of the name.

4 Now just load the list file but without the .L on the end of the name.

And HEY PRESTO! You should then see the first file on the list being loaded in. You can check which file you are in by looking at the file name on the OPTION PAGE. Press ◇O, the file name will be at the top of the right hand column alongside "file".

---

**TIP: Editing your .L file**
**If you need to edit your list file later all you have to do is load the file with the .L on the end of the name. YOU MUST LOAD IT AS PLAIN TEXT. If you forget your top margin will only show column A, and you may not be able to see any of the file names that go further than the begin-ning of column B. If that has happened press ◇BNEW, type "Yes" to overwrite text and start again - loading the file in as PLAIN TEXT this time!**

**When you have finished editing the file, carry on from instruction 3 above as before.**

---

Now we can get back to the Files Menu because this is where the rest of the commands come into their own.

## ◇FN

◇FN is the 'next file' command. Once you are in your list file you can use this to move you down to the next file down on your list. First PIPEDREAM will check to see whether you updated it. If you haven't changed anything it will immediately load in the next file on the list. But if you have done anything with the activity PIPEDREAM will automatically save it to the FILER for you before loading the next file.

## ◇FP

This is the 'previous file' command and will move you up to the previous file on the list provided you are not on the top one! Again it will automatically save the file you have been working on before loading.

## ◇FT

This is the 'top file' command. It will save the file you are in and load the file at the top of your list into the suspended activity.

## ◇FB

This is the 'bottom file' command and does the opposite to ◇FT! There are occasional problems with this one because it works sometimes and not others. It will get down so far and then put 'bad file name' in the comment line. As soon as a problem like this arises the machine automatically abandons the list file to preserve what is already there, so you will have to reload the list file in. Before you do that, load the list file in again with .L, as plain text, just to check there is not anything wrong about the file name that sent ◇FB round the twist! If you can't see anything wrong, load the list file without the .L again and take it down to the bottom file manually i.e., with multiple ◇FNs. If that works OK then you know that it was ◇FB putting a spanner in the works. If however, PIPEDREAM still chucks you out of the list file (you'll know it has happened if you try one of the above commands and PIPEDREAM puts 'no list file' on the comment line after telling you you've got a 'bad file name') you might have to do some research!!

Both ◇FT and ◇FB are slower than we expected because they do not go straight to the top or bottom of the list but load all the files in between first although you do not see them on the screen. But it is still quicker to do it that way than type in ◇FN or ◇FP as many times as you have files.

# LAYOUT

The layout menu has three quite separate sets of functions. The first group of commands control the columns' widths and the margins. The second group deal with the alignment of text. The third group are a group of miscellaneous spreadsheet commands.

Before we do any of these however, we want to talk about hard spaces! You can obtain a hard space by pressing ◇SPACE which tells the Z88 that you want a space which cannot be altered when all the other spaces are. For example, if you reformat a paragraph you may push a word onto the next line which should be linked to the one before and which is now stuck on the end of the previous line.

We believe that the place that hard spacing comes into its own is in sorting out the layout because, if you are using the aligning commands but these do not quite give you the desired effect, you can put in some hard spaces which will allow the aligning commands to think they are still doing what they were asked to do and at the same time give you the precise effect that you want.

For example, say on your letter heading you wanted to put your address on the right hand side of the page. The most straightforward way of doing that would be by moving the cursor to the position where you want each line to start manually. But that is quite a long-winded way of doing it and all those blank spaces sometimes cause problems - especially if you are searching for multiple spaces.

Another way of doing it is to type the whole address on the left hand side, mark it with ◇Z and then right-align the whole block with ◇LAR. You will then have the address at the right place, but it will be aligned on the last letters on the line rather than the first, which will give you a jagged left-hand edge to your address.

> Cats Whiskers
> Wishing-well Lane
> Adderbury
> Berks

like that - which is not what you need at all!   You can get the correct layout by putting hard spaces at the end of the shorter rows to bring the left hand edges level.

> Cats Whiskers
> Wishing-well Lane
> Adderbury
> Berks

By doing it this way you are ensuring that the layout will not be affected by any other command that you may use not realising that it may alter the layout. Unless of course you cancel the right- align command with ◊LAF

# Widths and margins

You have two separate commands here which are not linked together. We suspect PIPEDREAM's authors thought doing it that way would give us users a greater range of options, but it is a bit of a pain because you really have to use both the width and margin commands together.

## ◊W

◊W controls the amount of space a column takes up on a page, which we think is another way of saying that it alters the gaps between the columns - which is what we said earlier, we hope!

## ◊H

◊H alters the right hand margin of each column individually which is shown by the down arrow on the top border line of your displays. You can specify the column you want to change but if you don't it will change the margin of the column that the cursor is situated in.

You can also alter the margin with ☐ ⇐ and ☐ ⇒. ☐ ⇐ moves the margin one character's width to the left and ☐ ⇒ does the same thing to the right.

If you don't use the width command and the right margin setting commands together you are asking for problems. If your margin is set inside the column you will see the text that you have put in after the margin on the screen, but it will not appear on your page map and will not be printed. If your margin is set somewhere beyond the column width and there is text or figures in the adjacent column you will be able to edit it because the line will scroll to the left, but you won't see the bit that goes underneath the next column and it won't be printed. If there is nothing in the next column however, you will see through the empty column to your text and it will be printed. So the problems will only start if you are working with more than one column.

If you set 'wrap' to yes on the Options Page your problems will be compounded. For example, if you double the width without changing the margin setting for that column, you would end up with your cursor dropping to the next line half way across the column - which is particularly annoying if you are working in a database activity and only want the entry to take up one line! If you have wrap turned off you will, as mentioned above, still see it on the screen but it won't be printed.

# Aligning Text

The aligning commands help you to put the finer touches on what would otherwise be a boring activity - not content, just looks! You can re-align text and/or results of expression cell[slot]s over the width of the column.

You can use any of these commands in two ways. If there is a marked block when you call up one of them, the command will be actioned on the entire block. If there is no marked block the command will only be actioned on the cell[slot] that the cursor is situated on. So if you are only using column A then it will align the whole row that the cursor is on.

Text is normally left-aligned with the left hand side of the screen and expression cell[slot] values are normally aligned to the right hand margin.

Anything that has been aligned in any direction with any of the commands listed below will not be touched by ◇R, the Reformat paragraph command. This means that if you do not want a particular section's layout altered (even if it is already left aligned as normal), you can still ask PIPEDREAM to left-align it to ensure that it remains intact. It will remain unaltered even if you reformat all the paragraphs.

It is worth noting here that while the cursor is occupying any row that you have specified to be aligned, the row will revert to its normal position on the page and you will not see the effect of the aligning until you have moved the cursor off that row.

## ◇LAL

◇LAL is the left align command which means that either text or figures will be aligned with the left hand edge of the column.

## ◇LAR

◇LAR is the right align command which will align everything to the right hand margin in that column.

## ◇LAC

◇LAC is the centring command. It centres the text between the start of the column and its right hand margin

## ◇LAF

◇LAF is the free align command which cancels any alignment in the cell[slot] that the cursor is in. After using it text will be left aligned as normal but the values in the cell[slots] will be left aligned too as opposed to right aligned as they would be normally.

## ◇LLCR

◇LLCR is the left-centre-right align command. Do we hear steam coming out of your ears? It did out of ours when we first heard about this one! How can it align something in three different ways at the same time? Well the answer is it doesn't. You have to split whatever it is you are aligning up into three separate segments. These have to be separated in some way so that PIPEDREAM knows what you want put where. The system that was chosen was a spectacularly simple one. It says you have to use a character as a delimiter i.e., a character that PIPEDREAM recognises as a separator and not as a character. Where are we going to find one of those? Well PIPEDREAM's authors must have asked the same question because they came up with a solution that took them off the hook and put you onto it! They have left it up to you! They have written in a rule which says that the first character on the line, or all the lines of a marked block, will be the delimiter. It must be a character that you are not using as a character in that line. The easiest one to use is / unless you want it as part of the text but you can literally use any character you like.

The important thing to remember is that you must have your chosen delimiter, at the beginning of the line, after whatever you want left aligned, after what you want centred, and at the end of the line

So if you wanted to use X as your delimiter, and you wanted 'Z88 book' on the left, 'The Cauldron, Part Two' in the centre and 'Page 1' on the right, you would type in -

XZ88 BookXThe Cauldron, Part TwoXPage 1X

You would then type in ◊LLCR and you should end up with a line that looks like this -

Z88 Book                    The Cauldron, Part Two                    Page 1

---

**TIP: @ Fields - If this was a real header, or footer for that matter, you would not actually put Page 1 in like that because you would not want page 1 at the top of every page! PIPEDREAM has the facility to pull in - formation out of other places and insert it where you want. It can pull the current page number and title - from the current activity's option page, the current date - from the clock, and the value in any cell [slot] - from the current activity.**

**To do any of these you tell PIPEDREAM where you want to put them into the activity by enclosing it between @s So if you wanted the current page number inserted you would put @p@. If you wanted the title you would put @t@, and if you wanted the current date you would put @d@ and**

if you wanted the value of a cell[slot] you would enclose that cell[slot]'s co-ordinates between two @s.

We have just found out that to actually print out @p@ rather than the current page number, every @ you want to show as itself has to be doubled. It took us a couple of minutes to work out what the machine was playing at because 50 appeared in the above paragraph when we moved the cursor off the line! It then dawned on us, that it was just doing what it was told. We are actually on page 50 in the manuscript!

The most obvious place to use ◊LLCR is for headers or footers on a page and, surprise, surprise, PIPEDREAM has been pre-programmed to use that format - see Option Page.

# Fixing Rows and Columns

## ◊LFR and ◊LFC

These two commands allow you to either to fix a row or a column (or both together) so that they stay on the display while the rest of the activity still scrolls up and down as normal. These are very useful if you have a large table of columns because you can keep the headings and row labels in view even if they are really a long way off the screen. You can see when you have used this function by a solid line in the relevant row or column margin, but only if you are using the borders. You can unfix them again by calling up the command a second time.

These commands play havoc with the page map display on the right of your screen. They also disable the page counter which keeps track of what page you are on and puts it into the Option page. So these cannot be relied on while the fixing commands are in force. As soon as they are turned off however, these should go back to working normally - once they have been given time to recover! If you are working with a large activity it may help the page counter if you return to the beginning of the activity so that it can get its bearings!

This page intentionally left blank

# OPTION

The Options menu has only one command ◊O which puts you into the Options Page. You don't really need to go through the menu because the shorthand command is quicker to use.

The Options Page has two distinct functions. The first one, which takes up the left and the two middle columns, acts like a control box for that particular activity. There are a number of toggles and other forms of controls that allow you to say how you want the activity displayed both on the screen and on the printout. The second section takes up the fourth and fifth column. This is the notice board which contains important facts about the current activity.

## The Control Box

### Text/Numbers

This is normally set to T for text and indeed must be left like that if you are wordprocessing. If you change it to N for numbers the system will turn every cell[slot] into an expression cell[slot] and put everything you input up onto the Expression Edit Line. Which is definitely not where you want to see your text! But it is ideal if you are working solely with figures because it makes ◊X redundant.

### Borders

Borders are the markers on the screen which tell you where you are on the page, i.e. the column and row numbers. They are normally turned on - set to yes, and you get your normal screen layout with row numbers down the left hand side and the column labels across the top. When you turn them off you lose all these margins and release a larger area of the screen for you to work in. Normally the screen can show you six lines by seventy two characters wide at any one time. If borders are turned off, i.e. toggled to N, you can get a slightly bigger working area. You will have an extra line on view and you will be able to increase the right hand margin to eighty.

We feel the gain is minimal however although you, of course, may prefer the screen that way. Without borders it is more difficult to use commands like ◊CGS 'go to slot' because you have no idea of the row numbers!

## Justify

If Justify is set to yes it allows you to have the right hand margin as even as the left. PIPEDREAM achieves this by spacing out the words on each row so that all the last characters end at the same point.

The default setting is not to justify the text. Which means that PIPEDREAM will accept the spacing that you put in and wrap any word too big to fit onto the current row down onto the beginning of the next row. Which will mean that, although it will be as close as PIPEDREAM can make it, the right hand margin will be ragged.

## Wrap

This is normally set to yes. If you turn it off PIPEDREAM will not recog-nise when the right hand margin has been reached. Therefore even if the word you are typing in is too long to fit onto the line it won't move down. You have to take the decision to move down to the next row by pressing the ENTER key which takes on the role of a typewriter's carriage return key.

## Page Length

The normal page length if you are using A4 paper in your printer is 66 rows. This is normally divided up to give you fifty four rows for text and twelve rows which are spread between the top and bottom margins - which also have lines available for a header and footer. The Z88 can handle pages of up to one hundred and twenty seven lines - including top and bottom margins - provided your printer can! It can also cope with no page breaks at all. If you set the page length option to zero you will get a con-tinuous scroll of text.

## Line Spacing

This only affects the printout and the layout shown on the page map. It does not alter the row numbers and is not shown in your working area. It is normally set to 1 which will give you single line spacing. You can set it to anything from that to two hundred and fifty five lines between each line of text if you want to. Although we cannot imagine why you would want to waste so much paper!

## Start Page

This option means that you can tell the Z88 what page number you want it to start incrementing page numbers from. We suppose this could be useful if you have a large document which you have split into smaller activities. If, however, you have done that the ideal thing would be to join those activities together in a list file - see FILES MENU Section - which would automatically increment the page numbers of all the files in the list.

If the start page is set at zero however, it allows you to have the first page without a header or footer. When it gets to the next page - page one - the header and footer that you have asked for on the option page will be added to that and every other page. This is an extremely useful facility if you want to put a title page onto your activity because you would not normally want a header and footer on there.

## Insert On Wrap

This one you can toggle between R for rows and C for columns. The normal setting is R which means that when you reach the right hand margin and PIPEDREAM has to wrap the next word down onto the next line it will normally insert a new line for the text to go onto. Which is why, when you are typing text in normally, you are not up against the 'end of text' marker all the time. The only time that PIPEDREAM may not give you a clear line is if you are inserting text into an existing paragraph because you may only be adding a couple of extra characters and not a whole line. In this situation PIPEDREAM will put the cursor at the beginning of the next line of text and push the existing text along to accommodate the new text. If you are working with text that you have split into columns however, you may not want a new line to be inserted across the whole page because each column is a separate entity. So changing the insert on wrap toggle to C will add a line for the cursor to go down to, just in the column that the cursor is in.

## Calc. Auto./Man

This toggle determines whether the expression cell[slot]s in the activity are re-calculated every time an expression slot is altered. They can be altered directly by changing the figures or indirectly by changing an expression cell[slot] somewhere else which refers to, that cell[slot]s. If it is switched to Manual however it will only recalculate when you press press ◇A.

It is normally set to A, but if you are dealing with text you will find that setting this to M will speed the Z88 up no end.

## Columns/Rows

This determines in which direction the re-calculation is done first. It is normally set to C for columns. What you need to set this to really depends on the layout of your spreadsheet because there are some layouts that if you do them in the wrong order. you would get totally the wrong answers the first time round. If this happens to you try re-calculating with ◇A first and then change the column/row option.

The next four controls are similar to those on the Layout menu. They are:- Decimal places - normally set to 2 but you have from one to nine, or F for free, to choose from. Minus/Brackets - normally M, but you can have B for negative numbers to be bracketed instead of having a minus sign in front of them. Leading Characters - normally £, and Trailing Characters - normally % but you can insert up to 4 characters or your choice into either, which will be put before or after expression cell[slot]s.

Although these are identical options to the commands from the final column of the LAYOUT menu, if you change them here they will affect every expression cell[slot] in the activity. If you change them with any of the LAYOUT commands only the expression cell[slot] that the cursor is in or those in a previously marked block will be altered from what they have been set to here on the Options Page.

# Margins

The Margin options only affect the page layout when the activity is printed. They will not be visible in your working area although they will be represented on your Page Map.

If you have set your Page Length to 66 and you set all the other margins to 0, PIPEDREAM would give you 66 lines to put text into. The way the margins are normally set up however, will only give you fifty four lines for text. The other twelve lines are distributed between the margins that you have at the top and bottom of the page. If you use a header and/or a footer, the lines which they take up will also be taken out of the text area.

## Top Margin

The top margin is the area between the top of the page and the header - any heading that you want put at the top of each page - it is normally set to zero but as with all the margins you can set them to anything from zero to 255 blank lines - 255 seems to be one of the magic numbers when it comes to choices!

## Header Margin

The header margin is whatever gap you want between the header and where the text starts on the page. It is normally set to 0.

## Footer Margin

The footer margin is the area between the end of the text and the footer. It is normally set to 2.

## Bottom Margin

This is the area between the footer and the physical bottom of the page. It is normally set to 8, but the choice is yours!

## Left Margin

The left hand margin can be set here. It is normally set to 0 but as with the others above the maximum width is 255. You would however, need some very special paper sizes and printers to have it that wide! For a letter layout you may want a slightly bigger left margin. We think 5 or 6 looks good and it will also put the address in the right place if you are using window envelopes.

## Headers and Footers

Headfooters for short - sounds like someone got their "better footballing spell" a bit wrong doesn't it?!

Anyway headfooters allow you to give your activity real professional finishing touches. PIPEDREAM will print whatever you put into these spaces at the top and or bottom of every page - except page 0 if the start page option is set to 0. Both headers and footers have to be put into the Option page in the same format as you would use for ◊LLCR. Remember that one? If not, miss a go and go back three sections! No seriously, Layout is where it's all at so you might need to have another look.

The headfooters are divided into three sections so that you can specify what you want on the left, what you want centred and what you want on the right. This is achieved by splitting them up with delimiters, remember them? You can choose any character you like to act as a separator. If it's a "/" it has to go at the beginning of the line, at the end of what you want on the left, at the end of what you want centred, and at the end of your chosen headfooter. You of course cannot use "/" as part of the head-footer because it will treat it as a delimiter, count the first four "/" as the split points, and get the whole thing wrong! As you can choose any character we are sure that you will be able to find one to put at the beginning of the line as a delimiter that you are not using in the headfooter itself.

To put things like the title that are already on the OPTION PAGE into the headfooter you can use our old friends the @ fields. These are extremely useful for things like page numbers that are changing a great deal - see tip on @ fields.

# The Notice Board

## File

Where you give your current activity a name, it will be put into this space. A new activity can be named with ◊FC, or an activity that you have already stored in the FILER would have been named when you saved it with ◊FS.

PIPEDREAM will also put that name into 'your ref' against the relevant suspended activity in the INDEX, and insert it into the ◊FS 'file to save' slot.

Incidentally if it comes up with 'no file' in this space don't panic! It doesn't mean the activity you are working on has been spirited away, it just means you haven't named that activity yet. We reckon this space should have been called either File name or just Name. That might have made it clearer.

## Page

This shows you the current page that the cursor is on and how the pages will be numbered on the printout. It will not work properly, however -

a. If you are using the Fix Row command from the LAYOUT Menu;

b. If the page length option on the Option Page has been set to Zero.

The fix row ◊LFR command enables you to keep a row or a small group of rows from one page on view alongside rows from any other page in the activity. So it's a small wonder that PIPEDREAM gives up trying to decide which page you are really on!!

When you set the page length to zero, because you have asked for no page breaks, there will be no page numbers.

## Free

This normally displays an astronomical number! Our Z88 at the moment is reading 115465 which is pretty meaningless. It is supposed to indicate how much memory you have free for storing characters. But in practice it appears to bear little resemblance to how full the memory is. You can have thousands in the Free space but when you save the activity the Z88 comes up with 'no room' on the comment line. So we recommend that you use it purely as a very rough guide to the amount of memory you have left.

The only time you ought to take notice is if the figure is very low. Below 300 and you are then on the verge of running out of usable memory. You are then advised to start looking for activities and files that you can kill or erase. This will give you some more memory to work with.

## Title

A title, whether this is the same as the file name or something different, can be added here as long as it is no longer than 244 characters. This can then be picked up by @T@ - yes them again - and used either within the activity or in the headfooter.

## Insert/Overtype

The final column on this page normally just holds one word. Either 'insert' or 'overtype' and it tells you which of these modes you are currently in.

## Microspace

We said above that the final column only holds one entry. Well normally it does! The only time it doesn't is if you have asked for the printer to use microspaced print. Then microspace appears below insert/overtype.

# Page Layout

When you start a PIPEDREAM program, it loads in a set of 'default' values into the options page to allow you to start using the Program straight away. Sometimes however these options do not give the desired effect, if the text appears to be over to one side when printed, or the text from one page goes over to the next page before it should do and so on.

This section shows you how to design your very own page layout in just three simple steps.

Step 1 Print a page full of numbers to show where all the characters get printed.

Step 2 Designing your layout.

Step 3 Letting PipeDream know about your new layout.

## Step 1 - Print a page full of numbers

The first thing you need to do is to print a page full of numbers to show where the characters get printed on the sheet of paper.

PIPEDREAM actually has built-in margins that are initially set to default settings. Change all these numbers to 0 (zero) so that we can print everywhere.

Here is a 'step by step' account on how to do it.

   a) Get a new copy of PIPEDREAM

   b) Name the file ◊FC. We are going to use "PageLayout.doc"

   c) Select the Options page with ◊O and change the following:-

Page Length to 0            This will give an unlimited page length.

Margins:                    Top 0
                            Header 0
                            Footer 0

Bottom 0
Left 0

d) Leave the options page with ESC

e) Set the Right-hand margin to your printer width e.g. 80 or 132 with ◇H

f) Type across the first line a row of numbers starting with 1 and finishing when you reach the end of the line as indicated by the right-hand margin down-arrow mark on the top border line.

A....................B....................C....................D....................E....................↓F
1234567890123456789012345678901234567890123456789012345678901234567890

g) Copy this line 100 times with the Replicate command ◇BRE.

h) Check that you have a complete page of numbers on your Page Map. If you have:

i) Save the file with ◇FS . If not, start again!

j) Load your printer with paper, making sure that the top of the page is where you would normally load it.

k) Print the page with ◇PO.

You should now either have a page full of numbers or several sheets - well at least 100 lines worth. Number the lines starting with 1 for the top line.

## Step 2 - Designing your layout

Now that you have got a print-out showing where your printer puts all the characters you can design your layout using the following diagram that shows you which margins do what.

To find the Page length, you need to be careful that you have included any top margins your printer may use. The best way of measuring this, is to print two pages and count the number of lines from a point on the first page to the same point on the second page.

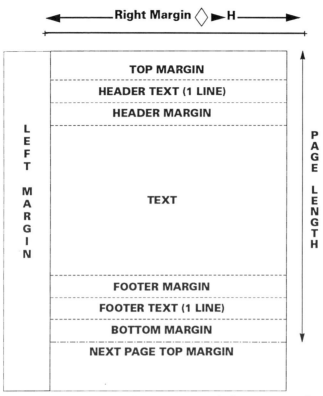

Using this diagram with the printout, you can design your page layout by resetting the margins.

For example, if you wish to use 'window envelopes' you could fold up the sheet of paper you have printed, and see through the window which line and character you see. If it was character number 10 on line 9 in the top left-hand corner of the window, you would make the left-hand margin 7. To get the printer to start on line 10, the total of the Top Margin, Header Line (which is always 1 line) and Header Margin, must add up to 9. This can be achieved in a number of different ways. If you make the Top Margin and the Header Margin the same, say four lines, the header text will be printed in between them.

You can change any of the margins to alter the layout as required - Why not experiment and see what happens!

## Step 3 - Letting PIPEDREAM know about your new layout

After designing where you want your margins to be you need to put this information into a PIPEDREAM file so that you can load it in when you want to use this layout again.

To do this you need to get another copy of PIPEDREAM by either select - ing ◇BNEW on the previous PIPEDREAM program or by getting a new copy of PIPEDREAM.

You should then name the file ( ◇FC) with a name that reflects what you would use the layout for. Taking the window envelope example again you might choose a name like "window.env".

Just put the numbers into the Options page ◇O for the following mar- gins:-

Page Length

Top
Header
Footer
Bottom
Left

leave the Options page with ESC and set the Right-hand margin ◇H to whatever you want it to be.

You should now have what looks like an empty PIPEDREAM file - with nothing on line 1. But there is something in it - your layout settings. Save it with ◇FS ENTER.

So there you have it. To use these settings in another file you need to load the layout file into PIPEDREAM before starting the new file. It is best to change the name of the file (with ◇FC) straight after loading the layout file. Doing this will prevent you saving the new file as the layout file name accidentally.

# PRINT

The PRINT MENU gives you the print command and its various options, which are on the first column. The second and third columns gives you the means to tell the Printer when you want something printed different-ly to normal. They are grouped together as Highlight Codes. We have already touched on these briefly in the section on Search and Replace. This is where we go into all the gory details!

## The Print Command and its Options

### ◇PO

◇PO is the main print command. It will print all or part of your current activity and allows you to access some of the extra features available on your printer.

You have three options with this command. They are all normally set to "No" and unless you change that PIPEDREAM will send the whole ac-tivity to the printer.

The first one is 'print only range of columns'. If you want to print a lon-gitudinal slice of your activity this option needs to be set to "Yes" after it. You can tell PIPEDREAM which columns you want printed by putting in two column labels, the one you want it to start at followed by the one to finish at, with a space in between.

## 'Select Rows To Print'

The 'select rows to print' option is not what it seems - Ah Ha more magic, and this lot is really powerful stuff! This is a not a block print command but a conditional one. It allows you to tell PIPEDREAM to ask a ques-tion about each row in turn and only print it if the answer is what you have told it to look for. Otherwise it will skip that row, move down to the next row and start the procedure all over again.

It might be worth noting here that you are unlikely to use this in a straightforward text activity. You are much more likely to use it on a database or spreadsheet where you have got lists of information in columns format. You will be able to pinpoint the information that you want to print easily with a cell[slot] reference.

To do this you first have to change this option from the normal 'No' set- ting to 'yes' and then you have to tell PIPEDREAM what you want it to look for. You can type this into the space after the Yes in the form of an expression or formula which can be as simple or complicated as you care to make it. When devising the formula you ask it to deal with the top line and PIPEDREAM will then automatically increment the row numbers so that it will cover every row in the activity. So if you were running a dating agency for witches and warlocks and a witch wrote in asking for a 45-year-old partner you would ask your Z88 to print out only those rows that have have 45 in column B by typing in B1 = 45 you would get a list of all the 45-year-olds on your books - provided column B was where you had stored all their ages of course! If your client also specified that she was looking for a good spellcaster and you had descriptions in column G you would put in B1 = 45 & G1 = "good spellcaster".

---

**TIP: Putting text into expression cell[slot]s**
**Please note that because this is a formula you have to tell PIPEDREAM that 'good spellcaster' is text and not figures. You do this by putting it into inverted commas.**

---

---

**TIP: Conditional And and Or.**
" &" is conditional "and".   " |" is conditional "or". Conditional "and"
tells PIPEDREAM to look for two things that you have asked for on the
row it is looking at before printing that row. Putting conditional "or" in
between will tell PIPEDREAM to print the row as long as it has one of
the things you have asked it to look for.

---

## Wait between pages

This enables you to get the printer to stop printing when it reaches the
bottom of every page. This will give you time to load the next single sheet
if that is what you are using in your printer. It tells you the page number
and waits your wishes. If you press M it will miss a page, C will continue
printing without any more waiting at the page breaks, any other key (except ESC) will start it printing the next page. ESC will tell it to abandon
that particular print run altogether.

There are two other options available which are not on the ◊PO option
display which are actioned depending on what you have done before
pressing ◊PO.

If you have a marked block in the activity when you have called up the
print option PIPEDREAM will only print that block - which is another
reason for clearing any marked blocks with ◊Q after you have finished
with them.

If you ask it to print when you are in a list file PIPEDREAM will first save
the activity that you have been working on and print all the files or activities in the list.  If you only want the file you are working on printed
rather than all those in the list, mark it with ◊Z.

## Microspace

Microspace is only used to enhance justified text.  It automatically
spreads the blank space on each row between the letters as well as the
words. This means that your printouts look more professional. Not all
printers are able to use this facility

When you request microspace from the menu or with  ◊PM the Z88 will
ask you whether you want 'microspace printed output'. If you say yes and
press ENTER the computer will tell the printer that you now want the

printing done in 120th of an inch spaces. Unless you tell it otherwise it will make each character 12/120ths wide and therefore give you ten characters to the inch. You also have the facility to put in another figure by the 'yes' to change the 12 to another number. PIPEDREAM will divide that by one hundred and twenty and give you that number of characters per inch. Therefore, in theory, if you put in 6 you would get 20 characters per inch.

The number you are inputting is called the horizontal motion increment (HMI) which will determine the microspacings. You may have to change these the settings in the PrinterEditor before you can use this command, because some printers require a prefix or suffix. Your printer's manual will tell you whether you can use microspace and what changes you need to make to your PrinterEditor. Your printer may require you to add a number in the "offset" field as well.

## The Highlight Commands

The first thing to note here is that YOU are very much in charge of these codes. Although you have been given a set for an Epson printer, you can change all the settings. This would mean that you have created your own printer driver. We will tell you more about how to do that in the Printer-Editor section.

Even if you leave them as they are you have the extended sequence code space which has not been given a job yet. It is waiting for you to find some - thing for it to do.

With all the highlight commands you must put them at the beginning and end of where you want them. You also ought to be aware that the default setting on the present printer driver is to turn off most of the commands when you reach the end of the cell[slot]. In a text activity where you are only in column A, the end of the cell[slot] is at the end of the line, other - wise it is the right hand margin of the column.

You can check to see whether this will happen on each of the commands or not by seeing if the CR option on page 1 of the PRINTERED is turned to "Yes" or "No". If its yes then it will stop the highlight command at the end of the row. You can do this by going into the INDEX and selecting PRINTERED with the cursor and pressing ENTER, or ☐ E.

While you are in the PrinterEd you can change the default setting if you want to, or you can cover yourself for every eventuality by remembering to put a highlight command at the end of the line and at the beginning of the next one if the area you want highlighted wraps down onto the next row.

The relevant codes will be shown on the screen when the cursor is on that line as a number in a reversed colour block - remember them! They were what you could look for in search and replace with the Wildcard ^ - but when you move the cursor off that row you will see a representation of the print format you have asked for.

## ◇PU

This has been set up as the underline command. It is printer code No.1. It will underline anything as long as there is something there for it to underline.

---

**TIP: Using The Underline Command to Draw a Line.**
**You have to use the underline command to draw a line, because PIPEDREAM won't let you underline an empty space. As a hard space ◇SPACE is treated as a character by PIPEDREAM, put one at the beginning and end of the row. If you underline the space between the hard spaces by putting ◇PU before the first one and after the second your line will appear with nothing on it at all when you print it.**

---

You can of course use the underline command together with other print commands. So you could underline part or all of for example, a bold or italic sequence. The only thing you need to remember is that if you re underlining the whole of the sequence the underline command should go in front of the other print command at the beginning and after the last one at the end. You can however underline the whole sequence and just put one or two words into bold in the middle if you want to.

## ◇PB

This has been set up in the PrinterEditor as the bold print command. It is code 2.

## ◇PX

This is called the extended sequence command. It is code 3. But, if you look in the PrinterEd you will find that there are no translation codes to send it to the printer. This means that if you look through all the things that your printer can do, choose one and (type in the on and off codes) you can make code 3 do what ever you like. For example our printer will print twelve different language fonts so we could decide that we wanted to do a lot of work in French and we wanted highlight code 3 to be the French character set.

---

**TIP: Changing the Print Codes in the PrinterEd.**

Page 1 of the PrinterEd is laid out with the highlight code number - the one you see in the inverted colour blocks on the screen - on the left. Their labels are in the next column followed by two columns of figures. The first column of figures is the code that PIPEDREAM has to send to the printer to tell it to start printing in the different format. The second column of figures are the codes to turn that off and put it into the nor-mal print mode again. So to change any of these all you have to do is decide what you want to change it to, look up the codes your printer needs to to do it and put them into the spaces.

There are three types of code that your Z88 and probably your printer know and can cope with. These are ASCII, DECIMAL and HEXADECIMAL. It does not matter which one you use but you must not mix them up.

So if we wanted to use the French character set in the extended sequence space we would find out what the codes were to turn it on. The decimal ones are 27, 82, 1. With most printer codes there is a specific code to turn it off but with this one there isn't so we will use the code to turn the printer back to the American character set which is 27, 82, 0.

The numbers might be different in you printer manual but the principle is the same.

---

## ◇PI

◇PI Will give you italic print. It is code 4.

## ◇PL

◇PL is the subscript command and is code 5

## ◇PR

◇PR is the superscript command, and is code 6

## ◇PA

◇PA is called the alternative font command and is code 7. However the codes that are already in the PRINTERED are the ones for condensed print mode on our printer.

## ◇PE

◇PE is called the user defined mode and is code 8. But if you look at your printer's manual and check the codes in there with the codes on the PRINTERED we think you will find they tie up. This one, according to our printer, is the letter quality mode. If we change the 1 on the end to a 0 our printer will then go into draft mode. What does your printer manual say?

---

TIP: Using highlighting codes together - You can use more than one of these codes at the same time so you could have something in bold underlined, or could you? Let's try it.

[1] [2] This is a bold sentence which is also underlined! [2] [1]

This is what the line will look like while the cursor is on it.

So how do you do it? There is one simple rule that you need to remember. You must get the codes in the right order. You have to treat them like brackets in maths - if you can remember back that far! The combination of codes you put in to turn the commands on, must be reversed at the end to turn them off. Therefore if you started at the beginning with the underline command then that must be the last one on the end, the second one must be the second last, etc. So at the beginning of the line, when the cursor is on it, you should see [1] [2] in reversed colour blocks. At the end, it should be mirrored so you should have [2] [1]. These numbers are for the highlight codes default settings. If you have changed those, the code numbers may be different, the principle however remains the same.

TIP: Using highlight commands with header/footers

Exactly the same rules apply here as above. The only thing you must do is to make sure that you get the highlight codes the right side of the delimiters. For example if you wanted the centred section in bold and you were using / as the delimiter you would type:

/what you want on the left/[2]centred[2]/what you want on the right/

If you get even one of the highlight codes the wrong side of a delimiter neither of them will work.

## ◇PHI

This is another way of calling up the highlight commands if you prefer to remember them by the code numbers. This would be very useful if you had been adventurous with the PRINTERED and changed all the codes so that they do something different. You cannot change the names of the commands however, either in the PRINTERED itself or on the PIPEDREAM Print menu. So if you change them more than once you might get a bit confused! Although you could make yourself a "hard" menu on paper and stick it..........well somewhere!

## ◇PHR

This is the remove highlight command. It will ask you which number code you want removed but it will only work with a marked block so without one it won't do anything. It will take out every one of the specified com-mands but you must mark the area you want to work with beforehand.

## ◇PHB

This is another block command and it will ask you which highlight you want to work with. This time however it will go through the whole block putting the highlight round each individual word in turn. That way it is not affected by the wrap point or anything else. It is a very quick way of doing what would otherwise be a very tedious job.

# USING PIPEDREAM TO CREATE AND MANAGE A DATABASE

A database is used to record information which is like a card index system. It stores information in such a way that it makes it easy to find what you want quickly.

A database could hold any information you want but it is likely that names and addresses would be part of it, if you are dealing with people. If you are recording something like the effectiveness of one particular spell against a potion that is supposed to do the same thing, you would still need an "address" or code number to identify that particular time of casting the spell as different from the next one. You can of course include a great deal of other information in this way. For example if you were doing research on your spells you would probably not only want to know whether the spell worked or not, but also where and when it was cast, at what strength, whether the person affected believed in your powers, whether the moon was in the right phase, or whether someone else had cast a counter spell to block yours!

When you are designing a database it pays to think carefully about how you are going to divide the information up. Use small enough bits to allow you to get to any part as quickly and easily as possible. At this early stage it is easy to change the format but once you have got any number of "index cards" filled out it may not be so easy and could become a major chore. As a general rule it is better to have everything broken down into small parts, e.g. a name could be split into three parts, title - Mr., Mrs, Sir, etc., first name and surname. You can then sort the surnames into alphabetical order with ◇BSO. You can mark a smaller block where the surnames like Smith are all the same and sort the first names into alphabetical order, and you could do a conditional save or print on the titles if you wanted to sort on sex, although the professional titles, such as Dr. or Prof., might cause a few problems. It is easier to put the sex in a separate column if it is likely to be of interest to you.

There is a problem with this general rule however, because although breaking everything down into the smallest possible pieces will help you cover most eventualities, even the ones you haven't come across yet, it will be extremely greedy in terms of memory. You might therefore have to settle for a compromise and just split it down to the bits you know you are going to need. This is why spending time at the planning stage will pay dividends later.

Since creating a database is essentially inputting and manipulating text and figures, if you have read the rest of the section on PIPEDREAM and used it - perhaps by doing the exercises at the back of the book - working with a database will be a piece of cake. We therefore don't intend to go into all the PIPEDREAM commands that you might want to use again but will just point you in the right direction, give you a push and hope there aren't any vertical cliffs for you to fall down!

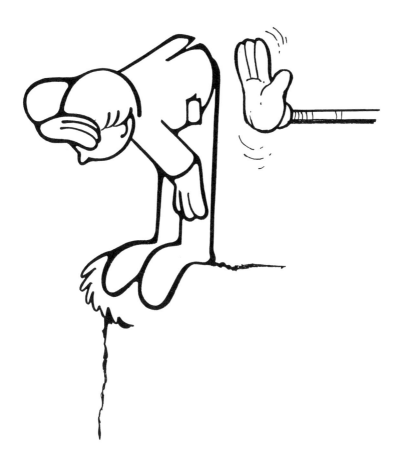

To set up a database within PIPEDREAM you must use one row per record. One of the first things you will have to do is stop anything being wrapped onto the next row. You therefore need to change the wrap option to 'no' on the Option Page. Instead of wrapping down it will just extend the line and push everything to the left as it needs to. If that happens you can either, shorten the entry or, alter the width of that column, or leave it alone. Leaving it alone means that you will only see, or be able to print, part of any columns that are overlaid.

It is then time to divide your page up into as many columns as you have separate pieces of information. Remember that you can change the column widths with ◊W and set the right hand margin of each column with ◊H and, most importantly, you must use these two together. If you need more than six columns you can add as many as you like - as long as it is not more than thirty four extra ones - on the right of your working area with ◊EAC, or you can insert columns to the right of the cursor with ◊EIC. You can have as many as 40 columns each with a maximum of 255 characters in each but you do not have to use all of either of these!

---

**TIP: Filling unused columns.**
**You may sometimes have less things to enter into the'"index card" than columns. Some addresses for example, have more lines then others. Normally that's O.K. but if you have to turn your entries into expressions for mailmerging purposes and leave the spare columns empty, tidy-minded PIPEDREAM will come along and fill them up with "0.00". You don't really need that in the middle of an address! To stop that happening you have to fool PIPEDREAM into thinking that there really is something there. Our old friend the hard space ( ◊SPACE ) does the job nicely although you may then end up with a blank line in the addresses. We think that that is still better than "0.00"!**

---

You may end up with a page wider than your printer can handle. You can always ask PIPEDREAM to print it out a few columns at a time so that you can put it all together with sticky tape afterwards. Your printer may be able to print a condensed font so that it will all fit on the page.

Since you will be putting each piece of information that you want to treat separately into one column of one row in database jargon the information has been divided into "fields". You are in fact using a cell[slot] for each "field" in your record.

You can use cell[slot] commands to help you do a mail merge. Mail merging enables you to write a letter and get your computer to send it to everyone on your database with the appropriate name and address on each one. You will also have to run a CLI routine to do a mail merge. There is a chapter on mail merge later. The combination of

PIPEDREAM and CLI is a very powerful one which will enable the more adventurous amongst you to carry out tasks that are normally only possible on a much larger machine. We will be explaining how CLI works in a later section.

Finally if you have a large database your search command ◇BSE will help you find any "field" if you know what it contains, but don't know where it is. Asking it to just search one column will speed it up.

# PIPEDREAM And Printers

The relationship between PIPEDREAM and your printer may not always be an easy one. PIPEDREAM sometimes gets positively snooty and doesn't take what the printer is doing into account at all. There are some situations where you may have to mediate between them! Otherwise you won't be able to get the effect you have asked for done at all.

PIPEDREAM doesn't take any notice of what size paper you are using or what font you have selected so even if you have selected too many lines - on the Option Page - to fit onto the paper size, PIPEDREAM will gaily carry on sending the text to the printer and it will spill onto the next page. The same thing happens if you ask for a larger font. If this happens to you then you have to take charge! You have to sort out what the printer needs to be sent and alter the page layout accordingly.

So, what sort of problems can you have, and how should you solve them? Let's look at two possible cases. It is assumed here that you have already given the Printer Editor the codes that tell the printer what font you want to use.

## Double Height Lettering

The problem that PIPEDREAM has with Double Height lettering is that it doesn't know - and doesn't want to know either - what font you have asked for. The fact that the double height font uses two lines for every line of text goes clean over PIPEDREAM's head. So it gets the page length all wrong, because if you are using 66 lines (which is 54 "active" lines) to a page, you would only be able to fit 27 active lines of double height lettering on it. The solution, is to count the lines yourself on the page, and insert a ◇EIP Insert Page Command, every 27 lines in this case. We've found that by printing the page first, it is often easier to see where the page breaks should go. If the whole document is being printed in double height, then you could just alter the page length option on the Options Page to 33, half the normal page length.

At the end of each page, PIPEDREAM sends a Form Feed code to your printer. This either ejects the page that you are printing and picks up a new one, or moves continuous stationary to the top of where it thinks the next page starts. If your printer gets this wrong, it could be because the form length has been incorrectly set up on the printer.

Remember that a number of printers can only deal with 11 or 12 inch lengths sheets, whilst an A4 sheet is nearer 11-2/3 inch. See your printer manual for details on what size paper you need to use and what settings you need to have for the page layout for your printer.

## Different Width Lettering

There is a similar problem with changing the width of each character. Your printer can normally fit 80 character on a line, but if you double the width of the characters you will only get 40 on a line. If you are doing a lot of work in this width it will be easier to reset the margin to 40 with ◇H. But if you are not going to do enough to warrant that then you will have to put the carriage returns in yourself. If you are only doing part of the line with the rest of the line in normal sized print the calculations get a bit more complicated. Just count the number of characters you have got, counting the double width ones as two. when you get to 80 split the line with ◇ESL.

# The Printer Editor

The PRINTERED is a separate application. It is used to link the Z88 to your printer. To select it, type ☐E or use the INDEX. It is the translator between codes that are used in the Z88 and the printer. The Printer Editor allows you to change any of these codes so that you can use them with any make of printer. There are two pages of codes in the PRINTERED. The first page of it is so closely linked to PIPEDREAM that we put that bit into the PIPEDREAM print section. So we will only deal with page two here.

But we'll give you the more general information first! All the settings on the PRINTERED are used to make up your printer driver. You can create as many of these as you need to carry out different printing functions or to enable your Z88 to work with different printers. There is a files menu for the PRINTERED to enable you to save a driver's setting. The file load, save. and name change commands are the same as in PIPEDREAM, but ◊FNEW and ◊FU are additional commands.

◊FNEW will reset all the settings to the default, which are the ones for the Epson printer.

◊FU takes the current settings in your editor, updates the printer driver from them and gets everything ready for printing with the new driver.

## Overprinting

Overprinting is where the printer goes over a character twice to achieve a specific effect. If you have got a daisywheel or similar type of printer they sometimes use this facility to underline or to put characters into bold by going over them twice. To achieve this effect you select which high-light commands you need to overprint and change the code. You need to put in a ? which tells the printer to carry out the command after every character - wildcards again - then the backspace and the underscore character codes. So instead of 27, 45, 1. which is the Epson 'ON' under-line code. You could use ?, 08,223 in decimal. This will take you twice as long as the underline command - if your printer has one - but there is nothing to stop you doing it that way. The same is true for bold. Instead of 27, 69 which is the decimal Epson code for bold you could just put ?,08,?. in the bold ON column of the PRINTERED, which would repeat each letter twice.

## Page Two

You can get here by pressing SHIFT + DOWN ARROW. As with the
highlight codes on Page One you will have to work closely with your
printer's manual to sort out the codes that need to be sent by your Z88.
We know it is tedious but it is the only way to get your printer to do what
you want.

Both the pages are set up to drive an Epson printer. So if you have got
one of those most of the work has been done for you. If not it is just a
matter typing in the codes from your printer manual, naming the file,
saving it and typing ◊ FU to update the Printer Driver. And hey presto,
another printer driver has been created.

Let's look at the settings available here in more detail.

## Printer On

This should be set to the code to initialise your printer. Some printers
can support different character fonts. You can therefore tell your printer
to print the whole activity in a particular font by adding these codes to the
initialisation. When you print anything from the Z88 it will first initialise
the printer and then select the character font you like to use. All you need
to do is put in the printer initialising code and then the code for the font
you want to use, not forgetting the commas after each group of figures.

## Printer Off

At the end of printing, this set of codes can be sent (yes that's right there
are no codes there because you don't normally bother!).

## End of Page

This is normally set to 12 or "FF" which is the "form feed" character. When
the end of the page is reached this option will motor the page straight out
of the printer. If you take the 12 out "Line Feeds" or blank lines are sent
until the end of the page is reached. FF is the quieter and quicker one of
the two.

---

**Tip - Form Feed and Page Length**
Some printers do not have this command. If you do use it, make sure
that the Page Length in PIPEDREAM is the same as the Page Length set
on the printer.

---

## Allow line feed

Line feed moves you down to the next line whilst a carriage return on its
own just puts the cursor back to the beginning of the line. So you would
normally want this option set to Yes. If it is set to Yes and the printer already does this for you automatically, you will get double-line spacing. If
that happens you should alter this option to No.

## Character Translations

This section of the PRINTERED gives you the facility to alter up to nine
characters in your printer's character set. The Epson printer uses an
American character set which is why you have already been given the
translation for the £ sign. It doesn't matter how long the code string is because although the "window" is only six digits wide the string will scroll to
the left to allow you to see and edit the rest of it a bit at a time.

To give you some idea of how translation works - if your printer's character set didn't have an ! you could tell your Z88 that when you press that
key you want the printer to print a single quote, then do a backspace and
print a full stop underneath it.

To do this you first find the Z88 code that you are going to redefine and
type that code number into the 'character' space in the translation table.
In this case we can use the ! key and the code for that - which you can find
in the newer versions of the User Guide in the Appendix on the Z88
character set - is 21 Hexadecimal or 33 decimal.

You then look up the codes in your printer's manual for:-

A full stop , (which is Decimal 46 or Hexadecimal 2E or just the ASCII
code itself ".")

A back space (which is Decimal 08 or Hexadecimal 08 or just the ASCII
code "bs"), and,

A single quotation mark (which is Decimal 39 or Hexadecimal 27 or just the ASCII code '''').

Then you put the whole lot into the 'change to' space, not forgetting to ensure that you are using the same type of code throughout. So if you start with the Hexadecimal code you must use it all the time.

---

**TIP: Translation Problems**
These may occur if you are transferring your activity to a different type of computer. Since different computers use different codes the character translations done in the PRINTERED may not get transferred. You may therefore have problems, particularly with the special characters which are variable depending on which character set you are using. So before you transfer a file for the first time check to see what the receiving computer will do with your characters by typing in your character set like this -

!@#$%^&*()_+¦ QWERRTYUIOP{} ASDFGHJKL;'~
ZXCVBNM? 1234567890-=\ qwertyuiop[] asdfghjkl;'# zxcvbnm,./

If you then compare what the other computer gives you with a copy from your Z88 you will be able to see at a glance where the problems are going to be.

Then, before you send a file to the other computer, you can search for the problem characters and mark them, e.g. if it s the pound sign mark each one with a double star which you could do very quickly with the replace command. Then after you have transferred the file onto the other machine you can ask it to search and replace the double star with a pound sign again.

You could also do the above test if you change the character set on your printer, to sort out any new translations that you have got to do.

---

This page intentionally left blank

# SPREADSHEETS FOR EVERYBODY

If you are saying "I would never use a spreadsheet - I'm not an account-ant," this is the section for you to read NOW.

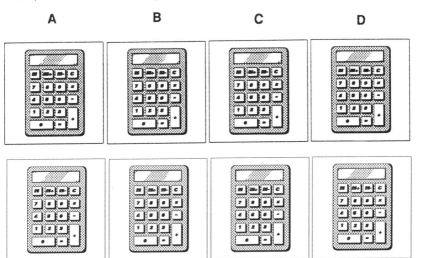

## First of all - what is a spreadsheet?

We simply regard it as a sheet of paper with little calculators all over the page. This means that whenever you need to work something out with numbers PIPEDREAM calculators do all the work!

## When should you use them?

They are not difficult to use - even for the inumerate mathematician! Whether you just want to add up a few numbers or want to work out the phases of the moon - PIPEDREAM can help you out.

How many times have you had a list of numbers to add up, (using a cal-culator) and then, just because you didn't have a print-out of what you did, you were unable to check the figures entered when they wouldn't balance at the end of it all. Perhaps a number was entered incorrectly by us humans! If you had used a spreadsheet, all you would have to do is to change the incorrect number and the spreadsheet would give you the correct answer straight away.

PIPEDREAM also has a super bonus. With a lot of other computers, calculations in spreadsheets had to be done with a different program PIPEDREAM can mix wordprocessing and spreadsheets together in the same activity. This is especially useful when writing reports or letters. (See the example later on).

## Why should you use them?

When working out numbers, a record of what calculations you have done is maintained. We all make mistakes, but with PIPEDREAM we can correct them before printing, so nobody knows.

## How do you use them?

What happens is that Columns and Rows become like invisible lines, turning your working area into a large piece of graph paper. The size of the squares on the graph paper are determined by the row height (which is always the same) and the column width (which can be altered).

## Setting up a spreadsheet for the first time

To start, put headings on the top line, describing what is in the different columns. You can always alter the width of them at a later stage. You should then arm yourself with the knowledge of the following commands:-

◇A - Recalculate the spreadsheet - see the word processing section

◇W - Changing the width of a column - see the word processing section

◇X - Entering an eXpression - tell's PIPEDREAM - "This is a Number, get one of your calculators ready NOW."

If you don't tell PIPEDREAM this, it will just assume that you are typing away in normal text mode and will not take any notice of any of the numbers or mathematical functions.

So what mathematics functions can PIPEDREAM perform? Well the easy ones are adding ' + ' (so you can put those fingers away!) subtract '-', multiply '*' (see the * on the 8 key) and divide '/' (next to the full stop key).

## Your first spreadsheet

To try this out, just put the cursor in any cell[slot], the cell[slot] number is shown on the top left-hand corner of the screen and type in "2 + 5" followed by ◇X and ENTER. You should see the answer of 7 in the cell[slot] and the eXpression '2 + 5' on the comment line of the display.

Work through the example below which uses text and numbers together. Remembering to use the ◇X command in the cell[slot] before or after putting in the numbers or expressions. If you run out of space in any of the columns, you can alter the width with ◇W - put a number in the option to say how many characters wide you want the column to be. The numbers and calculation in this example are in column C (see TAB sce-tion on how to move between columns), although we could use any free cell[slot].

Here is the screen view of what it looks like.

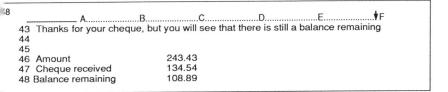

```
8
          A..............B..............C..............D..............E..............↓F
43  Thanks for your cheque, but you will see that there is still a balance remaining
44
45
46  Amount                    243.43
47  Cheque received           134.54
48  Balance remaining         108.89
```

and here is what you actually put into the spreadsheet.

```
8
          A..............B..............C..............D..............E..............↓F
43  Thanks for your cheque, but you will see that there is still a balance remaining
44
45
46  Amount                    243.43
47  Cheque received           134.54
48  Balance remaining         C46-C47
```

You will see that the "Balance remaining" number is not entered as a number at all, but is entered as an eXpression. C46-C47 tells PIPEDREAM to take the value of what is in cell[slot] C47 from the value of what is in cell[slot] C46. As this eXpression is in cell[slot] C48, this is where the answer is placed.

## More adding up

We can add numbers with the SUM command which is another really useful command to use for adding up loads of numbers. Take a look at this screenful for example:

```
B121    sum(A116A119,B116B119)
            .................. A................B.................C................D.....................E...................↓F
    116     123.45      543.56
    117     234.56      987.65
    118     345.67      876.54
    118     456.78      654.32
    120
    121     TOTALS      4222.53
```

By using the eXpression SUM(A116A119,B116B119) in cell[slot] B121 (which means get the SUM of the cell[slot]s A116 through to A119 and B116 to B119 inclusive) we get the answer of 4222.53 straight away!!

Easy isn't it? Would you like to know more about this in depth? - Alright then ... here goes...

# ADVANCED SPREADSHEETS

## Introduction

We went to a Parents evening at our son's school the other day and the maths teacher stood up and said "you can't teach anybody mathematics - they have to use it to understand it." We thought initially "Ah Ha - another teacher 'cop out statement on why our son is not getting on very well in maths", but on reflection this statement is very true. People who feel they are 'no good at maths' avoid it like the plague whilst those who begin using it go on in leap and bounds.

So in this section we want to introduce you gently to the wonders of using a spreadsheet for advanced applications without leaving those who are 'no good at maths' behind. How many of us know all about electricity but we are all quite happy using it to turn on the light switch or even a colour television!

It is the same with spreadsheets - there are a number of 'built in' tools or functions waiting for you to use. Use them simply on their own and you can get a few things done, but as you understand what each function can do you can use them with other tools and get the whole job done.

### Rounding Errors in Spreadsheets

Rounding errors are the black side of using all spreadsheets: they are usually forgotten about, nobody wants you to know about the bad things in life. If you are aware of them, you can get round the problem, so here goes....

Although you can change the Number of Decimal Places in the Options Page to effect the whole of the spreadsheet or use ◊LDP to change individual cell[slots]s, but this only alters the displayed number. PIPEDREAM itself always works to 9 places of decimals.

So if a calculation has come up with 1.123456789, ALL these numbers will be used in any future calculations. You will only see 1.12 if the default '2' places of decimals is selected, but the other numbers are still there lurking in the background. These can (and will) lead to accumulative errors being generated without you knowing anything about it.

The way round it is to use the Integer command to strip off unwanted numbers and avoid these errors from being accumulated in the first place. Integers strip off any numbers after the decimal point, so if you want two places of decimals all you do is multiply the number by 100, then get the integer of that number, and finally divide it back by 100 to give you back the right number again.

An example here may help. Suppose we have a "NUMBER" and we want to have it to two places of decimals. The formula to use is INT((NUMBER)*100)/100. If you want it to three places of decimals, then you replace both the 100's in the formula with 1000 and so on. Try this formula with a number on your Z88 and check whether you agree with it. You will have to change the number of decimal places to 9, so that you can see if the formula has stripped off the extra places or not.

The only problem we can see using this method is if the number needs to be rounded up before stripping off the numbers. E.g. supposing we had a number like 2.2397. Using the above formula you would get 2.23 when really 2.24 would be a lot closer. The way round this is to add 0.5 (a half) to the number before stripping off the unwanted numbers. This would automatically round up the number for you. To add the 0.5 into the formula use INT((NUMBER)*100 + 0.5)/100.

To show this effect, here is an example that exaggerates rounding errors, but it should be borne in mind that they will catch up with you unless you take the advised precautions.

To show that 1 + 1 = 3

Would you like to see how its done?

Get a new copy of PIPEDREAM.

Now put the following values into the spreadsheet.

```
A1    1.4
              A................B................C................D................E..............↓F
1        1.4
2        1.4
3        A1+A2
```

Change the decimal places to 0 on the Option Page - to show the effect. You will then get the following result.

```
A1    1.4
              A................B................C................D................E..............↓F
1        1
2        1
3        3
```

Which goes to show that $1+1 = 3$.

# Definitions

We are going to attack this part giving you an informal definition of what we think the definition means, followed by PIPEDREAM definition (as shown on the Z88's HELP pages).

Let's get the things we are going to be working with defined and then get on with something far more interesting - using spreadsheets!!

As well as reading this section, you may find it beneficial to work through the exercises at the end of the book.

## An eXpression

When using a spreadsheet you have to use eXpressions instead of just text in wordprocessing mode. There are four main sorts of eXpressions:- Numbers, Dates, Text, and Cell[slot] references.

## Numbers

Numbers can be written normally like 24, 0.235 and -1001 or in scientific notation which is like writing a number first with a fixed decimal point and then saying how far away you should move the decimal point to to get the right number. This is very useful when dealing with either very large numbers or very small numbers. Let's look at the following example.

100 is the same as 1.e2

this means you've got 1.00 and you should move the decimal point over to the right by TWO places

1000 is the same as 1.e3

this means you've got 1.00 and you should move the decimal point over to the right by THREE places

1234 is the same as 1.234e3

this means you've got 1.234 and you should move the decimal point over to the right by THREE places, you can also move the decimal point the other way.

0.01 is the same as 1.e-2

which means you've got 1.00 and you should move the decimal point over to the left by TWO places.

All PIPEDREAM calculations are accurate to 9 significant figures so 1.12345678945678 will only be calculated as 1.123456789 (what a shame) and the range of numbers are between 1e38 and 1e-38 which means between 100000000000000000000000000000000000000 (there should be 38 noughts there) and 0.00000000000000000000000000000000000001 which should give you plenty of scope!

## Dates

Clever PIPEDREAM can work with dates as well providing you put the number into the eXpression slot in the following format:-

DAY.MONTH.YEAR (if you are using the European format)

MONTH.DAY.YEAR (if you are using the American format)

You will get the "Bad date" message if you enter an invalid date like 30.2.89 - there are only 28 or 29 days in February! Valid Dates in PIPEDREAM lie between 1.1.42 and 31.12.99 European format.

## Text

Ordinary text may be used in the eXpression cell[slot] together with any spaces providing it is enclosed between double quotes. This can include numbers, but they cannot be calculated with in this form. Numbers in this form are just characters like A B C. So putting "Credit" into an e-Xpression cell[slot] will just put Credit without the inverted commas.

## Cell[slot] References

This is the most useful but the most difficult to understand until you use it. Instead of putting a number or text into the eXpression cell[slot] you can refer to what is in one Cell[slot] from another Cell[slot].

The maximum size Spreadsheet you can have on the Z88 (providing you have enough memory) is from A1 to BL32768 which is 32,768 rows by 40 columns, but beware that is 2.6 Million Cells!

Perhaps an example here may help.

Suppose you have put into Cell[slot] A1 the number 35 as an eXpression.

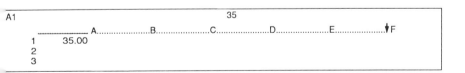

Now move to Cell[slot] A2 and put A1 into that cell[slot] again as an e-Xpression.

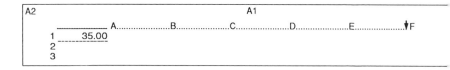

After pressing the ENTER key you should find you get 35 again as the answer in cell[slot] A2.

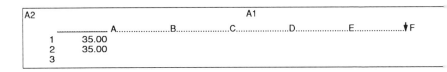

Changing the number (35) in cell[slot] A1 will change in two places automatically - A1 and A2 because you have referred A2 to A1. Got it? - Not yet. Well it might all fall into place once we start referring to cell[slot] with formulas:- Let's see.

---

**Tip. Putting PIPEDREAM into orbit!**

**There is a potential pitfall when using cell[slot] refernces if one cell[slot] references another cell[slot] which in turn references back to the original one.If you do that you will set up a never ending loop.**

---

# The Tools for the Job

When you want to use a PIPEDREAM spreadsheet function, you do not use the ◊ key and you will not find them in any menus. Instead, each function has a name which is typed as part of the eXpression. Most functions require brackets around the parts that you want the command to work on.

# Calculator Functions

All of the mathematical functions available are listed here and you can also get basic help on them (except Integer) from the HELP key (while you are in PIPEDREAM).

# Operators

PIPEDREAM uses the word operator to describe the mathematical functions that it can do. They are:-

Add: +
Subtract: -
Multiply: *
Divide: /

There is one you may not come across

Raise to power: ^

So a few examples would include:-

2 + 2 which would give you 4,

A1-A2 which would subtract the number in cell[slot] A2 from the number given in cell[slot] A1.

You can also use plus and minus with dates to find out the date in a week's time, you'd just type 30.5.89 + 7 which would give you 6.6.89.

Raising to the power is multiplying a number by itself the number of times you are raising it to. So 2^3 Two raised to the power of three is 2*2*2 (Two times two times two) which gives the answer of eight.

## Using brackets

Often a calculation doesn't only use two numbers - like 5*6 - but can have a number of calculations to do at the same time. For a complicated calculation we need to let PIPEDREAM know which part of the calculation we want done first, second and so on. PIPEDREAM does calculations in a predetermined order. As this may not be the order you want, using brackets forces PIPEDREAM to do it the way you want it done.

Let's look at this:-

$2 + 1 * 6/7$ (which means 2 add 1 multiplied by 6 divided by 7).

PipeDream calculates this as 2.857142857, because it does 1 * 6/7 then adds 2.

But if we calculate this step by step we come up with a different answer.

$2 + 1 \ = \ 3$
$3 * 6 \ = \ 18$
$18/7 \ = \ 2.5714285$

that is 0.3 less than the PIPEDREAM answer.

So how do we get round this little problem?

The answer is to use brackets. You put the brackets around the bit of the formula you wish to calculate first - in our example this would be around $2 + 1$:-

$(2 + 1) * 6/7$

then you'd put brackets around the second calculation which is the $(2 + 1) * 6$ bit:-

$((2 + 1) * 6)/7$

The last bit would be done automatically as the third calculation as there isn't anything else for PIPEDREAM to do. So checking the answer now with our bracketed formula - PIPEDREAM gives us:

$((2 + 1) * 6)/7 \ = \ 2.5714285$ The right answer!!

## Using the Calculator Functions

We're on holiday in Cornwall at the moment. How about a depressing list on where the money is being spent! Well not too depressing because it won't be very long!

Get a new application of PIPEDREAM and let's put some headings into the columns we've already got, at least to start with.

Remember, to move the cursor between the different columns you need to use the TAB key to move forward, SHIFT TAB to move back a column or ◇TAB to move to the first column (Column A).

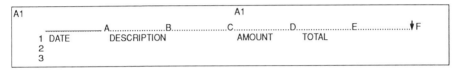

So in A1 we'll have the DATE, in B1 the DESCRIPTION of what the money was spent on, in D1 the amount and finally E1 for the running total.

---

**TIP - fix rows and columns- You can fix the top line with all the descriptions so that they do not roll off the top of the screen when we get past line 5.**

**Do this by leaving the cursor on the top line (A1) and selecting ◇LFR for Fix Row. A little line should appear on the top left hand side to remind you that the row has been fixed. However, doing this will stop the page map representing the page, so you will need to cancel Fix Row (by selecting it again!) to see the correct layout.**

**You can also fix the column in a similar way (for wide spreadsheets) by using the Fix column command ◇LFC.**

---

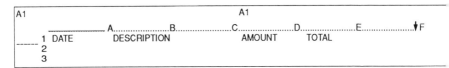

Now we can start putting in some figures, first the date - don't forget to make it an eXpression slot.

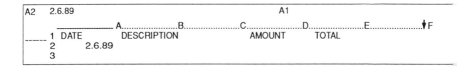

Then in the next column the description

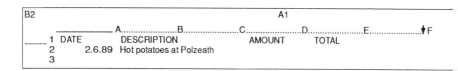

There is no need to make B2 an eXpression slot as we are not going to do any arithmetic with the description. We are not using column C, so the writing in column B can go across this column without penalty. In D2 we need to put the amount spent on the Hot Potatoes as an eXpression.

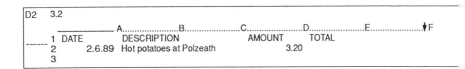

The Total in E2 is just D2 in this case as it is the first one in the spreadsheet.

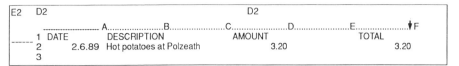

Now the next entry is for more Hot Potatoes at Polzeath (We're still hungry - that first lot wasn't enough!), so it will be the the same date (e-Xpression). But it will be a different description and amount (eXpression). Use the Block Copy command ◇BC to copy the date down to the next line. It should now look like this:-

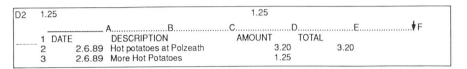

Now the running total to put into cell[slot] E3 is the previous total in E2 plus the amount in D3. This can be described as E2 + D3:-

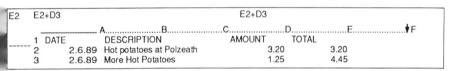

Using the ◇BRE Replicate function we can copy the formula in E3 (E2 + D3) right down to the end of the page.

      Range to copy from   E3
      Range to copy to E4 E47

You will notice that the Replicate function has automatically incremented the row number so that on row 4 the formula has been changed from E2 + D3 to E3 + D4 - Good isn't it.

Put some other ficticous amounts on the remaining rows and see how PIPEDREAM just adds up the numbers for you as you go along. If this is not working on your Z88 did you remember to put the numbers and formulas in as eXpressions?

## Integer & Date Functions

In this section we will look at the functions listed in the Integer & Date functions of PIPEDREAM. Remember to put the numbers in brackets when requested.

Let's do the easy ones first.

PI - $\pi$

This is for all those people who like dealing with circles and it just gives you the value of Pi.

The PIPEDREAM definiton is:-

PI returns the value 3.141592653.

## Absolute Numbers

The Absolute function is used to change negative or positive numbers into positive numbers. This could be used for changing a negative number into an overdraft amount like £135.00 O/D (you can get the overdrawn (O/D) by using the SGN and IF command see later on).

The PIPEDREAM definition is:-

ABS(n) returns the absolute value of "n".

Here are a few examples.

    ABS(-55) = 55
    ABS(67)  = 67
    ABS(0)   = 0

## Date functions

The date functions allow you to extract the day, month and year out of a number that has been written in the date format. Possible uses could be for monthly reports when you need to extract the months out of the dates you have in a list.

The PIPEDREAM definitions are:-

DAY(date) returns the day number in "date".
MONTH(date) returns the month number in "date".
YEAR(date) returns the year number of "date".

Here are some examples assuming European format:-

DAY(2.6.89) would be 2
MONTH(2.6.89) would be 6
YEAR(2.6.89) would be 89

## Square Root

Remember, a square is a number that is multiplied by itself. Well the square root is the number that if multiplied by itself would give you back the number you asked for! Confused? Just try it. Find the square root of a number (say 5), by typing "SQR(5)" into a cell[slot]. The answer is 2.236067978 (roughly!)

Now let's multiply it by itself. That is $2.236067978 \wedge 2$ (remember raised to the power of 2 - saves writing 2.236067978 again - whoops we've just written it again to explain it!) and that gives the answer of 5.000000001 (nearly 5).

The PIPEDREAM definition is:-

SQR(n) returns the square root of "n".

For example the SQuare Root of 4 is 2 because 2*2 gives you 4 and is writ-ten like this SQR(4).

## Sign

Sign is used to check whether a number is positive, or a negative number and is used with the Conditionals - see later. This could be used with the example shown above, Absolute Numbers, to check what the sign was.

The PIPEDREAM definition is:-

SGN(n) returns -1, 0, 1 depending on the sign of "n".

For example:-

SGN(-23456) = -1
SGN(-0.007) = -1
SGN(0)    = 0
SGN(35)   = 1

## Integers

This Integer function is a real must for getting rid of numbers after the decimal point.

The PIPEDREAM definition is:-

INT(n) returns the integer value of "n".

For example INT(4.99999999) is just 4.

This is very useful, for example, when working out VAT. Customs & Excise rules say that if the fraction of pennies is over 0.5p, they should be rounded up to the next penny.

So how do we work that out with integers?

If the total is in A419 the straight forward calculation if VAT is rated at 15% is:-

A419*15/100

But this would not use the Customs & Excise rule. It would just work out 15% of the total. The first thing to do is to add 0.5p to the amount. This would ensure that if the fractions of a penny in the VAT amount is over 0.5p they would be rounded up.

0.5 + A419*15/100

This is all very well but now we are left with the possibility of having a number, for example, like 3.7643367. What we want to do is to strip off the remaining numbers with the integer command so we are left with 3.76 dead. This is achieved by the following formula which works out the VAT amount in pennies then divide it by 100 to give the answer in pounds:-

INT(0.5 + A419*15)/100

We have shown earlier that this technique can also be used to get rid of any 'rounding errors'.

## List Functions

All list functions work with a "range" of cell[slot]s. It is a very useful way of selecting cell[slot] references without quoting them individually.

But before we look at these functions in detail, perhaps it would be use - ful to establish how to describe a "list" first.

A list is a range of cell[slots] which you want PIPEDREAM to work with. They can be in a row or column together, or scattered all over the place. You can describe a row or column or even a block simply by putting the top left-hand corner cell[slot] number followed by the bottom right-hand cell[slot] number. You can also add to the 'list' multiple rows, columns or blocks and individual cell[slot] as long as they are separated with a comma.

To clarify this look at this example:-

Suppose we wish to put the following marked cell[slot]s in the list.

```
XXXXX                          XXXXX
_____ A................B..............C...............D............E..............↓F
1    XXXXX                              XXXXX
2    XXXXX
3    XXXXX
4    XXXXX                              XXXXX      XXXXX
5    XXXXX
```

There is one block in the A column so let's start with that one. The first cell[slot] there is A1 and the last one is A5, so that can go into our list.

A1A5

There is another cell[slot] all on its own which is D1 so this is added to our list as follows:-

A1A5,D1

Finally there is another group in Row 4 in columns C to E or from C4 to E4 so we'd better put that into the list.

A1A5,D1,C4E4

The letters can be in UPPER or lowercase - PIPEDREAM doesn't care.

Now we know how to write the list let's see what we can do with them.

## Sum

The PIPEDREAM definition is:-

SUM(list) is the the sum of the items in "list".

## Count

This counts the number of used cell[slot]s in your list. Good uses include working out averages i.e. Total divided by the number of items. This would be written as SUM(list)/COUNT(list) - list being the list you wish to get the average of.

The PIPEDREAM definition is:-

COUNT(list) is the number of non-blank slots in "list".

## MAXimum and MINimum

MAX and MIN gives you the MAXimum and MINimum values in your list. You could use MIN in your bank statement to show whether you had overdrawn.

The PIPEDREAM definitions are:-

MAX(list) is item with max. value of slots in "list".

MIN(list) is item with min. value of slots in "list".

Both these functions return the value of the number in the list and not the cell[slot] number of where that value is.

## Choose

Choose allows you to select a number out of your list.

"How do you tell PIPEDREAM which number to CHOOSE?"

You tell it with the number called the index. The index will tell CHOOSE which number to pick. Index 1 will CHOOSE the first number in the list, 2 will CHOOSE the second number in the list and so on.

The PIPEDREAM definition is:-

CHOOSE(list) returns an element from "list", using the first element as an index into the remaining elements. eg. CHOOSE(3, 4, 5, 6) is 6.

Here are a few more examples:-

CHOOSE(2,A1A5) would choose the second value in the list from A1 to A5. CHOOSE(1,5,4,3)would choose the first value in the list - in this case 5.

To translate the months number in a cell[slot] A1 you could use the following expression:-

CHOOSE(A1,"January","February","March","April","May","June", "July","August","September","October","November","December")

## Slot Functions

The only Slot functions we have found useful is the Lookup one so far, but here are all the functions - starting (again!) with the easy ones.

## Col & Row

These pick up the number of the ROW or COLumn of the cell[slot] they have been used in.

If you ask for ROW in ROW1 you get 1, but in the COLumns the letters are transposed to numbers - so COL in column A will return 1, COL in column B will return 2 and so on... Possible uses include making up a quick multiplication table using ROW*COL as the eXpression and then using replicate to copy it to all the 144 cell[slot]s!

The PIPEDREAM definitions are:-

COL returns the column number in which it is evaluated. ROW returns the row number in which it is evaluated.

## Index

This INDEX function is another way of calling up cell[slot]. It works by calling the column by a number as well as the row. You would use this function if you want to change references to cell[slot]s using both rows and columns. It is similar to CHOOSE except now you can use this index to choose a number from a block.

The row numbers will remain the same, row1 will be 1, 2 will be 2, but column B will become 2, C will be 3, and so on  To use it you must put the column number in first, followed by the row number.

The PIPEDREAM  definition is:-

INDEX(column,row) returns the value of the slot referenced by "column" and "row".

For example if you wanted the value in cell[slot] A2 you could use INDEX(1,2) (column1, row2) to get this value.

## Lookup

When we first looked at this definition it meant absolutely nothing to us. Keys, Range1, Range2 and these Wildcards what are they?  What does Lookup really do?

It is used when you want to Lookup something (called the key) in one column or row and read the answer in another row or column. This comes into its own, when you use a table in a spreadsheet like looking up the time of a train in a railway timetable to something or a discount table - you know the sort, if you spend more than £5,000 per week you are entitled to 2.5% off for cash sales only!

The PIPEDREAM definition is:-

LOOKUP(key,range1,range2) returns the value in "range2" corresponding to the position the key occurs in "range1". Wildcards may be used in "key". If no match = "Lookup".

So how does Lookup work in practise?

Ranges work in a similar way to list, but you can only have one block of cell[slot]s a list can comprise of scattered blocks and/or a single cell[slot] - the Key - what you are looking for (aren't we all). So you put what you want to lookup in the Key, Range1 is what you are trying to match the Key with and Range2 is where you get the answer from.

For example let's build a table and use the Lookup function. The table is just the month of June (1989) with the days on it so we can Lookup the date and find out which day it was.

Get a new copy of PipeDream and Name it ( ◊FC) June89.

then set the following options (on the Options Page) to:-

> Text/Numbers N - saves us making the cell[slot]s eXpressions
> Decimal Places - 0 - get's rid of the decimal points (like 2.00)

Wouldn't it be useful if we didn't have to type in 1, 2, 3 and so on for the dates till we reach 30? We can do it by using the ROW command. Put ROW in cell[slot] A1 and then press ENTER. You should now see 1 in cell[slot] A1.
Using the Replicate function ( ◊BRE) the ROW command can be repeated down the rest of column A.

> Range to copy from A1 Range to copy to   A2 A30

| A1 | ROW | | | | | |
|----|-----|---|---|---|---|---|
| | | A............ | B............ | C............ | D............ | E............ ↓F |
| 1 | 1 | | | | | |
| 2 | 2 | | | | | |
| 3 | 3 | | | | | |
| 4 | 4 | | | | | |
| 5 | 5 | | | | | |
| 6 | 6 | | | | | |

The days can be now entered in column B starting with "Thursday" in cell[slot] B1 through to B7 "Wednesday." Because these days are strings i.e. text in eXpressions slots they need to be in"inverted commas."

This time you need to mark the block B1 - B7 and use Block Copy ( ◊BC) to copy this to the other cells[slot]s, with the cursor first in B8 and then repeat this in cell[slot]s B15, B22 and then finally, B29.

You will find that the words go down to B35 so you need to delete the 'overhang' by either marking the block you wish to delete and using the Block Delete command ( ◊BD) or delete the lines with ◊Y - usually a lot quicker.

Part of our completed table should now looks like this.

| B15 | Thursday | | | | | |
|-----|----------|---|---|---|---|---|
| | | A............ | B............ | C............ | D............ | E............ ↓F |
| 10 | 10 | Saturday | | | | |
| 11 | 11 | Sunday | | | | |
| 12 | 12 | Monday | | | | |
| 13 | 13 | Tuesday | | | | |
| 14 | 14 | Wednesday | | | | |
| End of text | 15 | Thursday | | | | |

Now its time to use the Lookup functions. Range1 is where the numbers are 1 to 30 from A1 to A30. Range2 is where the days are from B1 to B30 so it's just a matter of transposing this information into the definition:

LOOKUP(key,range1,range2)

LOOKUP(key,A1A30,B1B30)

This just leaves the key. Let's put the key into a cell[slot] so that we can change the value and see the result. How about A33? This gives:

LOOKUP(A33,A1A30,B1B30)

and we'll put this LOOKUP eXpression into cell[slot} B33.

By putting a value in A33 (say 4) you should see the answer appear in B33 like this:

Choosing invalid numbers, that is those that are not in the table (like 32) will put "Lookup" in cell[slot] B33 which indicates that Lookup has failed to find an answer in the table.


# Wildcards

As we have seen, PIPEDREAM can use Wildcards in Lookup e-Xpressions as well as in the Search or Replace command.

These are used when we don't want to put the full word down, but we've got a good idea of what bits of the word is like. So we can for example have a key of S ^ # which would match any words starting with an S, or ^ #ing would find all the words ending with "ing". You could use ^ ? wildcards which allow you to specify how many individual letters you 'don't know' about in the match. To find a string of say three characters beginning with W, you could use W ^ ? ^ ? to find it.

The PIPEDREAM definitions are:-

Any single character: ^ ? Any number of characters: ^ #

So you could use the wildcard in the following Lookup Table to save you getting a perfect match for the keyword. Look at the following example.

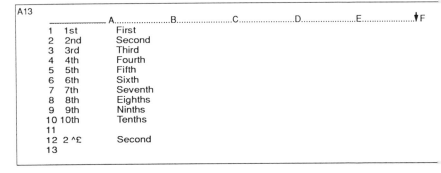

By putting $2 ^ \wedge \#$ in cell[slot] A12 and the Lookup command of LOOKUP(A12,A1A10,B1B10) in B12, you can see that a match is made with $2 ^ \wedge \#$ for 2nd.

## Relational Operators

These Relational Operators are usually used to ask a question. Does the expression follow a rule? There are only two answers. Either it does, a TRUE statement, or it doesn't, a FALSE statement.

When they are used with the IF function this gives you a very powerful tool that can actually make decisions in the spreadsheet.

The PIPEDREAM definitions are:-

> Less than: <
> Less than or equal to: < =
> Not equal to: < >
> Equal to: =
> Greater than: >
> Greater than or equal to: > =

These six operators can be separated into two groups as you can see from the table below:

| One way | The opposite way |
|---------|------------------|
| Not equal to: < > | Equal to: = |
| Less than or equal to: < = | Greater than or equal to: > = |
| Less than: < | Greater than: > |

So to compare two numbers say "is 4 greater than 1?" you would put 4 > 1.

The answer you would get will be a non zero number which means that the expression is true. If the result was zero, this would mean that the expression was false.

## Logical Operators

Logical operators are used with the relational operators to allow more than just one test to be made.

The PIPEDREAM definitions are:-

> Logical AND: &
> Logical OR: |
> Logical NOT: !

So how do these work?

The best way of explaining them is to use "truth tables" which do not require a bright light or tools of torture. They simply show the results from previous calculations - Result1 and Result2 together with the answer when using these operators.

There are always four states that need to be considered when comparing two results. These are if both the results are false, one is false whilst the other is true, then the other way round, one is true whilst the other one is false and finally when they are both true.

Let's start with Logical AND: &

| Result1 | Result2 | Overall Result |
|---------|---------|----------------|
| FALSE | FALSE | FALSE |
| FALSE | TRUE | FALSE |
| TRUE | FALSE | FALSE |
| TRUE | TRUE | TRUE |

This shows you will only get a TRUE result when Result1 AND Result2 are TRUE.

Now let's look at Logical OR: |

| Result1 | Result2 | Overall Result |
|---------|---------|----------------|
| FALSE | FALSE | FALSE |
| FALSE | TRUE | TRUE |
| TRUE | FALSE | TRUE |
| TRUE | TRUE | TRUE |

This shows you will only get a TRUE result when Result1 OR Result2 are TRUE.

and finally Logical NOT: !

Where is result2? With the others, you are combining the results to give you the overall result, but logical NOT only takes one result and reverses it - making FALSE TRUE or TRUE FALSE.

| Result1 | Overall Result |
|---------|----------------|
| False | True |
| True | False |

Here is one example using these operators:

To understand this you need a cold bath first! Then you work from the innermost brackets outwards. What we are testing is whether A1 is zero (A1 = 0) together with whether A2 is also zero (A2 = 0). We can do this by using logical AND (&) on these two results. We have now covered (A1 = 0)&(A2 = 0) which will give TRUE if both A1 and A2 are zero. We have reversed this result by using logical NOT.

## Conditionals

Conditionals are used to allow you to DO SOMETHING after doing a test which proves to be TRUE or to do ANOTHER THING if the result is FALSE.

It is like a signpost with two directions on it. One way shows what to do for a TRUE result, ELSE do the other way.

The PIPEDREAM definition is:-

IF(boolean,then,else).

If the value of the "boolean" is TRUE (non-zero), IF returns "then", otherwise IF returns "else".

eg. IF(5 > 1, "more", "less") is "more".

You will notice that there are three parts of the IF eXpression. These are:-

    boolean
    then
    else

The boolean part is where you put the test that you wish the IF command to perform. This can be made up from the previous "Relational Operators" and "Logical Operators".

Let's use PIPEDREAM's example and see what results it gives us.

IF(5 > 1,"more","less")

The boolean part of this eXpression is 5 > 1 (5 is greater than 1). Putting 5 > 1 into an eXpression cell[slot] gives us 1.000000000. As 1.000000000 is a non-zero number this means that it is a TRUE statement. Do you agree that 5 is greater than 1?

Moving on to the other parts of the IF statement, these do what you want, depending on what the boolean result was.

'then', contains the eXpression the IF command will perform if the test returns a TRUE result.

finally, 'else' contains the eXpression that will be performed if the test was FALSE.

## Trig. Functions

PIPEDREAM has got some 'built-in' Trigonometry functions. We are not going to attempt to explain what SINe CO-Sines or TANgents are; as that would require another book. PIPEDREAM likes to work in radians rather than degrees.

The PIPEDREAM definitions are:-

COS(radians),
SIN(radians),
TAN(radians)

return the cosine, sine or tangent of the argument.

ACS(n),
ASN(n),
ATN(n)

return the arc cosine, sine or tangent of "n" (in radians).

and finally the ever so important conversion radians to degrees (for those of us who only understand angles in degrees)

RAD(degrees) returns "degrees" converted into radians. DEG(radians) returns "radians" converted into degrees.

To find out the sine of 90 degrees (which should be 1) firstly convert the degrees to radians with RAD(90). This gives us an answer of 1.570796326 (Now you know why we prefer degrees). Get the SINe with SIN(1.570796326) which gives us the answer of 1.000000000. Good gracious it actually got it right!

You can put the conversion from degrees to radians into the main eXpression. Does it? Blowed if we know - lets try it.

SIN(RAD(90)) is 1.0000000.

Good, that saves writing in that 1.57079.. number doesn't it.

We'll leave all the other functions for you to try out, but we hope we have left you with a number of clues on how to use this trig section.

## Log. Functions

Time to throw away those Log books! PIPEDREAM deals with both Natural Logs, Logs to Base 10 and expenditials.

Our introduction to logs which was a long time ago said that they were used mainly for doing difficult multiplication or division when calculators were not around. When men were men and boys were boys!

They are retained in PIPEDREAM, as a number of formulas still require the use of both natural and logs to base 10 to be worked out.

The PIPEDREAM definition is:-

LN(n) returns the natural logarithm, (log e) of "n".

LOG(n) returns the logarithm to base 10 of "n".

EXP(n) returns the constant e, to the power of "n".

To multiply two numbers together with logs you simply look up the value of the log of one number and add it to the log of the other number. This answer needs to be changed back to an 'ordinary number' by using what is called anti-logs (which are logs the other way round and not a threat to logs at all) before you get the correct answer.

So how about these Natural logs then? They work the same way as the other logs except that the base is different, instead of it being 10 it is the value of e (which is about 2.718281829).

This page intentionally left blank

# THE CALCULATOR

## Arithmetic on Demand

The CALCULATOR is your ever available on board, arithmetic
machine. So you can throw away your abacus at long last. Have you, like
us, been round the calculator loop? If you were like us, you'd resisted
buying a pocket calculator until they were too small to see, and then suc-
cumbed to the salesperson's 'miracles of science' patter. Only to find that
it was too small to see in every sense of the word - you couldn't read the
display even with your glasses and it disappeared into the mire every time
you put it down! When it came to light again, somewhere around spring
cleaning time, it had stopped working. You took it back to the shop, the
salesman, a younger one this time hardly out of nappies, told you the batteries were flat. He then said that the batteries cost more than a new
calculator so why don't you buy one of our wonderful selection? You
declined, deciding that you would rely on your fingers.

Your Z88 is at least bigger! But having all the calculating facilities in PIPEDREAM has to some extent made the thing redundant. If you want to do a calculation outside of PIPEDREAM and BBC BASIC - the calculator is useful.

It has all the normal calculator functions and can be called up from any application with ☐ R - remember the three Rs! The conversion facility and ten memory locations are particularly useful.

Before you can use it you have got to know how to tell it what you want it to do. There are two ways of putting in figures and the instructions to tell the machine what you want done with them. The first one is selecting everything by moving the cursor to the appropriate square on the display and pressing ENTER. The second way is a great deal quicker - use the number keys and the first letter of the command. So C is clear, P is plus, M is minus, T is times, D is divide, U is unit, etc. The only exceptions to this rule are =, %, and the full stop (the decimal point), you have to use those specific keys.

## The magic squares

The magic squares are the other cursor locations on the calculator. With titles like StoM, Fix, and RclM they are enough to frighten anyone who hasn't been let into the magic circle! We will do our best to show you the way in.

## DEL

DEL will delete the last figure that you typed in. It will not however alter the arithmetic operator ( + .-.*,/). If you get that wrong all you need to do is type the one you wanted and it will change. If you hit the wrong operator twice you will get a K next to it on the display because you have turned it into a constant. If you put another operator it will change but the constant K will still be there. The only way to get rid of K is to press the same operator key again - a third time if you didn't change it, or a second time if you did, then K will disappear.

## StoM

StoM is the memory store. You have up to ten memory locations or boxes. Each will hold a number for you while you are working on another bit of the calculation. Put the number you want to store into the working area on the calculator display - if it isn't already there - and press S which will give you the 'StoM ?' prompt on the left hand side of the display. It is asking you which memory location you want it to use. You have a choice from 0 to 9. Once the StoM prompt has disappeared your number should be safely stored away and you can clear your working area for a new calculation.

You can still work with these figures even while they are stored away. If you press S for StoM and then +,-,* (multiply), or / (divide), before the storage location number it will add etc. the number in your working area to the number you have stored away.

## RclM

Use RclM to get the number you stored away back from its memory box and into your working area. All you need do is press R and the memory box number, and the number inside the box will be revealed.

When you have finished with that number you can start all over again by putting another number into that location. It will automatically erase anything that was in there before and insert the new one. So make sure you know which number you have got in which box otherwise you could erase a number that you really wanted.

## Unit

U or unit is your entry point into the conversion table. If you wanted to know how many miles are in five kilometres you would put 5 in your working area and then press U. The cursor will then move into the conversion table. You can move down or across until the cursor is over the one you want. There is a little arrow which moves down between the two sets of units to show you which way the conversion will be done. Here, because we are converting Km to miles, you should put the cursor over miles, the little arrow will then be pointing to miles. If you move the cursor over Km you will be converting miles to Kms and the arrow will be pointing the other way. When you press ENTER you will get the answer in your working area. In our example there are 3.11 miles in 5 Kms.

## Y< >x

Y< >x allows you to go backwards and forwards between two numbers in a calculation before you ask for the answer by pressing the = key. So if you ask for 2 + 3 and then realise you should have put in 4 + 3 you can press Y which will put the 2 back in the working area and then overtype this with 4 and the = key. The answer will be 7. If you are doing a longer calculation you can still use it because the machine gives you the answer to each bit of the calculation as it goes along. You will only ever be dealing with two numbers in your calculations. To take the above example further, if you wanted 4 + 3 + 4 when you type in the second +, 7 will appear on you screen - the answer to 4 + 3 - so the next calculation will be 7 + 4. You could still change the first number, 7, with the Y< >x command. You could also change the last figure you had entered, with the delete key, but there is no way of getting to the previous number like that.

Y< >x can also be used to give you the reciprocal of the answer to a previous calculation. To do this you divide the answer by 1. press Y and then the = key. The reciprocal of two is a half, so press 2, D, 1, Y, = The answer should be 0.5.

## Sign

I or Sign just changes a positive number to a negative one and vice versa.

## Fix

F or Fix allows you to say how many decimal places you want to work to. When you press it you get 'fix ?' on the left hand side of the display. You then have to type in a number between 0 and 8 and that number of digits will appear after the decimal point. If you need to work with very large numbers, the machine will automatically switch to scientific notation. See Advanced Spreadsheet Section for more details on this form of notation.

## %

The percentage % key is used with other operators +,-,x,/. You can use it to find what percentage one figure is of another (long gone are the days when you multiplied the figure by a hundred - or whatever it was!). You can also find 15% of a figure for VAT and then add or subtract it from the original.

So, to put 33 over 55 as a percentage you would type in 33 divided by (D or /) 55 % = 60

To find 25% of 3.504.56 you would type in -

3504.56 multiplied (T or *) by 25% (you don't need to put an = in be-cause it will give you the answer automatically).

The answer should be 876.14

If that was to be taken off your final bill as discount you would type -

3504.56 multiplied (T or *) by 25% minus (M or -)

According to our CALCULATOR that is 2628.42

Likewise if the original figure was subject to 25% tax you would add it on instead of taking it off so you would put a + not - at the end.

3504,56 multiplied (T or *) by 25% plus (P or +)

We make the final bill in this case 4380.70

## Constants

We mentioned briefly above that if you press either P. M. T. or D. (you should know these by now!) twice you get a K on the display which means you have set up a constant, so what does it do for you? Well, if you type in a number say 23 and then press T. T. the calculator would then times every number that you put in by 23. If one of the ingredients you need for your spells - say rats blood!- went up in price you would need to increase your charges for services rendered by the same amount. So if it had in-creased by 20p a pound and you need a quarter of a pound per spell, everything on the price list could go up 8p - well, when you live in an enterprise culture you have to show willing! All you then have to do is put 8 p,p, on the calculator and type in each old price on the list and it will automatically give you the new prices.

You should now know most of what there is to know about the calculator on your Z88. But there is one more thing we want to add: Because you are using the ENTER key as an execute key a great deal of the time when working in other areas of you Z88 it is very easy to try and use it in the same way here, typing in ENTER instead of the = sign. The problem is it doesn't work like that! Instead of getting the answer, you will just have added another figure onto the last figure you typed in. The ENTER key acts as a repeat key here because the cursor is still situated over the last figure you put in. If you do find yourself doing that there is no harm done because you can delete the unwanted figures with the DEL key, but we do find it extremely annoying!

# The ALARM

The Alarm clock will remind you of the time if you have an appointment you don't want to forget. The User Guide says that you can use it to wake you up in the morning, but we think the bell is a bit quiet for that. Maybe we are just heavy sleepers, or deaf, or both, but that little beep beep wouldn't wake us up in a hundred years!

Joking apart, this is a very useful application. You can set as many alarms as you like, and for each one you can specify the date, time and reason - to remind you why you set it in the first place. That might seem unnecessary but if you have set alarms for six months or a year ahead even you might need a reminder, we are positive we would! You can also put a CLI string in here instead which will be activated when the alarm setting is reached and cause something to happen! So if you see a Z88 attached to a whole load of wires and pulleys with a hammer hanging over your bed, beware! Someone might just have found a way to wake you up in the morning that might be more effective than the Z88's sound system!

When you call up the alarm with ☐ A the alarm display will pop down over the top of the activity you are working on. You will see the main display which will show the alarms that you have set - when you have set them!

At this stage the cursor will be over the Exit command and will only move to the Set Alarm command on its right and back again. The other two options will not be open to you until you have set an alarm. Which makes sense because if there aren't any alarms set there aren't any to view or clear either! Once you have set an alarm however, you can move freely between all four options.

# To Set An Alarm

To set an alarm place the cursor over the 'SET ALARM' option and press ENTER. The display will change to give you the current date, or if you called it up from the DIARY it will show the date you were on, and the time when you called it up. To change either of these, position the cursor over the individual numbers you need to change and type in the new number. The PIPEDREAM editing commands don't work here, so if you make a mistake go back over it with the cursor and type in the correct character. If you put a character over the / or : which act as delimiters between the different parts of the date and time, it will ignore them and put the delimiters back in their rightful place when you press ENTER to complete the setting. It will beep loudly at you and not allow you to do anything if the entry is invalid.

## The Alarm Options

Below the time there is a selection of options. To move around this whole area you can only use the LEFT and RIGHT ARROWS. The UP and DOWN ARROWS have been programmed as you will see below, to alter the settings within the bottom row of options,

The bottom row can turn the bell on or off with the UP/DOWN ARROWS. With the bell turned on you get seven loud beeps every time the alarm reaches the set time. You will also get the flashing bell symbol on the top right hand side of the screen just below OZ. The symbol will stay there flashing away until you clear the alarm so if you turn the bell off and you have several different alarms set you must cancel each one fairly quickly otherwise you won't know when a new alarm has been activated.

With the 'alarm type' option you can choose whether the timer will activate the alarm or whether it will execute the CLI routine which you have put into the 'reason for alarm' space.

You can also ask for the alarm that you have set to be repeated every second, minute, hour, day, week, month, year, or the default setting which is never. The DOWN ARROW will enable you to move between these until you get to the one you want. The UP ARROW will change the number. 1 to 2 and upwards, but if you go too far, you can use the DOWN ARROW to go backwards. So you could ask for the alarm to be repeated every 20 seconds or every two years. When that is set to what you want you can then move to the next option with the RIGHT ARROW.

The 'no of times' option allows you to choose how many times you want an alarm to go off. If you have asked it to go off every day to tell you that it is time to go and pick the Evening Primroses for your potions you might set it on Mondays to go off five times to cover your working week, always supposing that witches have the weekends off! Alternatively, you might set it to for ever, then you wouldn't have to worry about setting it every week. To set this option move the cursor over it with the RIGHT ARROW and press the UP ARROW which will change the setting from the default 'never' - which will let the alarm go off once to 1 and any number above that. If you press the DOWN ARROW you will go back down the scale again until you get back to 'never', when it will go to 'forever' before closing the loop with the highest number on the scale - 65534 - and go backwards from there.

---

**Tip. Every second forever spells trouble.**
**Don't set an alarm to go off every second, forever, because you will not be able to cancel it with the clear command and will have to resort to a soft reset.**

---

When you have got a number of alarms set you have two cursors to work with. The UP/DOWN ARROWS will move one cursor between the various alarms so you can select which one you want to view or clear. You cannot change an alarm that has already been set: you will therefore have to clear it and set a new one if you got it wrong the first time. The RIGHT/LEFT ARROWS will move the second cursor between the commands on the bottom row of the display. You must select the alarm you want to view or clear before selecting the command otherwise the command will effect whichever one the cursor is on, usually the top one.

**Clearing**

To clear an alarm select the one you want to cancel and the clear command. If it is one that you have set to go off more than once  pressing clear will cancel the last alarm that has been activated, leaving the next one ready to go off after the selected interval. If you want to cancel a repeating alarm altogether then press clear twice.

## Lock out

If your Z88 is turned off at the time when the alarm has been set to go off, it will turn itself on in LOCK OUT mode. This will mean that the screen will be turned on and will show the place where you were last working on your suspended activity and the alarm symbol will be flashing in its normal place. But instead of good old dependable OZ being above the alarm symbol where he normally is you will have LOCK OUT flashing. Your keyboard has been locked to stop you pressing keys accidentally. So OZ can safely stay asleep because you can't ask him to do anything for you anyway.

To unlock it all you have to do is turn it off and then on again, the machine should then be back to normal.

The ALARM will not go off, at the correct time, if you turn the Z88 off after setting an alarm but before you have left the ALARM altogether. Then the alarm will only be actuated when you turn the Z88 back on.

## Viewing

The view command allows you to see the present status of any alarm but you cannot do anything else with it. It shows you what all the options are set to. The 'no. of times' option will have been updated to show the actual number of times left. The machine will have subtracted the number of times it has already gone off from the original number that you asked for. When it has gone all the way back to 'never' you will know that you can clear that alarm completely.

# THE CALENDAR

The CALENDAR can be called up by pressing ☐ C from wherever you are in your Z88. It is invaluable as a quick reference tool because you can check dates without leaving the activity that you are working on.

## How to use it

When you first access the CALENDAR, either with ☐ C the square key or through the INDEX it will show you the current month. The cursor is larger than the one in PIPEDREAM and will be positioned over the current date. To move around the CALENDAR either in the current month or further afield you can use the cursor keys or a combination of cursor and function keys. The sequence that has been worked out is a fairly logical one and is easy to remember.

To move about in the current month you use the cursor keys alone. LEFT ARROW moves you back to the previous day, or days before that. RIGHT ARROW moves you to the next or subsequent days. UP ARROW will move you to the previous week and DOWN ARROW will move you on to the next week. If you move off that month, the page will automatically be turned and the display will show the appropriate month. SHIFT UP ARROW will turn the page and put you on the previous month. SHIFT DOWN ARROW will move you onto the next MONTH. Whilst ◇UP or ◇DOWN ARROW will turn over twelve pages and put you either in the previous or next year.

## Looking up a particular day

If you want to look up a date, to find out what day of the week it falls on, all you have to do is get the CALENDAR display onto the screen with ☐ C and press ENTER. You will get the 'look for' prompt with the current date. You can put in the date you want to check by positioning the cursor over the number that you want to change and typing the new number in - it works in a sort of overtype mode - not forgetting to put /s in between the day/month and month/year. If you put in just 66 for the year the CALENDAR will assume you mean 1966.

## Marked days in diary

All popdowns are affected by which application you were working with when you called them up. The calendar will assume a slightly different role if you call it up while working in the DIARY. It will then act as a quick reference point showing you what days you have got booked up. Any day that you have an entry in your DIARY will have a small arrow pointing to it. Any day marked like that is called an active day and you can move between them with ☐ LEFT ARROW or ☐ RIGHT ARROW depending on which direction you want to go in. See the DIARY for more details.

# THE CLOCK

The CLOCK is run by an actual hardware clock inside the Z88. This internal clock is almost as omnipresent as OZ the operating system and, like OZ, you are not aware of its presence very often. It is used in the INDEX, PIPEDREAM, and the FILER to time stamp when you enter an activity or save a file. The CALENDAR gets the current date from it and the ALARM uses it for the date and time.

So perhaps you can see now why setting the CLOCK to the correct time is one of the first things you need to do when you do a hard reset!

The CLOCK you see on the screen is your window on the inner world of the Z88. You can set it to the right date and time. It should be reasonably accurate but if you ever need to alter either the date or time the details are near the beginning.

As the CLOCK is a popdown you can call it up at any time from anywhere in the Z88 using ☐ T.

---

**Tip. Using the CLOCK - cancels timeout**
**One thing you must be aware of however, especially if you are running your Z88 on Batteries, is that while the clock display is on the screen your timeout option in the PANEL will be cancelled. The Z88 will not turn itself off after the selected number of minutes if you haven't used it in that time. So it will remain turned on until you either go into another activity where the timeout function will work, or you have to turn the machine off yourself by pressing the two SHIFT keys together. The**

timeout has been cancelled to enable you to use the clock as a timer but if you leave the clock display on the screen by mistake it could be awfully costly in batteries. You could lose all you files in RAM and all your suspended activities - so beware!

# DIARY

## Introduction

This section looks at using the built-in "Page a Day" DIARY. How you can layout the pages for maximum effect. What all the commands do and how you can use the DIARY together with the CALENDAR and ALARM.

The good news is that a large number of commands are the same as PIPEDREAM, some have the same name but do slightly different things whilst the last group of commands are on their own, being special to the DIARY.

To avoid duplication we have not covered all the commands so you may have to go back to the PIPEDREAM section for a full explanation of some commands.

## What is the DIARY

The DIARY is a book with nothing written on the pages except the DIARY Date. A Page looks like this:-

Even if you have not written anything in it, the Date and which mode you are using (either INSERT/OVERTYPE) will appear on the right-hand side of the screen. The rest of the screen is for you to use as you would a "normal" diary except that with this one you can have unlimited lengths pages on the days that you are really busy on. Whereas the pages with no entries (for the days you had to catch up on your sleep) will have taken no space in the activity at all!

## Selecting the DIARY ☐ D

To select the DIARY you can either select it from the INDEX or by using ☐ D. After loading in the Program, you should find yourself on today's date!! Unlike PIPEDREAM, you can only have one copy of the DIARY application open at any one time. If you try opening up another one, you will find that you go into the old one!!

## DIARY Commands that are the same as PIPEDREAM

### Blocks Commands

| | |
|---|---|
| Mark Block | ◇Z |
| Clear Mark | ◇Q |
| Copy | ◇BC |
| Move | ◇BM |
| Delete | ◇BD |

Next Match                    ◊BNM

## Cursor Commands

End of Line            ◊ ⇒
Start of Line          ◊ ⇐
First Line             ◊ ⇑
Last Line              ◊ ⇓
Save Position          ◊CSP
Restore Position       ◊CRP
ENTER                  ENTER
Next Word              SHIFT ⇒
Previous Word          SHIFT ⇐
Screen Up              SHIFT ⇑
Screen Down            SHIFT ⇓
Cursor Right           ⇒
Cursor Left            ⇐
Cursor Up              ⇑
Cursor Down            ⇓

## Edit Commands

Rubout                 DEL
Delete Character       ◊G
Insert Character       ◊U
Delete Word            ◊T
Delete to End of       ◊D
Line
Delete Line            ◊Y
Insert Line            ◊N
Insert/Overtype        ◊V
Swap Case              ◊S
Next Option            ◊J
Split Line             ◊ESL
Join Lines             ◊EJL

To find out more about these commands - look them up in the
**PIPEDREAM** section.

## Commands that are NOT in PIPEDREAM.

Here are the extra commands and the commands that have the same names in PIPEDREAM, but do different things!

## Blocks Commands

### List/Print ◇BL

This command is used to print what you have entered into your DIARY together with the Day and Date. When it is selected the following options are displayed.

LIST DIARY
LIST ON SCREEN                    Yes
LIST ON PRINTER                   No
LIST ONLY MARKED BLOCK            No

Just pressing ENTER will display all your entries on the screen. We haven't got anything entered in ours so all that has come up is today's date. We'll just put what we have done today in it.

0630   Write the Diary section of the Z88 book

If you want this sent to your printer, you should first connect the printer up and then change the "LIST ON PRINTER" to 'Yes'. Leaving the "LIST ON SCREEN"..........................Yes will display it on the screen as well, so you can look at it on the screen whilst sending it to the printer! Finally by marking a block first and using the "LIST ONLY MARKED BLOCK" option, you can list just part of your DIARY.

### Previous Match       ◇BPM

Previous match is like a backwards Next Match, so you can go Forwards and Backwards, looking for that appointment that you made under a particular name.

158

## Search     ◊ BSE

Search is similar to the one in PIPEDREAM, but it also has the facility of printing a list showing you on which days the word you are searching for occurs. Selecting Search gives you the following:-

------------------------SEARCH DIARY--------------------------

STRING TO SEARCH FOR

EQUATE UPPER AND LOWER CASE          Yes

SEARCH ONLY MARKED BLOCK          No

PRODUCE LIST                            No

PRINT LIST                              No

The line underneath the 'STRING TO SEARCH FOR' option (for a change) is where you put what you want to search for. You can't use wildcards (thank goodness,) but you can use a number of words together if you wish. 'EQUATE UPPER AND LOWER CASE' is normally set to 'Yes'. When you search for a word or a string of words, search will find it whether it is in upper or lower case. Setting this option to 'No' will only find what you asked for if you asked for "Word" it won't find "word"!

'SEARCH ONLY MARKED BLOCK' will just find the word in a pre-viously marked block if you set it to 'Yes'.

'PRODUCE LIST' is the extra option in search. If set to 'Yes', it will list on the screen the complete line where the searched word occurs, together with the date. This is a very useful facility as it could list all the different days you tried to contact "Fred Bloggs".

'PRINT LIST' does the same as 'produce list' except it sends it out to the printer. Remember to have a printer connected up rearing to go before using this one otherwise the Z88 will just stop until you plug a printer in. What no printer? Do not select this option in that case!

## Replace ◇BRP

REPLACE is again similar to the one in PIPEDREAM. But has a different layout so we will cover the options briefly.

Selecting the command gives the following:-

```
                  DIARY REPLACE
-----------------STRING TO SEARCH FOR ----------------------

------------------STRING TO REPLACE WITH -------------------
EQUATE UPPER AND LOWER CASE          Yes
ASK FOR CONFIRMATION                 Yes
SEARCH ONLY MARKED BLOCK             No
```

You put the word or words that you want to find in the line below the 'STRING TO SEARCH FOR' option.

Underneath 'STRING TO REPLACE WITH' you put what you want to replace the word or words with.

'EQUATE UPPER AND LOWER CASE' - See the explanation given in the Search section.

If you set the 'ASK FOR CONFIRMATION' every time you find the word you want, you will be asked "Replace Y/N". If you set this option to 'No' it replaces all the strings of characters it finds automatically without asking.

You can limit your search by marking a block first and then setting the 'SEARCH ONLY MARKED BLOCK' option to 'Yes'. This can save a bit of time especially if your DIARY is rather large.

# Cursor Commands

## TAB

This TAB is a 'trouble-free' TAB, different to the one in PIPEDREAM.
It does not work in columns, but puts a real TAB every eight characters.
There is no facility to change the Tab spacing - use it if it suits your layout.

## Today            ◇CT

◇CT puts you on the right page for Today. If you are on the wrong page,
check the date in the Clock (☐T).

## First Active Day      ◇CFAD

This command is not only for fitness freaks, because an "Active Day" is
a day with an entry in it. So an entry saying "Slept in the garden" would
still be an "Active Day!!"

## Last Active Day      ◇CLAD

This puts you onto the last page in your diary that has an entry in it.

## Next Active Day      ☐ RIGHT-ARROW

Moves you to the next day that you have an entry.

## Previous Active Day    ☐ LEFT-ARROW

Moves you to the previous day that you have an entry.

## Previous Day         ☐ UP-ARROW

Moves you back a day, even if you haven't got an entry in it.

## Next Day     □ **DOWN-ARROW**

Moves you forward a day.

## Memory Free    ◇**EMF**

The Memory Free command is just like the "Free" heading in the Options page in PIPEDREAM. It shows you how much memory you have left for this activity. But although you may appear to have lots of memory free, you can still run out of room when saving files. If you find this confusing, so do we.

# Files Commands

The files in the DIARY work in a slightly different way to PIPEDREAM. This is because a DIARY file is a list of dates together with your entries. The simplest way of using a file is simply adding entries into the DIARY and saving it with the File Save command.

But because the File load command actually adds the file (rather than overwriting it) to the DIARY, a number of tricks can be performed. If you become confused, don't forget you can just use the Diary with a single file to start with.

## Load    ◇**FL**

This load command is not the same as the one in PIPEDREAM because it actually "adds" the file to what you have already got in the DIARY rather than overwriting it. Selecting it gives you the following banner.

LOAD (APPEND) FILE INTO DIARY

------------------------ NAME OF FILE TO LOAD ------------------

START LOADING DATA AT DIARY DATE     NO

You type the filename underneath 'NAME OF FILE TO LOAD'.

The 'START LOADING DATA AT DIARY DATE' option is normally set to "No". Entries loaded from the file are added (or appended) to
your diary using the same dates as in the file. An appointment on the 1st
July 1989 would be added to the others on 1st July 1989.

For example, suppose you wish to add a file with entries on the following
dates:

12/4/89
16/6/89 - that is, 2 months 4 days later
23/10/89 - that is, 6 months 11 days later

If the 'START LOADING DATA AT DIARY DATE' option is set to
"Yes" and the DIARY date is 11th November 1989, these entries would
be added to your DIARY on the following dates:

11/11/89
15/1/90 - that is, 2 months 4 days later
22/5/90 - that is, 6 months 11 days later

## Save                    ◇FS

-------------------------SAVE FILE FROM DIARY-------------------

NAME OF FILE TO SAVE

SAVE ONLY MARKED BLOCK                    No


Just put the name you want to save your Diary as under the line 'NAME
OF FILE TO SAVE'.

Setting the 'SAVE ONLY MARKED BLOCK' to 'Yes' will only save the
Block that you have previously marked. This is useful for splitting up your
DIARY into smaller chunks as it naturally grows with all your entries.

# Using the Diary

This section encapsulates a few ideas that we have picked up whilst using the DIARY. This isn't to say that this is the only way to use it, perhaps you have a different way of working that's even better!

## Hints on page layout

You can put as many lines on the page as you need, so make each entry take up ONE line. Keywords are used within each entry to help organise your DIARY entries. By searching for the keyword using the ◊BSE command you can list separately these entries. We have used keywords like HOME and WORK, but you can choose your own

Then split the line into sections so that by using the "Search" ◊BSE command you can list separately the different headings like HOME WORK etc, but you can choose your own "keywords".

Here is an example of how TABs are used to space the Times, Keyword, Priority Rating and Description.

| Time | Sort of Entry | Priority Rating | Description |
|------|---------------|-----------------|-------------|
| 1000 | WORK | *P1* | Meeting with Sir Clive |
| 1130 | WORK | *P3* | Write report for the Rat Race Company |
| 1230 | SPARE | | Lunch - get the flowers for the evening |
| 1900 | HOME | | Dinner with Dick and Jean |

You can also put "Jobs" in as well, and if you don't get them done "today" then by marking the uncompleted jobs you can simply put them on to tomorrow by moving them with the block move command ( ◊BM).

## Putting in a list of dates

Often there are a list of dates that you wish to put into your diary. Using the DIARY to do this means that you would have to select each date by going to the appropriate page and typing the entry - which can become time consuming.

PIPEDREAM makes it easier by allowing you to enter the whole list in a single file. There is only one rule you need to follow when creating this file:

RULE - Make sure dates are on a separate line and have a '%' at the beginning.

Here is a PIPEDREAM file in DIARY format for you to look at.

```
%26/6/1989
000            HOME              Doris at Pat's
0800           HOME              book Colt MOT

%3/7/1989
2000           HOME              Doris Leaving Pat's

%25/7/1989
               HOME              GILLS BIRTHDAY

%26/7/1989
0000           HOME              Colt MOT runs out
```

After you have typed your list of dates in this format using PIPEDREAM, you need to save it as a Plain Text File before loading it (or adding it) to your existing DIARY. We have found this useful, especially since we all have Z88's. So when we want to meet up, we just need to type in one copy of these dates into a PIPEDREAM file, put it on EPROM, then circulate it between us. Then we all add these dates to our DIARY.

## Repetitive dates

We have seen before (in File Load) how it is possible to load the file "STARTING FROM DIARY DATE". This is useful for loading in repetitive dates like birthdays anniversaries and evenings at the club!

You need to build a file with all these entries in it for one year. Use PIPEDREAM as explained previously. You add the list to your diary by putting the cursor on the first date in the list.

## Pruning down the Diary from time to time.

If you are using your DIARY a lot, you will find that it grows!! A good way to make it smaller is by getting rid of the days that have passed. We have found however, that it is useful to keep a copy of what we have done in a printout, before deleting forever what we did.

You do this by using one word ◊CFAD "First Active Day". Mark the top line of this day (with ◊Z) then move to "Today" ◊CT and mark the top of that also. You can print the marked block with ◊BL after changing both the:- "LIST ON PRINTER" and "LIST ONLY MARKED BLOCK" options to 'Yes'. After that you can do a Block Delete ◊ BD.

## Making the DIARY, CALENDAR and ALARM work together

Using the CALENDAR you can move around your DIARY a lot quicker than by using the commands in the DIARY. So how should you use it? From within the Diary you can select the calendar with ☐ C. There will be a small triangle next to all the dates you have made an entry and the day that you currently have your cursor in. Don't worry about this because when you move the cursor to another date the mark will follow it! You can use any of the CALENDAR commands to select the date in your DIARY. When you press ESC, the CALANDAR date will become the DIARY date. MAGIC!

By selecting the ALARM ☐ A that date will be automatically entered when you SET the ALARM. So not only can you make an entry in your DIARY, you can also set the ALARM to the same date at the same time!

## When do the DIARY and CALENDAR start and finish?

You can start your DIARY from Tuesday 1st December, 4713 BC to Monday 31st December 18253 AD. Bear in mind that the Gregorian calendar did not start until the 14th of September 1752 (in Britain) or 14th October 1582 (continental Europe). Remember to adjust dates before those, to get the birthday of your favourite Pharaoh! The CALENDAR also knows about leap years, so you might get a few more centuries out of your Z88 yet!

# The FILER

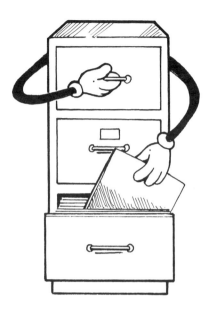

## Introduction

This section looks at the FILER in greater detail. You should already know something about it, but hold on - here is the authorised version!

The FILER works with a hierarchical filing system, which we have called "Filerarchy". This allows you to divide up the filing cabinet into smaller sections, rather than throwing them all into one large bucket! This can help you keep your files in smaller more manageable groups.

We look at all the devices you can use to store files, they range from RAMs, to the very popular EPROMs. With all this choice you may need to write the FULL filename - details coming up!

If you know anything about directories or sub-directories in computer terms, then this section is going to be easy. For those of you who don't, by the end of this section you will know most of what there is to know about designing, creating and selecting these directories.

Whenever you save a file, OZ - the operating system records the time and the date - the Catalogue file command reveals this hidden information.

You can make a copy of any files with COPY and TREE COPY (is this a special version for gardeners?) or just RENAME when you change your mind!

When memory becomes a premium, getting rid of your unwanted files is easy. No longer do you have to collect the rubbish and put it in the waste-paper basket. The Z88 filer ERASE command will get rid of files in an ozone-friendly way, and in doing so will free the memory for you to use again.

With all these files being generated, Name Match shortens your directory by 'hiding' files you are not interested in.

Finally there is a section on using EPROM to clarify the differences between them and RAM.

Although the Execute command is in the Filer, we are putting describing this off until we start working with the Wizard, which is where it really belongs, so you won't find anything about it.

## Selecting the Filer

To select the FILER whilst using an application, simply press ☐ F. It is important to note that as the FILER is a PopDown program, any changes you make to the settings (namely the Device Name, or the Directory Name) will only effect the application you are in.

This is a very useful facility, because it enables to have two activities running at the same time, using different memory packs. One activity could be using one RAM pack (set up by the FILER when in that application) whilst the other application could be using a different RAM, (also set up by the FILER).

### Selecting the Filer from the INDEX (This is a special case)

If you are in the INDEX, you can either put the cursor over the PopDown program named FILER on the left hand side or you can select the Filer directly with the ☐ F. The activity that you will be in, is the top one on the "Suspended Applications" list. Any changes you make here will only will effect that activity.

## Leaving the Filer

Pressing the ESC key when in the FILER, returns you back to the activity you were last in.

## Filerarchy

As mentioned before the FILER uses a hierarchical filing system. Here is a diagram to show what we mean.

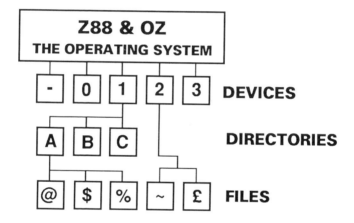

## OZ

Right at the top you can see the Z88's Operating System - OZ. He is in charge of running the whole show - so we can't leave him out!

## Devices

The next level down are the Devices. These are RAMs or ROMs, one of these MUST be selected. A full list of names are given in the Select Device section.

## Directories

Going down .... You can have a choice here, either to use directories, or not to bother. How can you make up your mind? What are the ad - vantages of using them? Well there is not a simple answer to that one, so let's just talk it through for a moment.

## The BIG bucket filecatcher

This is the easiest option to use, and probably the way you have started saving all your files in the Z88.

## The Selective smaller filecatcher

On the other hand you can use directories. If you are like us, using larger RAM packs and working with lots of files, it can help to group these files together into some logical order.

If you have created files of different settups for the Panel or Printer Editor, you may find it more convenient to put these together in one direc- tory. This will enable you to find them quickly.

When you are using Directories, you can have different filenames having the same name like read.me in the letters directory and read.me in your document directory. You could even have a file called "INFO" in each

directory with information about that directory and the files in it, just in
case you forget in six months time! You can have directories within directories. These are called "subdirectories". Use them in the same way as
directories.

# Files

And finally there are the files themselves. Like the Devices, you've got to
have a filename, but what you call it is up to you but follow the rules.

## Rules for naming Files and Directories

These are:-

Names can have up to twelve characters (a space is not a character, so
you can't use them), followed by an optional full stop and extension of up
to three characters.

Extensions are used at the end of the filename and can be used to remind
you what sort of file you are working with. Typical examples we have seen
in our travels are:-

.doc                    - for Documents

.ltr                    - for Letters

.v1                     - for Version Numbers 1, 2, 3, etc.

There are some special extensions that have already been used on the Z88
so you should avoid using these:-

.sgn                    - For ☐ + K and ☐ + S  - See CLI files
.CLI                    - For BOOT.CLI     - See CLI files
.L                      - For PIPEDREAM multi-file List File

So here are some examples of some good names - well we think they are
good anyway!

Z88book.v1

TheLongTitle.ext
Two-Names
Z88toPCfile1.V1
Z88toPCfile2.V1
Z88toPCfile3.V1

---

**Tip. Upper & Lower Case in Filenames**
When you save a file, the filename gets saved and displayed in whatever case you have used. When you load the file, case is ignored.

---

**TIP.  Bigger Computers Like Smaller Filenames**
Although the Z88 can cope with twelve character lengths filenames, there are a few computers out there, namely MS-DOS and CP/M ones which will only deal with eight.  So if you wish to transfer files to another com - puter from your Z88, you should bear this in mind when making up your filename.  In the example above, although the Z88 would not mind these names:-

Z88toPCfile1.V1
Z88toPCfile2.V1
Z88toPCfile3.V1

Using PC Link II - they would become

Z88TOPCF.IBM
Z88TOPCF.IBM
Z88TOPCF.IBM

All the same, so TAKE CARE.

If you only use filenames that use 8 characters you can use them for both the Z88 and most other computers.

# How to write a full filename.

The Full Filename is constructed the same way as the Filerarchy, so you need to know what order to put them in.

Firstly there is the Device - which RAM pack the file is in. Then there are the Directory or Directories which are optional and finally there is the file itself, which consists of the name.ext (and the optional extension).

Now you know what they all are, here is how you write it.

:DEVICE\DIRECTORY\DIRECTORY\FILENAME.EXT

To reinforce this lets look at one of the files from the previous diagram, say @.

The first thing to look for is which DEVICE is it in. There it is RAM.1, so put that in first together with the \ character at the end (not forgetting the colon at the beginning).

    :RAM.1\

Next, are there any DIRECTORIES? In this case Yes and it is A so that goes in next.

    :RAM.1\A\

Finally there is the filename so the full name is:-

    :RAM.1\A\@

Lets look at another one which is not in a directory. The full filename for the £ filename is:-

    :RAM.2\£

## Where to use full filenames

After reading this section, you may be tempted to ask yourself - why bother using these full filenames. The good news is that you don't always need to. This is because you already have the facility in the Filer to select which Device and Directories to use in the current application. The problem comes when you are in one device or directory and want to do something else in another one.

Let's take a look at a possible scenario where you would have to use FULL FILENAMES. You are writing away (just like we are doing) on your Z88

and you know that you are going to run out of memory in RAM.1 very
soon. You've put it off doing anything about it for as long as you can by
deleting all your old files, but it seems that you still need some extra space.
You read somewhere (in this book hopefully!) that you could save
memory by using a list file. Your list file (called LISTFILE.L) looks like
this so far:-

        Intro
        Part1
        Part2
        Part3

.... and you are running out of space in Part3.

You get another RAM and place it in slot 2.

There is now a little problem for your list file, because you have started
in RAM 1 and finished in RAM 2. Help is on the way. Changing the list
file to show which device the files are in as well, will cure the problem.

The list file should look something like this (Yes, we moved Part3 to RAM
2!):-

        :RAM.1\Intro
        :RAM.1\Part1
        :RAM.1\Part2
        :RAM.2\Part3
        :RAM.2\Part4
        :RAM.2\Part5
        :RAM.2\TheEnd

Another example. You are in a PIPEDREAM file and you would like to
insert another file that you had previously saved in another Device or
Directory. By using the FULL FILENAME, you can get to it without
changing the Device or Directory in the Filer.

Note / and \ are interchangeable, but the Z88 generates /.

# Filer Commands

This section looks at each of the Filer commands in more detail. There are THREE ways of selecting the commands here, because you have an extra menu on the left of your file listing area.

1. By moving the cursor up or down the COMMAND menu on the left hand side of the display.

2. By selecting the MENU first and then using the cursor keys to select which command you want.

3. By just using the short codes e.g. ◊CF. for Catalogue Files.

## Select Devices   ◊SV

This command tells the FILER which RAM to use.

## Legal Devices

You can select any one of these devices - provided you have them fitted. Don't forget the colon at the beginning!

| | |
|---|---|
| :RAM.- | Temporary RAM - can be anywhere - DO NOT USE IT until you have read about CLI. Delete any files before doing a soft reset if your operating system is older than 3.1. (See TIP) |
| :RAM.0 | 32K internal RAM |
| :RAM.1 | RAM in Slot 1 |
| :RAM.2 | RAM in Slot 2 |
| :RAM.3 | RAM in Slot 3 - if you use this for RAM you will have nowhere to put your EPROM and you will use more power than in slots 1 and 2. |

The EPROM is not a device - see the Fetch and Save from EPROM for more details.

---

**TIP. To find which version of the Operating System (OZ) you have, select the Index, then HELP and finally press the LEFT ARROW key. Our machine shows:-**

**The Cambridge Computer Z88 Portable Version 2.2**

---

Whenever you start an application, the device will be initially set to what you have set the Default Device to in your Panel.

RAMs are physically separate, so you are not able to load a file that starts in RAM.1 and finishes in RAM.2. If the file is too large to fit, you will get the dreaded message "no room" when saving the file.

# Directories

We have already talked about when you should use Directories - here are the codes on how you can make and select them. You should know by now what sorts of names you can have, so go on, be bold.

## Creating Directories      ◇CD

Type in the name you want to call your directory in upper or lower case lettering. The name will be displayed in "shorter capital letters" on the filelisting to show you that it is a directory and not a file.

## Selecting Directories      ◇SI

Now that you have created a directory, would you like to "come inside!"

There are two ways of selecting your directory, one way is to select   ◇SI and type in the directory name, or you can just move the cursor over the directory name and the SHIFT + DOWN ARROW.

You will find that the first time you enter a new directory, all your files seem to have disappeared! Fear not, they are still there, but not in this directory. The other thing to note is that on the top of the file listing area the directory name will be shown to tell you which directory you are in. Don't forget, you can always put more directories into directories.

Just to make sure, you can go "back up" to where you were, by using (you guessed it right) SHIFT UP ARROW. You will then see all the other files again and the directory name, but not the files in that directory.

# Wildcards - Not again!

Although we have talked about wildcards before, in Blocks - PIPEDREAM) just to confuse you, the FILER uses different characters to do the same thing. We are not sure why there is a "character change" in the Z88 - perhaps two different people wrote the programs. We have got three people writing this so we know the problem. These special wildcards are:-

* which means any characters (or none)

? which means any single character /

/ which means any number of Directories (or none)

Note / and \ are interchangeable but the Z88 generates /.

You can use wildcards when "doing things" on a number of files - like CATALOGUE FILES, SAVE TO EPROM, RENAME, ERASE, COPY and NAME MATCH. Put them in place of or as part of the filename.

Really there is only one way to understand wildcards, and that is just to use them and see what happens. Lets just work through a few examples to clarify what wildcards can do. Firstly, let's just use a list of names, which would normally be filenames but in this case we are using A List of Everyday Things that the Z88 User might need.

| | | |
|---|---|---|
| Batteries | Eprom-Packs | Paper-Clip |
| Printer | Ram-Packs | Spare-Batt |
| Spare-Paper | | |

S* (all names beginning with S) would give:-

Spare-Batt     Spare-Paper

?a* (names with an "a" as the second character, don't care about the rest!) would give:-

Batteries          Paper-Clip          Ram-Packs

*Packs (All names ending with Packs), would give:-

Eprom-Packs Ram-Packs

?p?????a* (second character "p", and the eigth character "a", don't care about the rest), would give:-

Eprom-Packs    Spare-Batt          Spare-Paper

If you are using Directories, you can use the // wildcard to find a file even if you have forgotten which directory you put it in. For example supposing you had a file called "letter1" somewhere, by using :*//letter1 it will find the file, even if it is in another device or RAM pack.

**Tip. Selecting Files**
**Before using any of the commands listed below, you are able to select the file or files that you wish to use. This is achieved by moving the cursor over the filename you want, and then press the ENTER key. A triangular mark will appear to the left of the filename, to show that this file has been selected for use. Further files may be selected, by pressing SHIFT ENTER.**

**If you forget the SHIFT key, you will find that you can only mark one file, the last one selected. We had a great time "chasing around" some files before we realised what was happening. Did this happen to you as well?**

## Using Multiple Files

If you use the wildcard or have marked a few files you will see "SELECTED FILES" come up in the "Name" part after selecting your command.

## Catalogue Files     ◊CF

This command is used to show you when you created or last saved a file. You can either select the files you wish to find out first by marking them, or just press ENTER at the 'Name' prompt to select all the files in the current directory you are in.

To see all the files on your Z88 simply do Catalogue Files  ◊CF and then put :*//* in the filename.

If you would like a printout of your filenames, please refer to the CLI section.

```
*** WARNING -   PLEASE NOTE THIS   ***
```

There is a minor bug in this part of the program.

When running Catalogue Files you will see on the left hand side of the screen. PAGE WAIT, SPACE CONTINUE and ESC RESUME.

At this point ONLY SELECT ESC or SPACE. If you press the INDEX key for example, you will leave the last file displayed "open." You will only notice this when you want to erase that file and find that you can't!!

The only way to cure this "open file" problem is to ◊PURGE the Z88. Please read the implications of doing this first BEFORE doing it... please(!)

## Copying Files     ◊CO

This command is generally used for making a copy of an existing file and giving it a different name. This copy can either be in the same directory or in a different directory. You should use Full Filenames if you wish to Copy a file into a different directory or Device.

To copy "Thisfile" to "Thatfile", select ◇CO and you will get the Name prompt. Put in "Thisfile," then after pressing ENTER, you would type in "Thatfile" next to the New Name:

Name :                       Thisfile

New Name :                   Thatfile

You should automatically get a question after pressing < ENTER > you will be asked to confirm your command with a Yes/No response. You can change your mind before committing the Z88 to carry out your instructions!

If you mark a number of files before using the copy command, Copy will join the files selected in the same order, and copy them into the new file. For exmple by marking file1, file2, and file3 before selecting copy ◇CO you will get:-

Name :                       SELECTED FILES

New Name :                   FILES1-3

Putting FILES1-3 in New Name you will get a copy of those three files in that order (file1,2 and 3) in the "FILES1-3 file. Very useful!

NOTE: You can't copy a file to itself!

Copy is often overlooked as a convenient way of copying or sending files to different parts of the Z88. We will be dealing with this in more detail in "Talking to Other Weirdos", later on but here is a taste of what you can use copy for.

Making up some blank files to use with a list-file you are going to use.

Name :                       :NUL.0

New Name :                   :Intro

This would give you an empty file called "Intro" in your current directory. You could build up a number of these files, put them all in a list file and then start writing. The files will be waiting for you to fill them all up.

Here are the remaining Devices with helpful comments.

:ROM.0                   The ROM - This is where all the application
                         programs are.

:SCR.0                   The Screen

:PRT.0                   The Printer, using the printer driver

:COM.0                   The RS-232 port without the printer driver

:INP.0                   The Keyboard

:OUT.0                   The Output, normally directed to the Screen.

:NUL.0                   NULL - Nothing.

There is more information on some of these Devices in the 'Talking to Other Weirdos' section.

## Tree Copy  ◇TC

This command is used when you want to copy a number of files from one device or directory to another device or directory. Wildcard names are not used here, nor are selected files. You will have to use Device and/or Directory Names to get the desired copy.

To copy all the files you have in :RAM.0 into :RAM.1 you just do

Source :              :RAM.0

Destination :         :RAM.1

If you want to copy files from different directories e.g. THISDIR to THATDIR then you would do.

Source :                  \THISDIR

Destination :             \THATDIR

But REMEMBER you must create the Destination directory first, other-wise it won't be found!!

## Changing Names of Files    ◇RE

This is a straightforward command to rename a file. When used with Wildcards and Selected files, prompts come up for the individual files, to confirm what you want the new name to be for each one.

To change "Oldname" to "Newname":-

Name :          Oldname

New Name :    Newname

## Changing the name of a Directory

You can't use ◇RE to change the name of a directory. Use Create Direc-tory ◇CD first and then Tree Copy to copy all the files into the new directory. Check that you have copied all the files, before finally deleting them from the old directory, and then delete the old directory itself.

## Erasing Files - throwing them away ◇ER

WARNING - Once you erase a file, there is no way of getting it back again!!

Use erase file to get rid of unwanted files. This will release memory for your Z88 either to use as working memory, or for new files.

To erase "Oldfile" simply type in the name of the file:

Name :          Oldfile

When using wildcards or selected files, the prompt 'Confirm each file?' will be shown. Press ENTER for Yes.

You will then be prompted at each of the individual files, asking you if you want that file to be erased. There will already be a 'Yes' there for you to use if you press the ENTER, or by changing it to 'No', the file will not be erased.

This is a very useful facility, since it saves you from remembering all your filenames. By putting the wildcard "*" in the Name, you can work through all the files, and decide which files you will erase as you go along. Be careful!

For example if you just wanted to get rid of a file called "Oldfile1" but you couldn't remember its name at the time - you can use the Wildcard '*' and confirm each file. Make sure that you only erase 'oldfile1' by changing all other erase prompts from 'Yes' to 'No'. Press ESC to leave after you have found and erased the file.

## Name Match     ◇NM

Name Match is used to reduce the number of files shown on the screen by using wildcards in the Name.

Selecting Name Match gives you the following:-

Name : *

This is normally set to *, which means "everything" in wildcard terms at least. If we changed this to S*, we would only see the files listed in the directory that started with an "S."

You would also notice that an ◇NM will appear on the top left-hand side of the screen, to remind you that you are using Name Match and that there could be more files in the Directory than you can see!

You can see all your files again by changing the entry in Name Match back to the "*" again.

# EPROM

You CAN SAVE files to the EPROM from your RAM device.
You CAN FETCH files from the EPROM to your RAM device.
You CAN SEE what files you have saved into your EPROM.
You CAN ERASE the COMPLETE EPROM - all the files, at the same time.

You CAN'T ERASE INDIVIDUAL FILES in the eprom. When erasing EPROMs, you expose the whole pack to ultra-violet rays in an EPROM eraser, which boldly goes and destroys all the files you have.

You CAN'T LOAD FILES from the EPROM directly into an application - like PIPEDREAM. You have to "Fetch It" first, put it in the RAM and then load.

## Catalogue Eproms ◇CE

This is a similar facility to the ◇CF command. You use it to see what you have got in your EPROM. If you have not saved any files to the EPROM you will just see *END* on the listing. However, there is no time or date stamp recorded in the EPROM.

This command also puts a header onto your EPROM either when it is a new one, or after you have erased it. Without the header, you will find that the INDEX ◇CARD command will not show that you have an EPROM fitted, even if you have! So when you first fit an EPROM - Catalogue it.

## Fetch from EPROM ◇EF

You should make a note of all the files that you wish to "Fetch from EPROM" in the "Catalogue Eprom" command before you start using this as there is no facility to mark the files and then copy them to RAM.

Selecting this command you will get the following:-

Source :

Destination :

The source is the filename that is on the EPROM. When ENTER is pressed, the same filename will be copied automatically to the Destination. You can change the "Destination" to a different filename if you wish, or even change which RAM or directory you wish to save the file to by using the FULL FILENAME.

## Save to EPROM ◊ES

Prepare yourselves for a 'orrible shock! Whenever we use the "Save to Eprom" command, and that is even after we have used it loads of times it still makes us jump. It flashes the screen in a most alarming way to conserve battery power. Although we are warning you now in writing, its not quite the same as experiencing the real thing - so DON'T PANIC, everything is alright, even when the display goes out - just wait, or better still don't look at the screen!

Saving files to EPROM is easier than fetching the files, because you can either put in the individual filename you wish to save, or mark the files before hand or even save everything in the current Directory by using the "Wildcard." So lets see how that works in more detail. When the command is selected you get the Name: prompt where you should now put the filename that you want to save.

If you had previously marked some files in the Directoryor have used Wildcards, you will get no prompt at all, it will just save the files and flash the screen with SAVE TO EPROM on the screen.

## Execute - Doing office chores ◊ EX

This command is used for starting CLI files - Look at "Working With the Wizard" section for more details.

# The Summary

We hope that this section has helped you to understand how the files should be named, where you can put them (politely) and how you can use directories. Remember, the FILER can and should be used with all the applications to set which Device and Directory you want to use, so that you don't have to use the full filenames all the time.

# Talking to Other Weirdos

## Introduction

This section deals with how the Z88 communicates with other computers and accessories. The Z88 has been designed to be able to send and receive data easily to other 'computer like' products. We will be showing you a number of different ways that these connections can be made.

There are usually a number of different steps you need to make before the Z88 can communicate. It might be a good idea to make notes as you go along. Then if it doesn't work, you know you've got to do it differently next time and if it does work, you will have a permanent record for all other times.

It is essential that you know what you want to do. Are you sending a file to a Printer? Transferring a file to another computer, or using the Z88 as a terminal?

You will need a cable and you may need some software.

Finally you need plenty of time to do it in, because only a few things work the first time. You just have to try, try and try again, double checking everything as you go.

Do not be afraid of damaging your weirdos or the Z88, because of wrong settings or such like. We have never experienced any situation that this has happened. All you find is, that if you've done it wrong, it doesn't work!

# Cables

Buy your cables - don't attempt to make it up yourself, unless you are an electronics expert and know what you are doing. There is a Z88 Cable wiring guide in the Appendix for those of you who are cable makers.

There are several sorts of cables available. These are (to name just a few)

> Parallel Printer Cable
> Serial Printer Cable
> PC - Z88 Computer Cable
> Macintosh - Z88 Computer Cable

## Connecting it all up and adjusting the controls

To connect up your Z88 to your "weirdo" use the socket on the right-hand side of the Z88 called the RS-232 port.

The driving controls for this socket are in the Panel ([ ]S) and appear on the right-hand side of the screen. These set up the speed at which the data is sent up and down the cable (called the baud rate) and a couple of other things that checks the data and slows it down. We will be looking at these in more detail later on.

---

**Tip. Sharing your Z88 with lots of weirdos.**
**If you find that you are plugging different weirdos into your Z88 at different times, why not use a 25 way RS-232 switch box.**

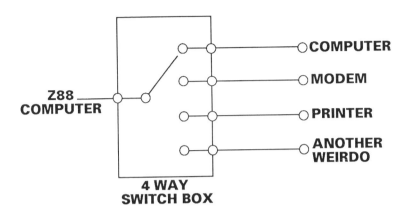

Now you do not have to keep unplugging and connecting up different weirdos to your Z88 everytime you need to change. Just select it with the switch.

# Talking to your printer

## Setting up

There are basically two different ways to communicate with a printer. One way is called Parallel (or Centronics) and the other is a Serial (or RS-232). You can tell the difference by either looking it up in the printer manual, or by looking at the socket that the connecting cable plugs into the printer. The Parallel connection is a tongue and groove connector whilst the Serial connection is a 25 socket pin and hole connection. Let's deal with each one in turn.

## Parallel

If you have a parallel printer, this is the easiest type of printer to use. Just follow these simple steps:-

1. Get a parallel printer cable,

2. Plug one end into the Z88, the other into the printer. You can't plug it in the wrong way round because the plugs are totally different.

3. Check that the PANEL ☐ S settings are set up as follows:-

> Transmit baud rate 9600 Receive baud rate 9600

> Parity None

> Xon/Xoff No

> and don't forget to press ENTER to update any of the settings, otherwise the changes will not be made!

You should be ready to print now.

## Serial

If you have a serial printer, there are a few more combinations to get right. If you do a bit of research first, from the printer manual and follow the steps given here, you should be up and running in no time.

1. Get a serial printer cable,

2. Plug one end into the Z88, the other into the printer. You can't plug it in the wrong way round because the plugs are totally different.

3. Now you need to match:

a) the speed or baud rate of the printer
b) the parity bit and
c) whether the printer works on Xon/Xoff

You can do this two ways, either by changing the settings on the printer, or changing the settings on the Z88. It doesn't matter which way round you do it as long as they are the same!

You can find out from the printer manual what these settings are already set at. We've found it is easier to set the Z88 to match the printer setting rather than the other way round. If you need to change the settings on your printer, there is normally a table of different settings that you can set your printer to. These are set with either switches in the printer or by a setup procedure which may also printout the current settings.

So let's check out the different settings in turn. We can't help you with your printer settings but on the Z88 you need to look at the PANEL ☐ S settings. Here are the normal settings.

> Transmit baud rate 9600/Receive baud rate 9600
> Parity None
> Xon/Xoff Yes

## Baud Rate

The "Transmit baud rate" and "Receive baud rate" are normally set to the same values. You can see all the different values available on the Z88 by placing the cursor over the number (e.g. 9600) and pressing ◊J for the next value. With all these different numbers, you should find one of them that match the speed of your printer.

## Parity

Just to make life interesting, some earlier versions of the Z88 did not display the setting correctly. This is not a problem because if you select the wrong parity setting, all that happens is the printer does not work correctly. A bit of black magic is called for here (i.e. trial and error). So initially, set this to what you think it should be (again you can use the ◊J to change the settings). After all you can always return to the PANEL later on and change it. If your printer prints lots of funny looking characters, it is likely that changing this setting to a different one will give you different funny looking characters until you hit the jackpot when the printer just prints boring old text properly!

## Xon/Xoff

This little function has only two states - either it's On or Off, but what is it?

To understand what it does, you need to be aware of a little problem that computers have with weirdos. To be frank, some weirdos are just not fast enough to keep up with the speed that computers can send the data. The weirdo must be able to say to the Z88 "STOP, Hang on, wait, give me a break" whilst it catches up. Printers can fall into that category. Perhaps it runs out of paper, or it is unable to print 960 characters a second! So there are two ways this STOP signal is handled.

The first way is using one of the signal lines on the RS-232 cable to act as a simple ON/OFF traffic light signal from the printer to the Z88. If it is "ON" the Z88 sends data to the printer. If it is OFF, it stops, until the printer turns it on again.

The other way is to use another facility that RS-232 has. Not only can the Z88 send data to the Printer, but the Printer can send data back to the Z88. Thinking about this, Printers in general are not notorious for sending lots of data back to the Z88 Connecting two computers together would be a better example. The Printer can still use the data line to send a message to the Z88 to say STOP (Xoff) and then another message later on to say START AGAIN (Xon)!

This data signal is called Xon/Xoff. How do you know what to set it at? If your printer is expecting an Xon/Xoff signal, and this is not turned on in the Z88 or (visa versa) - you will in effect loose bits of your text to the printer. You should be ready to do a print now.

# How to Print from Different Applications

We will now look at the commands that you use to print from the different applications. It is assumed that the file has already been loaded into the application before the print command is given.

## PIPEDREAM

To print a complete file from PIPEDREAM, it should have no marked blocks (otherwise you will only print the block).

The command ◇PO will give the following options:-

| | |
|---|---|
| Print only range of columns | No |
| Select rows to print | No |
| Wait between pages | No |

If you have to either load in single sheets, or your printer does not manage to stop the Z88 for a rest, there is a useful option here that can help you and it is called "Wait between pages."

Changing this option to 'Yes', will just send the data a page at a time, stopping at the end of each page sent and inviting you to tell the Z88 when to send the next page. This can give you time either to change the paper sheets, or let the printer catch up with the Z88, or both!!

After selecting the options you want press ENTER to start printing.

## DIARY

To print your DIARY, you need to use the List/Print ◇BL command. Selecting this gives you a different set of options. These are:-

| | |
|---|---|
| LIST ON SCREEN | Yes |
| LIST ON PRINTER | No |
| LIST ONLY MARKED BLOCK | No |

Change the option LIST ON PRINTER to 'Yes'.

You can also print using the Search command. See the Diary for further details.

## FILER

Would you like a printout of what files you have got in your RAM, now that your printer is working? Let's use the CLI command that allows a copy of the screen, to be sent to the printer as well. First of all select the Filer with the ☐F command. Then after checking that your printer is plugged in and turned on correctly, you need to turn on the special command to send to the printer with ☐ + P. You should now see a "CLI" symbol at the top right-hand corner of the screen.

Select the Catalogue Files with ◇CF or just press ENTER again. You should now see the names of all your files on the screen and your printer printing your catalogue as well. When it is finished, deselect the printer with the ☐ -P command. The "CLI" symbol should now disappear.

You can use this command to get a printout of all the files on your EPROMS as well by doing the same thing with Catalogue EPROM.

---

**Tip. Printing without a printer?**
**Do not use the ☐ + P command if you have not got a printer connected. If you do, you will find that your Z88 may go to sleep, because it is wait - ing for your printer (which isn't there) to respond! How can you wake it up then?  Press SHIFT ESC!**

---

# BBC BASIC

To print from Basic you use the same PRINTER DRIVER as PIPEDREAM.  You are now responsible for sending the correct codes to the Printer Driver.

1)  You must select the Printer Driver Device by opening :PRT.0

2)  Send the Printer Driver ON command CHR$(5) + "["

When you've finished, send the Printer Driver OFF command CHR$(%) + "]"'. With these Printer Driver ON/OFF commands, there are a number of other codes that interface the Driver to BASIC and the other programs on the Z88 that uses the Printer.  These are listed in the Printer Driver Section below.

## Printer Editor ☐E

We feel that we should add a note here to remind you that the Printer Editor has already the driver installed for an Epson Printer.  If your printer uses different codes for underlining and so on, you will have to change them.

See the PIPEDREAM section for further details on how to do this.

# Printer Driver

It must be a bit confusing at first sight how Application Programs, Printer Editor and the Printer are connected together. To help you, here is how we think they work!

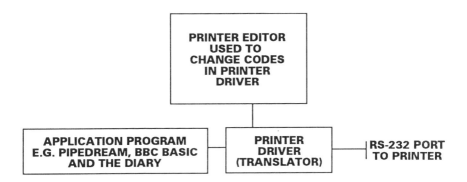

## Using the Printer Driver from Applications

The Printer Driver uses special common codes so that it can be easily interfaced with all the application programs that use the Printer, like PIPEDREAM, DIARY, BASIC etc.

If you are using BASIC, then YOU have to send these codes to the Printer Driver when you want to use the printer. We have already seen how you can turn the Printer Editor ON and OFF in the previous section, but here are the full list of codes, should you want to use these printer codes.

You MUST switch the Printer Driver ON or OFF, when you start and finish using it. Sending it those codes will automatically send the "Printer On" and "Printer Off" codes to the Printer, (so make sure the Printer is connected before using it!).

All the codes start with an ENQ (ASCII code 5) so we will put all the codes in that format.

## Control Codes

| | |
|---|---|
| 5,'[' | Printer Editor On |
| 5,']' | Printer Editor Off |
| 5,'2','P',32 + n | Set page length to 'n' lines |
| 5,'2','P',32 + n | Microspace 'n' units |
| 5,'S' | New slot, reset highlights that would be reset on CR |
| 5,'3','$','x','y' | Send &xy to the Printer |

## Toggle display modes

| | |
|---|---|
| 5,'U' | Underline |
| 5,'B' | Bold |
| 5,'X' | Extended sequence |
| 5,'I' | Italics |
| 5,'L' | Subscript (lowered text) |
| 5,'R' | Superscript (raised text) |
| 5,'A' | Alternate font |
| 5,'E' | User defined |

The following codes are also sent to the printer together with SP to DEL (Hex Code &20-&7F).

NUL (&00)
BEL (&07)
BS (&08)
HT (&09)
LF (&0A)
VT (&0B)
FF (&0C)
CR (&0D)

# Talking to Other Computers

Let's look at an example of why we should be interested in doing file transfers.

## Sharing data

This file you are reading now, started life on the Z88 in our back garden. Unfortunately, it started to rain, so in came the Z88 and we transferred the file to the PC computer and continued writing the same file on that.

Now the future of this file (depending on when we finally finish it) will be to transfer it back to the Z88. It will then go next door and be loaded onto Ann's PCW computer to have the typing errors removed. After being reloaded on the Z88 again and then back to the PC computer, it will be put onto disks and then sent to the publisher.

## Backing up files

In the previous example we finally put the files onto a disk. This can serve as our backup copy, just in case the batteries on the Z88 go flat, or if a flash of lightning hits our power lines again and leaves this PC computer in a bad way.

# Different types of Files

There are two types of files that you will come across. These are ASCII and BINARY files.

## BINARY Files.

The only application on the Z88 that creates and uses Binary files is BBC BASIC. If you want to transfer a BINARY file you need to use one of the following programs to do the transfer.

> Import/Export
> Z-Term using X-Modem protocol
> PC Link

Notice that this list does not include the BBC Computer so if you want to transfer a BASIC file to your BBC Computer you need to make sure that it is an ASCII file first - See Working with the Wizard for this.

## ASCII Files

Most applications on the Z88 use ASCII files

> DIARY
> PIPEDREAM
> PRINTER EDITOR
> PANEL

If you wish to transfer an ASCII file you can use:-
> BBC Link
> PC LinkII
> MacLink or any other programs that use the PC Link EPROM.

Bear in mind that you can always transfer an ASCII file in BINARY, but you can't transfer a BINARY file in ASCII.

## An Example using an IBM PC and the Z88

## Installing on the PC

First, you need to make a copy of all the files that are supplied with the package on either 3.5 inch disks or 5.25 inch disks. If you've got the wrong sort, send the disk back to Cambridge Computer for a replacement.

Read the instructions - and use the setup program especially if you have a floppy disk computer because it makes up a working disk of PC Link together with some system programs that it needs.

## Plug in cartridge

Returning to the Z88 you need to plug in the Link Popdown EPROM into any available slot (after putting the Z88 into the INDEX first).

## Using PC Link II

You should start running the Link Popdown on the Z88 with the ☐L command. This program when running will inhibit the time-out feature on the Z88, so it is a good idea to use the mains adapter here, otherwise you may find your batteries are flat before you've got your files across to the PC!!

Type 'pclink' on the PC. If communication is made, then you will see a picture of the PC and Z88 on the screen of your PC. If not, see the problems page. All the commands for file transfer and file conversion, will then be handled on the PC.

## File conversions

File conversions are extremely useful. PC Link II can convert PIPEDREAM files into WordStar (for word processor files) or Lotus 1-2-3 (for spreadsheet files). There is normally a conversion program available to convert from Wordstar and Lotus 1-2-3 to the wordprocessor or spreadsheet you are using.

You cannot have a mix of wordprocessing and spreadsheets together, as you do within PIPEDREAM. If your file has both, you would first have to separate them on the Z88 before transferring them to the PC. Then you would convert the spreadsheet one to Lotus 1-2-3 and the wordprocessor file to WordStar separately.

If the package you are using can handle both spreadsheet and wordprocessor together, then you can 'import' the two files that you have converted into the package using the facility of loading in a Lotus 1-2-3 and a WordStar file.

Of course, if you like PIPEDREAM, with the facility of mixing the two together, why not get a copy of PIPEDREAM for the PC or Archimedies, then you don't have to worry with any file conversion - just send the file to and from the Z88.

# Using your Z88 as a terminal

Having a TERMINAL on your Z88 is quite useful when you wish to con-nect your Z88 to another computer or use it with a Modem

Remember, you may need to change the baud rate and the other values for the serial port to that you used with your printer. Use the PANEL ☐S to change these. You can use the explanation given previously in the

Serial Printer section if you have forgotten how to use this. You may decide to save these values in a file from the PANEL, so that you can just load your terminal set-ups and your printer set-ups when required.

## Terminal □V

The TERMINAL is VT52 compatible. This means that although you are using a Z88, the weirdo you have connected to it will think that your Z88 is a VT52 Terminal.

### Commands

The commands that are available are shown by pressing MENU. There are only a few so we've listed them here.

Cursor movement - use the arrow keys

Function keys - These are special to the VT52, and are used to do different things in different programs - look in the manual of your weirdo for details.

| | |
|---|---|
| Function 0 | SHIFT + LEFT ARROW |
| Function 1 | SHIFT + RIGHT ARROW |
| Function 2 | SHIFT + DOWN ARROW |
| Function 3 | SHIFT + UP ARROW |
| Rubout | DEL |
| Backspace | SHIFT + DEL |
| EXIT from the Terminal Program | SHIFT + ENTER |

There is no direct facility to save or send the text to or from a file in the TERMINAL program. You can use the COPY command in the FILER to send a file and CLI command □ + S to receive a file copy of what is sent to the Z88's screen. Read the "Working with the Wizard" BEFORE USING IT (please!!).

To enable your Z88 to talk to another computer you will need a communications package. These packages will include a program to run on the 'other' computer and a cable to link it to the Z88. They will either use software already on the Z88 (Import Export) or they will provide their own program on ROM.

---

**Tip. Check PANEL Settings are Correct**
**Before doing file transfers check your PANEL ☐S. Your other computer, like your printer may need different Baud rate, Parity and Xon/Xoff settings.**

---

## Computer Linking Packages

To summarise, there are a number of 'ready-made' packages already available, here are a few of the more popular ones.

| | |
|---|---|
| PC Link-II | Z88 to PC compatible computer |
| Mac Link | Z88 to Apple Macintosh |
| BBC Link | Z88 to BBC computer |
| PCW Link | Z88 to PCW computer |

## IMPORT/EXPORT

This is a built-in PopDown in the Z88 that allows you to transfer files across to other computers.

Other communicating packages use IMPORT/EXPORT on the Z88. This program uses special characters so that the name of the file can be transferred as well as the file itself. Programs that use this include the PCW Amstrad Link, the BBC Link and the old PC Link program.

Before you start ...... Are your customs papers in order?

What we mean is that there are several steps you should take before using this program.

1. Make sure that the other computer and your Z88 are set up to the same baud rate, parity bit and that Xon/Xoff is set to 'Yes'. To set these use the PANEL ☐S and press ENTER to update these new values.

2. You should have got a copy of a program for the other computer to send and receive files in the IMPORT/EXPORT protocol down the serial (RS-232) port. See IMPORT/EXPORT Protocol for full details.

3. You should get the correct cable to connect the two computers together.

---

**Tip. Filenames in IMPORT/EXPORT**
**If you are using different devices and directories you have to use "Full Filenames" with the IMPORT/EXPORT program. You are unable to set it up with the FILER, as in the case of PIPEDREAM, because both the FILER and IMPORT/EXPORT are PopDown programs, only one of them has complete control!**

---

To select IMPORT/EXPORT use ☐X or select it from the INDEX. You will get the following response:-

    Imp-export B)atch receive, E)nd batch, R)eceive file or S)end file?

There are four commands and two modes of operation.

You can send and receive files either individually or as a batch.

Let's look at Sending a file (and a batch of files) from the Z88 first.

After selecting S for Send and then pressing the ENTER key you should see:- Filename?

Now you have a choice of either entering a single "Full filename" name or you can use a wildcard to select several files to send at the same time.

Let's look at the single name first which should be in the form of :DEVICE\DIRECTORY\FILENAME

Set up the other computer so that it is ready waiting to receive the file from the Z88 and then press ENTER on the Z88. You should see the line numbers appear on the Z88 as they are being sent together with the file name.

After the file has been sent the Z88 returns to the main menu for more instructions.

If you want to Send more than one file, you just put them one after the other in the Send filename? line or you can use a wildcard. For example, ":DEVICE\DIRECTORY\*" would send all the files in the :DEVICE\DIRECTORY\ to the other computer without you having to type the file names individually.

When sending several files, however you need to tell the other computer when you have finished and you do this at the end by selecting the E)nd batch command. The other computer should then finish saving the file(s) and then wait for further instructions.

Receiving files is very similar. Use R)eceive file for single files. You can either put in the name that you want to save it as on the Z88 when you get the Filename? prompt, or by pressing the ENTER key with no filename, the Z88 should pick up the filename sent by the other computer.

To receive a batch of files use B)atch receive. Remember it is now up to the other computer to tell the Z88 when it has finished with the "End Batch" command.

## Suspended - Trouble on the border

If the battery goes low, the card flap is opened or the Z88 is switched off the display will be turned off. If this occurs whilst sending or receiving a file using Import/Export, a "Suspended" message will be displayed when the display comes back on. You then have to start the transfer again.

## Import/Export protocol

To cross the frontier you need a program on the other computer that
sends and receives the file in the following protocol. For programmers
this is quite an easy task, but for us mortals without the gift of programming this can be a "Pain in the Neck!" Fear not, for the Z88 Users Group
have a library of programs that have already been written by the chosen
few for other computers, and you might be lucky in finding "The one for
You!" For further details of this dating service, join the Z88 Users'
Group, then pose the question!

For all those programmers out there, you are not going to be disap-
pointed. Here are the codes you've been waiting for. Good Luck!

| Code | Function |
|---|---|
| ESC N | Start of the Filename |
| ESC F | End of the Filename and Start of the File |
| ESC E | End of a File .. more to follow |
| ESC Z | End of a File and End of the Batch |
| ESC B x y | A Hex byte is to follow in the form of two ASCII characters in the x y. For example the byte &C8 will be sent as ESC B C 8 |
| XON = &11 | Receiver sends to the transmitter to re-start the data. |
| XOFF = &13 | Receiver sends to the transmitter to stop the data. |

All characters after the ESC code must be in UPPER CASE.

# Transfer protocol

First file, and subsequent files: ESC N filename ESC F data ESC E

Last file: ESC N filename ESC F data ESC Z

where data is a sequence of characters between &20 and &7E, characters in the range of &00 to &1F and &7F to &FF should be transmitted
using the ESC B Hex code sequence.

If all else fails and you still want to send a file over to your favourite com-puter try using the Copy command in the FILER. It is unlikely that you would be able to do any file conversion i.e. PIPEDREAM to Whatsit wordprocessor, so first you should save the file in PIPEDREAM as a "Plain text file". This will remove all the special characters that PIPEDREAM uses to underline words, or define how many lines you can get on the page and so on, but retains the text.

Remember to check the PANEL ☐ S settings to see that the baud rates are the same as the other computer. Check that you know how to get the data from the serial port to a file on the other computer before you send the file from the Z88. Look at the other computer's manual to find out what to do under "transferring data" using the RS-232 Serial port. Also look up what is used for the 'end of file' character. This character is &1A ( ◊Z) for MS DOS ans CP/M computers or &04 ( ◊D for UNIX com-puters. See the ASCII table, at the end of the book, for other characters.

Select the FILER ☐ F and mark the file you want to send. Select Copy ◊CO and you should see:-

Name :                     SELECTED FILES

New Name :

Put :COM.0 in the new name press ENTER twice and your file should then get sent to the other computer.

When the Z88 has finished the other computer is waiting for more! You have got to tell it that you have finished and you do this by sending the other computer and 'End of File' character from the Z88. How do you do that? I hear you ask - simple - just go into the Terminal with ☐ V and then press the code you found earlier. The other computer should now burst into life by saving the file you have sent it onto disk.

To send a file to the Z88 you should be able do the reverse, putting :COM.0 in Name and the filename in New Name, but this DOES NOT WORK because you can't send the Z88 an "end of file" command. You have to use the CLI command ☐ +S to receive a file copy of what is being sent to the Z88's screen. Read "Working with the Wizard" BEFORE using it Please!

## The Problem Page

What? Isn't it working? What a surprise!! Here are some useful hints. If it doesn't work it is normally something quite simple.

Has the cable been plugged in correctly?

If you are using a switch box, is the switch in the right position?

Is the power turned on?

Are the weirdos turned on?

Has the Z88 timed out?

If all else fails, try another weirdo, cable or even another Z88.

## Modems - Remote connections to computers

Modems allow "remote" connection to other computers, using the telephone line as the cable. This facility can allow you to connect your Z88 to your computer at work, home or even "Electronic Mail" computers like Telecom Gold or Mercury.

If you wish to connect your Z88 over the telephone line, the other computer must be equipped with a modem and a communications program. There are a number of battery-powered modems available including one that is designed for use with the Z88 and comes complete with connecting cables and an EPROM program to allow you to store the telephone numbers to dial on the Z88. If you wish to use another modem as long as it is "Hayes compatible" then you could Z-Term, a program produced by Wordmongers.

# Z88 Basic

## Introduction

This chapter introduces you to the wonderful world of Z88 BASIC. Our aim is simple - to show you how to write a BASIC "program" - even if you've never even thought of writing one before.

Since we've got only one chapter to cover a topic that normally takes a complete book, we've had to leave out a lot of interesting stuff. But you'll find that there's enough to get you started and to give you enough insight to write quite complex applications and to understand the description in the User Guide - there's a lot to cover!

To provide a framework for the chapter, most of the examples are taken from a real application - a program for a double glazing salesman.

Reading this chapter without having a Z88 beside you will probably lead to confusion... BASIC requires you to learn quite a few new concepts which are easier to absorb if you can put them into practice as you learn them.

## Why use Basic?

As we've seen, the Z88 already includes a powerful set of applications which cover the majority of things that you might want to do with a computer. The main reason for using BASIC is to persuade your Z88 to do something special just for you. But, before you leap in and begin generating your application, bear in mind that most of the things that can be done by simple BASIC programs can be done with PIPEDREAM.

But, suppose you've got to work with statistics (the kind of which Disreali said "there are lies, damned lies and statistics") that are not easily expressed in a PIPEDREAM spreadsheet. If you know the formulae, then you can write a BASIC program to perform them for you.

That's a classic application of BASIC, to perform mathematical calculations, and it's all that lots of people think Basic can be used for. Not so... We've written quite of few Basic programs over the years and only a few have involved solely mathematics - the rest have been processing text.

Let's be clear - we're not suggesting that you try and rewrite PIPEDREAM in BASIC. But it's surprising how many tasks can be accomplished by simple BASIC programs. For example, the "core" of the double glazing program - the part that calculates the quotation - is only about ten lines long.

There are, of course, limits to what you can do with BASIC. We don't think you could use it to control a nuclear power station, but, within reason and with a little thought, it's amazing just what you can do.

There's another reason which, for some people, is just as important as getting the job done. Programming is good fun - most people get a thrill out of persuading an inanimate lump of plastic called a Z88 to behave just as they want it to.

A word of warning - programming is certainly addictive and should probably have a government health warning. You should either be strong willed or have plenty of time and patience.

## What's Programming?

We've used a term - "programming" - that you've probably heard quite a few times when people are talking about computers. In passing, the noun is spelled "program" - one of the gifts of the American language to us Europeans. You've probably heard some other phrases as well - "a computer must be told how to do anything" and even "garbage in, garbage out" (we'll cover that one later).

Well, it's true that computers don't understand anything but they are provided with a kind of "toolbox" which we can use to describe to the computer what we want it to do.

What we'll be doing is explaining how you describe what you want to do in language that BASIC can understand. In other words, how you use the BASIC toolbox. The job is a lot easier if you plan what to do and decide what tools are needed.

## How to decide what to do

It's all too easy to dive straight in and begin typing in the program (an activity called "coding" for historical reasons) but, unless you're a genius, or very lucky the result will be frustration as well as a program which suffers from the following:

> a) It will be difficult to get it working properly - you'll spend a lot of time thinking "I wish I'd thought of that earlier".

> b) It probably won't do what you want it to - either because you'll run out of time or patience or both.

> c) It won't be easily changed - so the next time you want to do something similar, you'll end up starting again.

If you aren't completely put off learning BASIC, the solution is as simple as it is obvious:

**Always spend some time designing what the program is going to do and how it is going to do it before you start coding.**

This process is known as "specification". Note that it consists of two parts - we'll call them "what" and "how". The "what" part typically includes such things as what you expect to type in and what output you want to see. The "how" part explains the details of the steps by which the program operates.

Now for some bad news - and it's taken twenty year's experience to say this - the ONLY way to be sure that you are clear in your own mind about the specification is to write it down. Since you've got a Z88, why not use PIPEDREAM?

In techie talk, this is called "The Specification and Design Phase" (so now you can really impress your friends) but don't worry - the written descriptions don't have to be very detailed - just so long as you understand them yourself.

For reference, we've included the specification of the Double Glazing program.

This has two sections, Object and Functions, which say 'what' the program is going to do and two sections Operation and Error Handling, which show how the program is going to operate.

## Double Glazing Program Specification

### Object

The object of the sales program is to allow a double glazing salesman to prepare quotations and record orders on his Z88 and then to pass data on sales to a PIPEDREAM spreadsheet for statistical analysis.

### Functions

The program performs the following functions:

> a) Allows input of customer's name and address or recalls existing customers

b) Allows entering of customer's requirements, in the form of a list of windows.

c) Calculates the price of the double glazing

d) Allows the salesman to enter a "quick order discount" - after all, this will be used by the typical double glazing salesman!

e) Record the order and the method of payment

f) Send the details of the order to a PIPEDREAM spreadsheet for statistical analysis.

**Operation**

The program is assumed to be left as a suspended activity between each call.

It will ask for the customer's name, check if it is already known and, if so, will recall the address together with an indication of the total value of orders that this customer has placed. Otherwise, it will ask for the address.

Next, the sizes of windows (entered as width and height) will be requested. The list of window sizes will be terminated by entering a width of zero. Negative widths and heights will be regarded as errors.

Upon completion of the list, the program will display the total cost and allow the salesman to enter a discount amount. Negative discounts are regarded as invalid. This will be applied and the program will display the discounted price and the "saving".

The salesman may confirm the order and then enter a method of payment. This may be "credit card", "cheque" or "finance deal". (In a real application, it is liable that this part of the program would be greatly expanded to deal with other options as well as satisfying the many government regulations that apply.)

The generation of the data for exporting to the PIPEDREAM spreadsheet will be automatic as soon as the order is confirmed.

### Error Handling

The error handling in the program will be limited to picking up invalid input data. The response of the program to invalid data will be to issue an error message and request that the user re- inputs the correct data.

------------------------

See, it really isn't that bad and at least we know what the program is supposed to do even if, as yet, you don't have a clue about how to write it. Don't worry if your specifications aren't as "formal" as this one. All that's important is that it records the essential details of the program.

## Ensuring that your Programs work

In the late 1980's, you should, even though you are just beginning to write Basic, try and ensure that your programs have some feel of "quality" to them.

Let us explain: When you go shopping for a tool, would you choose a dirty old tool that was twenty years old and didn't really do the job or choose the latest tool which did the job in half the time and with less effort? Put like that, it's easy to choose, isn't it!

OK, so what's this got to do with BASIC? Well, over the twenty year life of Basic, people have discovered some fundamental does and don'ts which apply no matter what the application. You've already met one of them:

> 1. Always plan what your program is going to do.
>
> 2. When a program gets some data, always check that it's valid before using it.
>
> 3. Always try and produce code that can be re-used within different programs - this saves "re-inventing the wheel".
>
> 4. Always include "remarks" in your program to explain to yourself and others what it's doing.

5. Always ask yourself whether you will remember what the program did in six months time - and, come on, be honest about your memory.

If you obey these simple rules, you'll write programs you can be proud of, instead of making excuses like "Well, it sort of works but you mustn't type more than three letters because that crashes it".

# How you use BASIC

We've now going to write and then run our first BASIC program...

It's not going to be very long - in fact it's only one line - but it gives us the opportunity to cover lots of the mechanics of using Basic.

To start a copy of BASIC, either type ☐ B or select it from the Index page. Like all the other Z88 application, it can be suspended and then restarted either by selecting it from the list of suspended applications or by typing ☐ B - which selects each copy in turn.

When you start BASIC it displays:

```
BBC Basic (Z80) Version 3.00
(c) 1987 T.J. Russell
>
```

The ">" is the so-called "command prompt" which is nothing to do with theatres but is BASIC's way of saying "Ok, tell me what to do next".

You may notice how BASIC has selected Caps Lock for you automatically - shown by the "CAPS" legend in the OZ window. Leave it set for now, BASIC tends to prefer most things in upper case.

Right, we're now ready to write our first program, so type:

```
10 PRINT 1+2
```

If you make a mistake, correct it by using the DEL key - which will delete one character to the left of the cursor. Remember to make sure that "CAPS" is still selected. In passing, the left and right arrow keys operate as you'd expect, Basic uses the Insert/Overtype setting set up in the

PANEL However, the UP ARROW and DOWN ARROW keys are not used.

Let's explain what this line means:

"Call this line 'Number 10'. Work out the sum of 1 and 2 and print the answer on the screen."

You might be surprised that you just got another prompt when you hit ENTER. This is because BASIC realises that most programs are longer than one line and so doesn't execute each line as it is typed in.

## RUN

To tell BASIC to run your program, type:

```
RUN
```

Now, Basic "executes" your program to display the answer, which should be 3.

If the result is a message such as:

```
Mistake at line 10
```

You have made a typing mistake. Simply re-type the line. Basic always automatically looks through your program (which consists of the single line at the moment) to find a line with the same number as that you have just typed and will replace it with the new line. We'll cover this in more detail later.

## LIST

You can always look at your program by asking BASIC to "list" it. The command is:

```
LIST
```

You should see a copy of the program that you typed.

Don't be surprised if you find that the format that the program is listed in may be different from that you used when you typed it in. BASIC compresses your program to save space in memory, the listed version is recreated from this compressed version, not your original.

When you are listing a long program, you can either use just LIST to display the complete program (it will stop at the end of each page) or you can give a range of line numbers. The listing will include all the lines between these (or the ones nearest to them if the one you give don't exist). For example, the following command will list the first section of the double glazing program even though line 900 doesn't exist:

```
LIST 100,900
```

## ONE LINERS

Most BASIC "statements" - that is, the lines that make up a program - can also be entered without line numbers.  For example, type:

```
PRINT 3+4
```

This time, the result is displayed immediately - the name for this mode of execution is "immediate".  Unfortunately, very few useful programs can be written in one line but Immediate mode is invaluable when getting a program to work.  We cover this later on...

## NEW AND OLD

Before you type in a new program, it's a good idea to type:

```
NEW
```

This says "I'm writing a new program and I want a clean slate so please forget any other program that may be hanging around". NEW generally ensures that things are neat and tidy for the new program. Luckily, there's an antidote to NEW but it only works if you've not typed anything else. The magic word is "OLD".

Earlier, we mentioned that you should leave Caps Lock selected.  You can do this all the time, but there are certain things that can be in lower case in Basic programs.  You can select an "Inverted Shift" mode - where

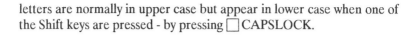

letters are normally in upper case but appear in lower case when one of the Shift keys are pressed - by pressing ☐ CAPSLOCK.

## SUMMARY

To start BASIC, use "☐ B" or select it from the INDEX.

BASIC lets you know it's ready for a command by displaying " > " as a prompt.

A BASIC program consists of lines, each one beginning with a line num- ber. Each line number in a program is unique, so entering another line with same number replaces the original.

You instruct BASIC to execute your program with the RUN command.

You can display the program by using the LIST command.

BASIC statements entered without line numbers are executed im- mediately.

Prepare BASIC for a new program by using the NEW command. Enter ☐ CAPSLOCK to select Inverted Shift mode.

# What's in a Variable?

So far, we've met three Basic statements: PRINT, RUN and LIST. Before we cover some of the others, we're going to look at "variables" which are really the key to the power of Basic.

In our experience, the concept of variables is one of most difficult for new- comers to Basic to grasp. Unfortunately, its also difficult to describe because of the "Eureka!" factor - once you do grasp it, it's so obvious that it's impossible to put yourself in the shoes of someone who hasn't grasped it.

We suggest that you settle down with your feet up and a large glass of your favourite tipple by your side...

Imagine a set of boxes, each with a name on the outside (which must be unique) and each just big enough to hold a sheet of paper with a number written on it.

At the start of a BASIC program, there are no boxes available, they are all in a storeroom. The first time you refer to a box, BASIC goes to its storeroom and fetches an empty box (actually, it puts a piece of paper with 0 written on it but that's just to be helpful).

Later, your program can read the piece of paper in the box (this is called "reading the variable") or it can replace the piece of paper with another with a different value (or even the same value as the one being replaced) written on it - this is called "writing to a variable".

Since each box can only hold one piece of paper, each variable can only hold one value at a time. When we replace one value with another, the old value is completely lost.

In passing, BASIC has quite a large storeroom of variables - you can create about one thousand variables even on an unexpanded Z88, so there is normally always room to create the variable.

OK, let's write a simple program using variables to see the concept in operation:

```
10 REM A demonstration of Variables
20 LET Amount = 580.50
30 LET Discount = 127.75
40 LET Price = 0.0
50 LET Price = Amount - Discount
60 PRINT Price
```

Before reading the description below, you may like to type the program in and RUN it. See if you can guess the result.

Line 10:                          This is "Remark". A remark always begins
                                  with the letters "REM" but can include any
                                  text to remind you what the program does.
                                  We'll see lots of them in this chapter.

Line 20:                          This loads a box called "Amount" with a piece
                                  of paper with 580.50 written on it. Since this

is the first reference to "Amount", Basic will get a empty box and write the "Amount" label before putting the piece of paper into it.

BASIC is rather naughty using the " = " symbol here. It does NOT mean "equal to" (although as we'll see later, Basic does try and confuse you by using the same symbol for that purpose.) This statement should be read "Let Amount become 580.50".

Line 30:

This repeats the process above, loading "Discount" with 127.75.

Line 40:

Repeats the process, loading "Price" with 0.0. (Actually, this line is not necessary in a real program, as BASIC will always create a variable whenever it is first used, we've included it so we can show how the value is overwritten by line 50.)

Line 50:

This is where things get interesting... The computer examines the contents of the "Amount" variable (it opens the box and reads the sheet of paper - which has the value "580.50"), repeats the process for "Discount" (which contains 127.75) and subtracts the VALUES. Basic always looks inside variables to get their values, it never tries to "subtract" the boxes. Having calculated the answer, 452.75, the program then puts that value in the "Price" variable. In effect, it replaces the sheet of paper in "Price" with a sheet with the value of the "expression" (580.50 - 127.75).

Line 60:

The latest value of the variable "Price", 452.75, is printed on the Z88 screen. Notice how the original value, which was 0, has been forgotten.

If you've not already tried this program, type NEW to clear any previous program, enter the program and then RUN it. It will display either 452.75 or an error message. If you do get an error message, welcome to the real world of computing... Later, we'll cover a number of ways of solving such problems. For now, you'll probably find your mistake if you look through the program having LISTed it. Retype the offending line.

## VARIABLE NAMES

The names you choose for your variables is very important to you - BASIC doesn't care if you called all your variables "A001", "A002" and so on but you would. We'd better explain...

It's all to do with Quality again. The names you choose can help you explain what your program does. Suppose we'd called the variable which held the discounted price "Percent". The program would still work: go on, try it and see (remember to change it all the times it appears - you'll need to re-enter lines 40, 50 and 60).

It's now six months later: you need to alter this program and LIST it. Line 50 would now read:

```
50 LET Percent = Amount - Discount
```

Help! That certainly doesn't look like a calculation of any percentage, does it?

We know that this example probably seems a bit far fetched but it's a very common problem. It's not the fault of BASIC, it let's you have variable names with up to 31 letters (and digits) long. It even let's you mix upper and lower case letters so the examples below are valid names:

InterestRate
CapitalInvested
Distance_Squared

The "_" character can be used as a letter in a variable name and is useful (as in the above examples) to separate words. A space cannot be included in variable names. One word of caution: Z88 BASIC is slightly unusual in that it treats upper and lower case letters as different in names of variables. So, a variable called "Count" is distinct from ones called "count" and "COUNT".

As well as variables that can hold numbers, BASIC also has two other sorts of boxes - "Integers" and "Strings".

## INTEGERS

An integer can only hold whole numbers - so, for example, it can hold 122 but not 122.1. It's just the same as a Real variable but it has a name which ends in "%". So, for example, the following are Integer variables:

Item_Count%
Total_People%

As these examples show, Integers can be useful when counting things, after all, it's normally difficult to have (say) 1.25 men. That's not to say that ordinary variables - the sort without a "%" - can't hold whole numbers at times, as the variable Price did at line 40 of our demonstration program - it's just that Integer variables can ONLY hold whole numbers.

There are two benefits of using Integer variables. First, they don't suffer from our old enemy "Rounding Errors". Second, they are processed much faster than ordinary variables - this is particularly true on the Z88.

## Strings

Strings can be understood by going back to our description of variables as boxes. The piece of paper that a String can contain has characters written on it. The box has "elastic" sides so it can hold Strings with any number of characters.

For example, if Customer$ is a String (yes, the "$" designates it as a String), then:

```
LET Customer$="Vic Gerhardi"
```

means that the contents of the string Customer$ will be set to 'Vic Gerhardi'. You can test this by typing this line - it will be executed immediately as there is no line number. To display the String, use the PRINT command

```
PRINT Customer$
```

As we said, Strings can hold any number of characters, so try the following little program:

```
10 REM Demonstration that a String can hold a
varying number of
20 REM characters
30 LET TestString$="A string"
40 PRINT LEN(TestString$), TestString$
50 LET TestString$="A longer string"
60 PRINT LEN(TestString$), TestString$
```

We're deliberately increasing the pace now so this example introduces
two new aspects of Basic:

1) More than one variable (or expression) can be printed by one PRINT
statement. See line 40 and 60.

2) The expression LEN(TestString$) is a "function call". LEN examines
the contents of the given string (in this case TestString$) and determines
the number of characters actually stored in the string.

BASIC provides a wide range of functions, ranging from the standard
mathematical functions like "COS" and "SIN" through "TIME$" (which
returns a String holding the current time). Later on we'll show you how
to write your own functions.

## ARRAYS

Sometimes, it's convenient to refer to one of a set of variables by number.
For example, you might have a list of customer names. Programs would
quickly get unworkable if you had to store each one as a separate variables.

In BASIC, the set of variables can be stored in an "Array". Unlike other
variables, this must be "declared" - this tells BASIC how many boxes to
set aside. Suppose we had twenty customers, we would use:

```
DIM Customer$(20)
```

"DIM" is an abbreviation of "Dimension". To refer to a particular "element" you write an expression like:

```
Customer$(15)
```

This opens the fifteenth box in the array Customer$ - in BASIC terminology, the value of 15 is used as a "subscript" to select an element of the array. You should note that the type of the array is declared, just as with other variables, by whether it's name ends in '%' (for an Integer array), "$" (for an array of Strings) or neither (which creates an array of numbers).

If your program refers to an element outside the declared size; as in:

```
Customer$(23)
```

Basic will complain by displaying the rather cryptic error message "Subscript". This is confusing as the number in brackets is also the subscript. Actually, Basic is rather generous because, for free, it creates another element which it calls element 0. Supposedly, this can be useful although we always forget about it...

The real power of arrays comes when you discover that, as well as referring to the elements of an array by number, you can use a variable (actually, any expression) as a subscript. Therefore, the following BASIC program will display "Gill". We've commented it so you should be able to understand it from the code alone:

```
10 REM Declare an array of 3 Strings
20 DIM Names$(4)
30 REM Set up some names
40 LET Names$(1)="Vic"
50 LET Names$(2)="Gill"
60 LET Names$(3)="Andy"
70 REM Set up an Integer to access the 2nd name
80 LET Second%=2
90 REM Now, print the accessed element
100 PRINT Names$(Second%)
```

Line 20 declares the array as having four elements but we've only used three. The others, that is, Names$(4) and the "free" one - Names$(0), contain so-called "null" strings which have no characters in them. If you declare arrays which have more elements than you're actually using, Basic doesn't mind. Don't declare all the arrays you use a lot larger than they need to be as the spare elements still occupy memory.

There is one question you may like answered: What happens if I use an ordinary variable or a number like "3.5" as a subscript? As always, Basic tries to be as helpful as it can and "truncates" the value to the next lower Integer. So, Names$(3.5) is treated just as if you'd typed Names$(3).

## 2-D 3-D or more

Try to picture the simple array described above as a straight line of boxes labelled from 1 to the number declared in the "DIM" statement. In mathematical terms, it's one dimensional.

It's possible to declare two-dimensional arrays which can be pictured as a grid (rather like the array of PIPEDREAM cells), or a three-dimensional array - picture one of these as a box full of little boxes. It's even possible to declare four dimensional (or even higher) arrays but these become rather difficult to visualise.

For example, the statement below declares a two-dimensional array with twenty rows of four String variables:

```
DIM Address$(20,4)
```

To access a particular element, say the second one of the fifth row, the subscripts are written as shown below:

```
Address$(5,2)
```

This example illustrates one of the reasons for using multi- dimensional arrays - they allow you to relate groups of variables together. There could be one row of the array for each customer and each element in that row will be a String holding one line of the customer's address.

## SUMMARY

Basic uses variables to hold values during the execution of a program.

There are three kinds of variables. Ordinary variables hold decimal numbers and have names which end in no special character. Integer variables can only hold whole numbers and have names that end in "%". String variables hold strings of characters - any number from one to about 250 - and have names ending in "$".

You must decide how many elements there are going to be and declare it, using a DIM statement in an array before you start using it. You tell BASIC which element of the array to look at by using a subscript. Multidimensional arrays can be created and used.

Names for all variables in your program should be chosen to reflect what they all going to hold. There's rarely a good reason for re-using the same variable for two different purposes and never a good reason (or even a remotely good excuse) for using cryptic names. If in doubt, always make the names you use longer rather than shorter.

## Being Expressive

So far, we've only shown examples of LET statements where the "right hand side" (that is, the value to be assigned to the variable on the left of the equals sign) have been simple "constants" (such as 580.50 or "Gill"), other variables or simple arithmetic expressions (such as Amount - Discount).

But Z88 allows much more complex expressions - similar to those you can create in PIPEDREAM spreadsheets. For example:

```
10 REM Take a percentage discount from a price
20 LET Price = Price -
(PercentDiscount/100)*Price
```

The expression in line 20 first divides the PercentDiscount by 100 to yield the fractional rate, then multiplies this by the Price which yields the amount of the discount. This is then subtracted from the original price to give the discounted price. Finally, the discounted price is stored in the variable called "Price". Remember, the " = " symbol in a LET means "becomes".

An interesting example of expressions using functions is shown below:

```
10 REM Get the current date
20 LET Date$ = LEFT$(TIME$, LEN(TIME$)-10)
```

When you RUN this program, you will notice that it doesn't display the results of this expression because there is no PRINT statement. To see the values, you can use an immediate mode PRINT statement after RUNning the program - that is, you type a PRINT statement without a line number:

```
PRINT  Date$
```

Line 20 shows how complex expressions can become... See if you can work out what's happening before you follow the description below.

The TIME$ function (which is a little unusual in that it's not followed by brackets) reads the internal clock maintained by the Z88 and returns a String which contains the date and time. Because we want only the date, we must remove the time portion from the string.

Unfortunately, day names have different lengths so we can't just take the first "n" characters from the string. Instead, we get the length of the string (via the LEN function) and then, because the time portion of the string is ten characters (assuming European format), we subtract 10 from the length of the TIME$ string to yield the length of just the date portion. Finally, we apply the LEFT$ function which creates a string which is a copy of the TIME$ string for as many characters as specified - in our case, just the length of the date.

In fact, this example contains a subtle mistake. Because TIME$ is called twice in one expression, it could return different answers. However, this only matters around twelve midnight - we might get two results which have strings of different lengths because the day names have different lengths (say "Monday" and "Tuesday").

There is a special use of the " + " operator for joining strings (in BASIC terminology, this is "concatenation"). For example, the program below:

```
10 REM Example of string concatenation
20 LET Forename$="Gill"
30 LET Surname$="Gerhardi"
40 PRINT Forename$+" "+Surname$
```

will display "Gill Gerhardi". Notice that we had to insert a space between the names, BASIC treats Strings as blocks of characters, not as separate words.

A full list of the operators and functions that you can use in expressions can be found in the User Guide.

# Further into the Basics of Basic

Before looking at some of the other statements, other than LET, PRINT and DIM, that make up Basic programs, there are some details that are important.

Statements usually begin with a "keyword". Because most programs have lots of LET statements and Basic can recognise them easily anyway, it allows you to miss the LET keyword. Therefore:

```
10 LET InitialValue = 0.0
```

and:

```
10 InitialValue = 0.0
```

Both perform exactly the same operation - setting the value of the variable "InitialValue" to zero.

There's another short-cut: more than one statement can appear on a single line if each statement is separated by a ":". This means that our sample program can be written:

```
10 REM A demonstration of Variables
20 Amount = 580.50 : Discount = 127.75
30 Price = Amount - Discount : PRINT Price
```

It would even be possible to write the complete program on one line although that generally not a good idea as it would make the program more difficult to read.

## Line Numbers

By now, we expect you're wondering why the line numbers at the beginning of each statement mean and why they always seem to increase in steps of ten. These little numbers actually control the order in which most of the program is executed...

As you enter a program, Basic is continually checking the statement numbers on each line. It's aim is to ensure that the lines are numbered in ascending order. It doesn't mind if there are gaps in the numbers but each must be unique.

Can you guess what happens if you enter two lines with the same number in a program? If you made a mistake in one of the examples and corrected it by retyping the line, you already know. BASIC forgets about the old line and uses the new one.

All these points will probably become clearer if you type NEW (to clear any program that's already there) and then type the following lines:

```
12 Test2=1.2
23 PRINT Sum
18 Sum=Test1+Test2
9 Test1=1.3
12 Test2=1.5
191 REM this will be at the end
5 REM this will be at the beginning
```

Before you try a LIST command to sort out this mess, see if you can fathom out what the result will be. Remember, BASIC sorts the statements into ascending order and uses only the latest copy of any line.

When you do list the program, you should see:

```
5 REM this will be at the beginning
9 Test1=1.3
12 Test2=1.5
18 Sum=Test1+Test2
23 PRINT Sum
191 REM this will be at the end
```

Because BASIC automatically sorts the statements into order, it's a good idea to leave some gaps in the line numbers so you can insert lines without worrying about a block of lines running into another. It's for this reason that the examples in this chapter all use steps of ten - you could then insert up nine lines between each statement and still maintain the correct order.

## Auto and Renumber

Just for completeness, we'd better mention two rather special commands which allow you to handle line numbers. The AUTO statement automatically fills in the line numbers for you and the RENUMBER statement does just that - it renumbers all the lines of your program.

## Saving and Loading

When you have written a Basic program, you will want to save it so that you can re-use it later. The command to do this is "SAVE" and it is followed by the name of the file in ""'s. So, for example, our double glazing program might be saved on RAM.1 with:

```
SAVE ":RAM.1/Glazing"
```

If you don't specify a cartridge, the one specified as the Default Device in the PANEL is used.

To retrieve a program, the LOAD command is used. As with the SAVE command, the file name is enclosed in double quotes. To retrieve the double glazing program, we would enter:

```
LOAD ":RAM.1/Glazing"
```

If you want to load a program and then immediately RUN it, use the CHAIN command:

```
CHAIN ":RAM.1/Glazing"
```

As an aside, this command can appear in programs, so you can build programs which are larger than the available memory by splitting them into sections and then CHAINing them together.

## Naming your program

BBC BASIC provides a whole series of "star commands" - that is, commands beginning with "*" - for providing access to the operating system.
The Z88 implementation provides only a few of these but the "*NAME"
command is useful as it allows you to choose a name for your program
which will be displayed in the INDEX page when your program is a
suspended activity. For example:

```
10 *NAME Glazing
```

will display "Glazing" when the program is a suspended activity.

## Summary

BASIC statements normally begin with a keyword, except that "LET" can
be left out.

More than one BASIC statement can appear on a line if they are
separated by colons.

Normally, BASIC programs are executed from top to bottom after sorting the statement numbers in ascending order. If a line with a duplicate
statement number is entered, it replaces the existing line.

To save a Basic program, use the SAVE "filename" command. To run a
saved program, use either LOAD "filename" followed by RUN or CHAIN
"filename".

The *NAME command can be used to identify the program in the list of
suspended activities in the INDEX.

## Talking to the User

In this section, we're going to introduce an important person into the picture - the user of your program. Even if you are going to be the only person
using the program, it's still vital that it should be easy to use.

We've already seen how you can display the results of your programs using
the PRINT statement. Later in this section, more details of the PRINT

statement are covered to allow you to format your displays so as to make the output from your programs clearer.

## Input

Let's explain how the user can provide input for the program to use. In the simple examples so far, we've always used LET statements to assign values to variables but this requires that the user knows BASIC and knows which lines to alter.

A better way is to use the INPUT statement as shown in the program below:

```
10 REM A demonstration of INPUT
20 INPUT Amount
30 INPUT Discount
40 LET Price = Amount - Discount
50 PRINT Price
```

If you enter this program and RUN it, you will see that it displays a "?" - it's asking for the amount of the sale. Type 580.50 and then Enter. The program displays another question mark - it's asking for the discount amount. After typing 127.75, hit ENTER and the program displays "452.75" which we know is the discounted price.

The best you can say of this little program is that "It works!" - it's certainly not user-friendly and it requires the user to know what data to enter when the "?"'s appear.

Now, look at the example below:

```
10 REM A demonstration of INPUT with prompts
20 INPUT "Please enter the value of the
Order",Amount
30 INPUT "Please enter the Discount ",Discount
40 LET Price = Amount - Discount
50 PRINT Price
```

We've asked BASIC to display a message prompting the user for the appropriate figures - the user no longer needs to understand the program itself - he merely follows the instructions given to him.

We've padded the string on line 30 so that the output aligns with that from line 20 - a small touch but one which can make a great deal of difference to the "feel" of the program.

You've probably noticed that the "?"'s still appear even though they are not included in the prompt string - this is because the strings are separated from the variables by a comma. If you don't want the question marks, don't use commas; as in:

```
20 INPUT "Please enter the value of the Order "
Amount
30 INPUT "Please enter the Discount " Discount
```

Sometimes, you may want to combine the input of two variables in one INPUT statement:

```
20 INPUT "Please enter Value",Amount,"and
Discount",Discount
```

However, this makes formatting of the display and verification of the value of each variable (covered in the next section) difficult and is not recommended.

In passing, if you are reading strings which are likely to contain characters such as commas, quotes or leading spaces (data such as addresses) then you should use the INPUT LINE statement. For example:

```
90 INPUT LINE "First Line of Address :-"
Address$(CustomerNo,1)
```

## Print

So far, the program still displays the discounted price with no text and no control over how many decimal places are displayed. First, let's modify the program to add some text before the value is displayed:

```
10 REM Program to calculate discounted price
20 INPUT "Please enter the value of the
Order",Amount
30 INPUT "Please enter the Discount ",Discount
40 LET Price = Amount - Discount
50 PRINT "The Discounted Price is ",Price
```

As in the INPUT statement, the comma in the PRINT statement has special significance. In a PRINT statement, a comma causes the Z88 to assume that the values are to be aligned to ten character tab stops. If you want no spaces between items, separate them with ";"s. If the last item in a PRINT statement ends with a ";", the next display position is used for the next PRINT statement; otherwise, printing will continue at the beginning of the next line.

## What is @%

To gain control over the number of decimal places and the precise format of the displayed value you must use the special variable called "@%". You set this to a value and then PRINT the variable.

Decoding the documentation in the User Guide and setting up this variable is not a job for the faint-hearted (particularly as it's coded in "hexadecimal") and so we've included a list of useful values. Just type one of these statements:

Default Value: LET @% = &0000090A - displays numbers with up to nine decimal places in a ten character field.

Currency Values: LET @% = &0002020C -displays numbers with two decimal places in a twelve character field.

Scientific Use: LET @% = &0001090E -displays numbers in scientific notation (ie, 100 would be displayed as: 1.000000000E2) in a fourteen character field.

Using the suggested value of "@%" specified for currency values, our sample program becomes:

```
10 REM Using the format control variable
20 INPUT "Please enter the value of the
Order",Amount
30 INPUT "Please enter the Discount",Discount
40 LET Price = Amount - Discount
50 REM Set up the format control variable to
force two d.p
60 LET @% = &0002020C
70 REM Display the price
80 PRINT "The Discounted Price is",Price
```

To get really professional looking output, you can use two other state-ments. "CLS" clears the text area on the Z88. "TAB" allows you to control the position of output on the display.

TAB behaves like a function in that it is called from within an INPUT or PRINT statement and can be used to position within the current line; as in:

```
10 PRINT
"Beginning";TAB(35);"Middle";TAB(70);"End"
```

Or, to position text anywhere on the screen, as in:

```
10 PRINT
TAB(0,0);"Beginning";TAB(35,4);"Middle";TAB(70,7);
"Bottom";
```

Characters are numbered from 0 to 93 (ie, the Pipedream map area can be used) and rows are numbered from 0 to 7. If you access the screen with this form of TAB you must remember to end every PRINT statement with a ";" or the display will scroll as each PRINT statement is executed.

Let's apply these commands in the sample program, notice how TAB can appear in INPUT statements as well as in PRINT:

```
10 REM Using CLS and TAB
20 CLS
30 REM Display a title
40 PRINT TAB(40,0);"Discount Calculator";
50 INPUT TAB(20,2),"Please enter the value of
the Order",Amount
60 INPUT TAB(20,3),"Please enter the Discount
",Discount
70 LET Price = Amount - Discount
80 REM Set up the format control variable to
force two d.p
90 LET @% = &0002020C
100 REM Display the price - remember to stop at
end of line
110 PRINT TAB(20,5);"The Discounted Price is
";Price;
```

## Summary

Your aim should be to help the user work with your programs.

To get input from the user of a program, use the INPUT statement. Remember to include a prompt message identifying what data is required.

Variables are displayed using the PRINT statement. If more than one item is included they will be displayed aligned at tab stops if they are separated with commas or without if they are separated by semi-colons, they will just follow on, one after the other.

After a print statement the next print position will be the beginning of the next line unless the final item ends with a ";".

The format of the values displayed by PRINT statements is controlled by the "@%" variable.

The CLS statement clears the text area on the Z88 display.

TAB function calls can be used to position output in both INPUT and PRINT statements. Normally, you should use a ";" at the end of PRINT statements which use TAB(character,row) calls.

## Who's in Control?

So far, all the sample programs we have seen have executed one statement after another from the first line to the last line. Such programs are frequently found as exercises in books on Basic (as in this chapter) but are rarely found in real applications.

To understand why, we must look at what computers do... Let's begin with one of our "important statements". By now, we expect that you know the routine - settle down with a large glass, etc.!

Most computer programs make "decisions" based on the data they are processing as they are executing.

## If Then Else

There are a wide variety of types of decisions to be made during the processing of a typical program but they can all be expressed as combinations of:

```
IF some condition
THEN do something
ELSE do something else
```

Let's begin with an example. Suppose we wished to introduce a rule that said the discount could not be more than the order amount in our double glazing program - this seems reasonable because otherwise we'd have to pay people to accept the double glazing! Let's assume that if the discount was greater than the price, we ignore the discount and charge the original amount.

In terms of "IF-THEN-ELSE" this can be expressed as:

```
IF Discount > Amount
THEN LET Price = Amount
ELSE LET Price = Amount - Discount
```

In BASIC, we write the complete statement in a single line:

```
10 IF Discount>Amount THEN Price=Amount ELSE
Price=Amount-Discount
```

This is a major limitation because there are only eighty characters to a line. A partial solution exists for simple situations - using ":" to write multiple statements on the line. But for more complex sequences of statements, there's only one answer - the dreaded GOTO statement.

## GOTO

Those of you who are new to programming are probably wondering "what is this GOTO statement and what's wrong with it?"

For the answer, we must retell a little story from the history of computers - past the Z88, past the IBM PC, even past such monsters as the PDP-11, until we reach nearly the beginning. The early pioneers realised that all computation could be reduced to a very simple set of operations - in which the GOTO instruction (or, rather, its ancestor) figured very strongly. Almost every program used them extensively - not least because they were "efficient" and allowed very clever programs to be written.

All was well until the mid-sixties when a Dutch computer science professor realised that all was not well when using lots of GOTOs in programs which were becoming increasingly complex. It is extremely easy to end up with a program which resembles a plate of tangled spaghetti and which is almost impossible to follow. For example, our example program could become:

```
10 REM A very bad program using GOTO statements
20 GOTO 100
30 GOTO 200
40 PRINT Price
50 REM The END statement stops the program
60 END
100 LET Amount = 580.50
110 LET Discount = 127.75
120 GOTO 30
200 LET Price = 0.0
210 LET Price = Amount - Discount
220 GOTO 40
```

We're sure you guessed by now that a GOTO statement alters the normal top-to-bottom execution of a Basic program by allowing you to specify which line number will be executed next.

We need the END statement to avoid "running into" the lines following line 50. Can you see what would happen without it?

The program would execute the following statement numbers:

```
10 20 100 110 120 30 200 210 220 40 50 100 110
120 30 200 210 220 ...
```

There is no way out of this "infinite loop". The program will continue until you ◇KILL that copy of BASIC or until the batteries run down...

This situation is quite common - particularly if you are developing complex applications. There is a "no-hassle" way of stopping a program - you simply press ESC and BASIC displays a message saying "Escape at line X", X is the line number which happened to be being executed when you pressed ESC.

The relationship between the IF-THEN-ELSE statement and the GOTO statement is that one of the things to do (either the "do something" or "do something else") can be GOTO statements.

**Warning: Unless you use this feature carefully, your programs will resemble a 1960's program and look like our old friend - a plate of tangled spaghetti...**

Let's give an example to illustrate the proper use of IF-THEN- ELSE and GOTO. We'll extend the example above to include printing a message when the discount is greater than the amount ordered:

```
10 IF Discount>Amount THEN GOTO 20 ELSE
Price=Amount- Discount:GOTO 40
20 Price=Amount
30 PRINT "Discount ignored as it's more than
Amount ordered"
40 REM the next statement...
```

When reading line 10, remember that there's an implied "LET" just before "Price" - we've had to leave it out because the line was becoming too long to fit on the page.

You will probably begin to detect the spaghetti tangling already in this example but it's really all right because it obeys the "Golden GOTO Rules" which are:

GOTOs should always be to higher statement numbers unless they are accompanied by comments (as REM statements) explaining the purpose of the statement.

If possible, the destination of any GOTO statement should be "close" to that statement.

The destinations of the GOTO statements should appear in the same order as the statements themselves.

In passing, the statement structure found in line 10 of the above example, where one outcome of the test points to the very next line is so common that there is a shortened form of the IF-THEN- ELSE statement; namely, the IF-THEN statement.  If the example is rewritten using this, the resulting code is:

```
10 IF Discount>Amount THEN
Price=Amount-Discount:GOTO 40
20 Price=Amount
30 PRINT "Discount ignored as it's more than
Amount ordered"
40 REM the next statement...
```

Note that this example used "Discount > Amount" rather than the conditional "Discount < = Amount".  We've had to "reverse" the conditional to ensure that the right code is executed when the conditional is tested.

Ensuring that you use the correct conditional operator is one of the most difficult aspects of coding a program.  It's worthwhile to "play at being a computer" and follow the execution of the statement through for a number of pairs of sample values to ensure that you've used the correct operator.

The table below lists the six conditionals that can be tested for and gives their "reversed" versions:

| Conditional | Operator | Operator for Reverse |
|---|---|---|
| Equal To | = | < > |
| Not Equal To | < > | = |
| Greater Than | > | < = |
| Less Than | < | = |
| Greater Than or Equal To | > = | < |
| Less Than or Equal To | < = | > |

All three types of variable (Ordinary, Integer and String) can be used in conditionals.  Note that two Strings are equal only if their lengths (as calculated by the LEN function) and the characters they contain are equal and that rounding errors can occur when comparing numbers for equality. The safest way to compare two numbers is to test for "near equality" using a statement like:

```
10 REM Compare two numbers using "near equality"
expression
20 IF ABS(Value1-Value2) < 0.00001 THEN PRINT
"Equal"
```

This calculates the difference between the variables, takes its absolute value and then compares this to a tolerance value (which will depend on the application).

Just as in arithmetic expressions, expressions can be formed of conditionals. The operators are: AND, OR, NOT and EOR. NOT is applied to just one conditional and reverses it; ie, if (A = 1) is True, then (NOT A = 1) is False. EOR is nothing to with donkeys (get it?) but stands for "Exclusive OR" which is true if one or other of the conditionals, but not both, are true.

As an example of using conditional expressions, look at this example:

```
100 REM See whether it's lower case
110 IF NOT(Letter$ >= "a" AND Letter$ <="z")
THEN GOTO 140
120 REM It's lower case, turn it into upper
130 Letter$=CHR$(ASC(Letter$)-32)
140 REM ...
```

Line 110 tests whether a letter is lower case by seeing whether it is between "a" and "z". If not, then the program skips the rest of the code. Line 130 is an expression which converts the lower case letter to upper case - it uses the ASC function to return the ASCII character code (all character on the Z88 have an equivalent ASCII code), then subtracts 32 (the difference between the codes for lower case and upper case letters) and re-converts this code back to a String using the CHR$ function.

## Summary

Processing data by computer requires that programs make decisions based on the contents of the data.

Basic allows decisions to be made by using the IF-THEN-ELSE or IF-THEN statements.

Conditionals can test all three variable types and can be combined to form expressions.

In some circumstances, you may be forced to use GOTO statement to pass control to other points in the program but always remember the Golden GOTO Rules.

## Going Round and Round...

Most computer processing involves doing the same sort of thing many times. Basic provides two different types of "loops" for controlling this.

In the first, the FOR-NEXT loop, the number of times you wish to repeat the task must be known. In the second, the REPEAT-UNTIL loop, the number of repetitions is unknown but the finishing point is known.

Let's look at how we might use a FOR-NEXT loop for displaying a table of discount rates for the double glazing program:

```
10 REM Print discount rate table
20 FOR Amount=500 TO 900 STEP 100
30 PRINT "Discount on ";Amount;" is ";Amount/5
40 NEXT Amount
50 REM Execution continues here after loop is
complete...
```

Line 20 sets the Amount variable (Amount) to 500 and notes that a loop has begun. The "loop control" variable is used to control the number of times the loop is executed but can also, as you can see from line 30, be used in the program as a normal variable.

All the lines of the program down to the NEXT statement on line 40 are executed and the first line of the discount table is displayed. Basic then goes back to the FOR statement.

It adds the value following "STEP" and then tests the new contents of the Amount variable (now, 600 being 500 + 100) against the "TO". If it is less than that value (as it will be when the first pass though the loop is executed), the statements inside the loop will be executed again. Otherwise the loop is exited and program execution continues from the statement after the NEXT statement.

This program would display:

```
Discount on 500.00 is 100.00
Discount on 600.00 is 120.00
Discount on 700.00 is 140.00
Discount on 800.00 is 160.00
Discount on 900.00 is 180.00
```

If the STEP value is 1 it may be omitted. Negative STEP values are allowed but the initial value should be greater than the final value as the STEP value is then subtracted from the loop control variable on each pass. For example:

```
10 REM Print discount rate table in descending
order
20 FOR Amount=900 TO 500 STEP -100
30 PRINT "Discount on ";Amount;" is ";Amount/5
40 NEXT Amount
50 REM Execution continues here after loop is
complete...
```

## Repeat - Until

Now, let's look at a REPEAT-UNTIL. This time, we'll use a new example - we want to get a "customer number" which is unique for each customer name. If the customer names are stored in an array (called Customers$), we could use the subscript of each name in this array as the customer number. Let's assume that the customer name which we are looking up is stored in a string called CustomerName$.

If we ignore the process of loading the Customers$ array, our first attempt at this program might look like:

```
10 REM Get customer number from customer name
20 DIM Customers$(100)
30 INPUT "Please enter customer name",
CustomerName$
40 Number=0
50 REPEAT
60 Number=Number+1
70 UNTIL Customers$(Number) = CustomerName$
80 PRINT "Customer Number is ";Number
```

In this program, line 50 merely records the fact there is a REPEAT-UNTIL loop. Each time Line 60 is executed, one is added to the number, so its value will be 1, 2, 3, etc. It's line 70 which actually contains the conditional to be tested. If the names don't match, then executing line 50 will cause the loop to be repeated.

We called this a first attempt as that's just what it is - it won't work if the name we're looking for doesn't appear in the Customers$ array. The Z88 would go round the loop again and again, adding one to Number until it was 101. At that point, BASIC will stop the program because the 101st element isn't there.

To correct this, we ensure that the loop terminates on the hundredth pass by changing line 70 to:

```
70 UNTIL Customers$(Number) = CustomerName$ OR
Number = 100
```

This sort of conditional expression is common in most real applications of REPEAT-UNTIL loops. Frequently, the conditional includes two parts: a test which is true when the loop is successful and another which "catches" error conditions.

Sometimes, you might be tempted to use a GOTO statement to leave a loop. Z88 BASIC may give you strange error messages if you do this. It's a good idea to learn to express your ideas without using these GOTOs.

## Summary

Loops repeat a sequence of operations.

FOR-NEXT loops repeat all the program lines between the FOR statement and the NEXT statement a fixed number of times. A control variable is set to an initial value and, at the end of each repetition, the STEP value is added and the value is compared with the TO value.

REPEAT-UNTIL loops repeat all the lines between REPEAT and UNTIL statements until the conditional specified in the UNTIL statement is true. The number of times that the statements in the loop are executed is irrelevant.

You should not use GOTO statements to exit from loops.

# How to write a thousand line program

By now, you know enough Basic to write programs that can perform some quite complex applications. What happens when your programs grow...

Well, one thing that happens is that you'll appreciate all the comments you've put in about how the program works when you come to change it. In fact, writing a large program is not too difficult; changing one is!

It's always sensible to design a program so it can be easily changed - never assume that a program will not need to be altered.

The best way to "design for change" is to divide the program up into manageable pieces - each of which performs a defined task. Basic provides three ways of doing this - we're going to cover only two because these offer significant advantages over the older method, GOSUB.

## "Procedures"

A procedure is a section of Basic program which looks like a mini-program in it's own right. To indicate that it's a procedure, it's preceded by a "DEF" statement which includes the "name" of the procedure and it's followed by a "ENDPROC" statement. For example:

```
1000 DEF PROC_Discount
1010 REM This procedure calculates the discount
on a sale
1020 Discount=0.20*Amount
1030 IF Discount <100.00 THEN Discount = 0.0
1040 ENDPROC
```

This procedure calculates a discount at 20% of the order amount but doesn't give any discount if the discount would have been less than £100.00.

In BASIC, all procedures have names beginning in "PROC" and we've adopted the convention that the next character will be an "_". We've done this to make the programs more readable.

You'll notice that this procedure has line numbers which range from 1000-1040 - this is because we're going to use it together with our original discount program and we don't want any of the line numbers to clash between the proccdure and the program which is going to use it. It's a good idea to begin the line numbers in each procedure on, say, a multiple of 1000 as this will help ensure that there are no clashes.

Now, let's use the procedure in our sample program instead of asking the user for the discount:

```
10 REM Program to calculate discounted price
with a procedure
20 INPUT "Please enter the value of the
Order",Amount
30 PROC_Discount
40 Price = Amount - Discount
50 PRINT "The Discounted Price is ",Price
```

Using procedures is as simple as that!

## Parameters and local variables

Z88 BASIC provides two rather neat extensions to this concept - "parameters" and "local variables". Let's use both in a rewritten version of the above program:

```
10 REM Program to calculate discounted price
with a procedure
20 INPUT "Please enter the value of the
Order",Amount
30 PROC_Discount(20)
40 Price = Amount - Discount
50 PRINT "The Discounted Price is ",Price

1000 DEF PROC_Discount(DiscountPercent)
1010 REM This procedure calculates the discount
on a sale
1020 LOCAL DiscountRate
1030 REM Use the local to hold the discount rate
as a fraction
1040 DiscountRate=DiscountPercent/100
1050 Discount=DiscountRate*Amount
1060 IF Discount < 100.00 THEN Discount = 0.0
1070 ENDPROC
```

As you can see, parameters can be used to pass data to a procedure. We've underlined "to" because you cannot pass data back from a procedure to the calling program via a parameter - it acts like a one-way valve.

Local variables are used to create variables which can be used freely inside the procedure but which are not known about outside the procedure. They are useful to avoid clashes with variables in the calling program. For example, you could have added another local variable called "Amount" inside the PROC_Discount procedure - and then used it for holding the amount of the discount. It would not have clashed with the "Amount" variable in the main program.

## Creating your own functions

If you want to pass data back to the calling program, you can use a "function" which will behave just like one of the built-in functions such as SIN. For example:

```
10 REM Program to calculate discounted price
with a function
20 INPUT "Please enter the value of the
Order",Amount
30 Price = Amount - FN_Discount(20)
40 PRINT "The Discounted Price is ",Price
50 END


1000 DEF FN_Discount(DiscountPercent)
1010 REM This procedure calculates the discount
on a sale
1020 LOCAL DiscountRate, Discount
1030 REM Use the first local to hold the
discount rate as a fraction
1040 DiscountRate=DiscountPercent/100
1050 REM Use the Discount local to hold the
discount amount
1060 Discount=DiscountRate*Amount
1070 IF Discount < 100.00 THEN Discount = 0.0
1080 REM Return the amount of the discount
1090 =Discount
```

Line 1090 is not a printing error, it's the method Basic uses to say "Return this variable as the result of this function".

You can only return one value from a function but it can be either an Or-dinary one, an Integer or a String. If you want to define a function which returns either an Integer or a String, it's advisable to remember to terminate the name with "%" or "$" respectively. Z88 BASIC does not insist on this itself but it could cause somebody reading your program to wonder why, for example, a function called "FN_Name" (without a "$") was returning a String.

A procedure or function might grow and grow until it becomes too complex to understand. It's easy to avoid that happening. For example, suppose we wished to check that the value of the discount percentage value was valid (ie, between zero and one hundred), we could write a function:

```
2000 DEF FN_PercentRate(Percent)
2010 REM Return percentage expressed as fraction
2020 REM Test whether in range
2030 IF (Percent) OR (Percent100) THEN PRINT "%
Out of range":STOP
2040 =Percent/100
```

By creating this function as a separate entity, we can use it anywhere (either in this program or in another program for a totally different application) that requires us to deal with percentages. To use it in our sample program, we modify the procedure which calculates the discount:

```
1000 DEF PROC_Discount(DiscountPercent)
1010 REM This procedure calculates the discount
on a sale
1020 LOCAL DiscountRate
1030 REM Use the local to hold the discount rate
as a fraction
1040 DiscountRate=FN_PercentRate(DiscountPercent)
1050 Discount=DiscountRate*Amount
1060 IF Discount  100.00 THEN Discount = 0.0
1070 ENDPROC
```

We've now got the following "structure" to the program:

Main Program calls a procedure:
PROC_Discount which, in term, calls a function:
FN_PercentRate

The standard way of describing this structure is in terms of levels. Procedures (or functions) which are called through fewer levels of inter-mediate procedures from the main program are called "higher level" while those which are called through more levels are called "lower level". FN_PercentRate is at a lower level than PROC_Discount.

## Summary

Use functions and procedures to allow you to split your programs into more understandable pieces.

Each procedure or function should perform one clearly defined task. The name you choose should reflect the task that it is performing.

As a rule of thumb, if a procedure or functions grows beyond about twen-ty to thirty lines of code, you should split it into separate parts.

Remember, there's no reason why one procedure can't call another - in-deed, almost all application programs use the technique of higher level procedures calling lower level ones.

## What to do when your Program Fails

"None of us are perfect but programming requires perfection."

In this section, we'll look at some ways to reconcile human imperfection to the perfection required to write programs that function correctly. This topic is rarely covered in introductions to Basic because most people believe that there are no useful hints on getting programs to work - "it's all a matter of experience" - but we will show that, although it's difficult to give a step-by-step guide, there are some techniques which can help find problems quickly.

How will you know that the program has an error? In simple cases, the program will either stop after reporting one of the standard error mes-sages (such as "Subscript" or "-ve root at line X" - which occurs when you try to take the square root of a negative number) or will generate results which are obviously invalid - like the classic one million pound gas bill. Not all errors are so obvious and may appear in few circumstances when running the program with particular data.

To pick up errors of this kind before you use the program "live", you must spend some time testing it with various inputs and check its outputs - it's never enough to run one test (with the same test data as you always use) and then say that the program works.

There are a number of sources of errors. The ones that most people worry about are coding errors (the techniques given in this section can help) but these are not as important as the ones which occur earlier on in the design of a program. Typically, a coding error will involve altering one or two lines while a design error may require throwing away a large section of the program and/or writing a completely new section. It is essential to avoid this kind of error - which is why the Specification and Design phase is so important.

The task of finding errors in a program is called "debugging". This is reputed to be because some of the errors which occurred in the first computer programs were caused by flies which were attracted to the computers by the heat of all the valves!

# Principles of Debugging

Always investigate any error message.

Always remember that all errors have logical explanations.

Patience and a systematic approach are as important in debugging computer programs as they are in detective work.

Errors due to Z88 Basic itself (as opposed to those in your own program) will be rare.

## TRACE

Basic itself provides a tool which can be used to debug programs, the "TRACE" command. After a TRACE or TRACE ON statement, Basic will display the line number of each line in the program as it is executed. At first sight, this may appear to be the ultimate answer to debugging as you can see each line being executed.

Unfortunately, programs typically go wrong for reasons which are related to the contents of variables and, on its own, TRACE provides no information on what values are in variables. Not only this, but it tends to produce large amounts of output - of which only a small portion is relevant to the problem being investigated. It's one of the features of Basic which will be used more by beginners than by experienced programmers.

Z88 BASIC does, however, provide two rather clever ways of making TRACE more useful.

First, you can include TRACE ON (and its complement TRACE OFF - which disables tracing) as statements within your program. This allows you to trace just a small section of your program - say, just one procedure.

Second, if you type a line number following the TRACE command, as in TRACE 1000, then only those line numbers less than the value you specify will be displayed. If your program is written so that the main program (and higher level procedures) occur before the lower level procedures, then this allows you just to trace higher level procedures without cluttering the display with trace information from lower levels.

We've just said that most problems will be caused by the values of variables. The way to display the values of variables in a BASIC program is, as we've already seen, to use PRINT statements. "How do I know which variables to display and when to display them?"

If an output from a program is incorrect, it's because one of the components that went into making it was incorrect. Therefore, it's always worthwhile PRINTing these components as this will reveal which of them is wrong. This will, in turn, lead to other variables which make up to faulty component and so on. When you identify the first component that has an incorrect value, it's usually a simple matter to locate the cause of the problem.

You can either add the PRINT statements to the program or you use ESC to stop the program and then use immediate mode PRINT statements to display the variables.

More subtle problems can occur where IF statements or FOR/REPEAT loops are involved. In these cases, it may be necessary to track the values of variables as they change before and after the IF statement or during the execution of each pass through the loop. This may reveal that the condition was not being tested correctly (a " < " test should be a " > " test, for example) or that the loop is not being executed the correct number of times - a very common mistake is the so-called "off-by-one" errors where a loop is executed either once too many or once too few times.

Remember that BASIC always executes statements in ascending order unless there's one of these "control" statements. There's no need to keep checking the same variable unless it's been altered or a GOTO statement "jumps into" the section of code under investigation.

If the problem can't be identified by PRINTing variables or TRACEing the program it may be necessary to extract the code which is failing. You can incorporate it into a "test bed" which is a short piece of code which allows you to set up all the variables and then print all the results. Here is a Test bed for the PROC_Discount procedure:

```
10 REM TEST BED FOR PROC_Discount
20 REPEAT
30 INPUT "Type TEST amount", Amount
40 REM CALL THE PROCEDURE
50 PROC_Discount(20)
```

```
60 PRINT "Discount calculated is", Discount
70 UNTIL Amount <0
80 END
```

This technique can also be used where you are not sure how a particular feature of BASIC operates or where you suspect a problem with Z88 Basic itself.

When you take a program section with an error and run it separately, you'll be surprised how often an error in your code will immediately become apparent as you can concentrate on just one little section of your program. If it doesn't, then at least you have the opportunity to find a "work-around"; that is, an alternative way of doing the same function that does work.

Finally, two topics which may appear rather "academic" but which we have found important. First, record how many errors are found in each procedure of the program and, if the number exceeds about three, consider rewriting the module from scratch. Second, it's a good idea to keep a "programming log" in which you record any errors you make (keep this private so that you can be frank with yourself) so that you can learn what sorts of errors you make (we make "off-by-one" errors) and thereby take extra care to avoid them.

## Summary

Always test your programs to ensure that they work with a range of test data before you use them "live".

The TRACE command provided by Basic is useful if it is used selectively.

Most problems are caused by errors in control statements. PRINTing the variables affected and tested by these statements will uncover these errors.

Don't be afraid to write little test programs to find out how particular BASIC features operate.

If you find that a particular procedure has more than three errors, give serious consideration to rewriting it from scratch.

Keep a "programming log" so that you can get to know what types of errors you make and so give yourself the opportunity to learn to avoid them.

## Storing your Data

We have already seen how you LOAD and SAVE BASIC programs. The files contain the statement together with the line number, but do not include the contents of any of the variables. If you wish to save the contents of a variable you must use the statement described in this section to create your own files.

Now, we'll show you how to store your variables that data in the Z88 File system and how to retrieve them for further processing. See the chapter on the Filer for more information on Z88 files.

This section covers the "basics" of using files. We'll begin by introducing the concepts behind files, then go on to describe the Basic statements used and, finally, show an example of a file handling program which translates a file to upper case.

To BASIC, individual files are like the tape in a tape recorder. You write one item of data after another - just as you might record one piece of music after another.

To retrieve information, you begin at some point in the file and replay the data in the same order as it was recorded - just as playing a tape on a tape recorder would play back successive pieces of music. As with a tape, you normally begin at the beginning and play the file through.

## Channel Numbers

Rather than continually refer to the full file name each time you read or write to a file, Z88 Basic uses "channel numbers" held in ordinary variables as shorthand. The actual channel number (that is, the value held in a channel number variable) is of interest only to BASIC, all that's important is that wherever a reference to a file is made, the appropriate channel number variable is used.

You associate a channel number with a particular file by using an OPENIN or OPENOUT statement. You use OPENIN if you are reading data from a file and OPENOUT if you are writing to an existing file or are creating a new file. For example:

```
10 REM Open the file called ":RAM.1/InputData"
20 InputFile = OPENIN ":RAM.1/InputData"
30 REM Open a file for output
40 OutputFile = OPENOUT "OutputData"
```

If the file cannot be opened, Basic sets the channel number to zero. Since there is no point in processing files which cannot be opened, the proper way to open a file is always to test the channel number before doing any further processing:

```
10 REM Open the file called ":RAM.1/InputData"
20 InputFile = OPENIN ":RAM.1/InputData"
30 REM See if file could be opened
40 IF InputFile = 0 THEN PRINT "Input file
couldn't be opened":STOP
```

It is essential that every channel is closed after all the data has been transferred to or from the file. In common with other statements except OPENIN and OPENOUT which use channel numbers, the channel is prefixed by a "#" so that the format of a CLOSE statement is:

```
10 REM Close both channels
20 CLOSE #InputFile : CLOSE #OutputFile
```

Once a channel has been closed, the channel number variable can be re-used either to hold another channel number or for other purposes.

Reading data from and writing data to a file is normally done with modified versions of the INPUT and PRINT statements which include the channel number of the file. For example:

```
10 REM Read a line from a file
20 INPUT #InputFile,Line$
30 REM Write a line to a file
40 PRINT #OutputFile,Line$
```

Files can be any length but are terminated by an "End-of- File" marker. When a file is read, this marker can be detected by using the EOF# function. All data has been read when "EOF#(ChannelNumber)" returns a value of -1. When writing to a file, this marker is automatically moved each time more data is added to the end of the file.

The example program given below reads a file and writes another file, replacing all lower-case letters with their upper-case equivalents:

```
10 REM Lower case to Upper case Converter
20 REM
30 REM Open the two files
40 InputFile = OPENIN ":RAM.1/InputData"
50 REM See if input file could be opened
60 IF InputFile = 0 THEN PRINT "Input file
couldn't be opened":STOP
70 OutputFile = OPENOUT ":RAM.1/Outputdata"
80 REM See if output file could be opened
90 IF OutputFile = 0 THEN PRINT "Output file
couldn't be opened":STOP
100 REM
110 REM Repeat this loop until End-of-File
detected
120 REM
130 REPEAT
140 REM Read a line from the input file
150 INPUT #InputFile,InputLine$
160 REM Perform case conversion
170 PROC_CaseConvert
180 REM Write a line to the output file
190 PRINT #OutputFile,OutputLine$
200 UNTIL EOF#(InputFile)=-1
210 REM
220 REM Close both channels
230 CLOSE #InputFile : CLOSE #OutputFile
240 END

1000 DEF PROC_CaseConvert
1010 REM Convert a string from lower to upper
case
1020 LOCAL Char, Letter
1030 OutputLine$=""
1040 REM
1050 REM For each character in line
1060 REM
```

```
1070 FOR Char=1 TO LEN(InputLine$)
1080 REM Extract letter
1090 Letter$=MID$(InputLine$,Char,1)
1100 REM See whether it's lower case
1110 IF NOT(Letter$ = "a" AND Letter$ <= "z")
THEN GOTO 1140
1120 REM It's lower case, turn it into upper
1130 Letter$=CHR$(ASC(Letter$)-32)
1140 REM Append to output string
1150 OutputLine$=OutputLine$+Letter$
1160 NEXT Char
1170 REM
1180 ENDPROC
```

## Summary

BASIC program access files in the Z88 file system by OPENing them for reading (with an OPENIN function) or for writing (with an OPENOUT function).

Once opened, files are referred to by channel number.

Data is read from a file using "INPUT #channel" or "INPUTLINE # channel" statements and writing is achieved using "PRINT #channel". The EOF#(channel) function is provided to test whether the End- of- File marker has been reached.

It is essential to CLOSE each file after it has been read or written.

## More on Files...

This section covers more advanced topics which allow you to gain greater control over the contents of files. We've included this information as you may need it to read and write files which can be shared with other Z88 applications such as PIPEDREAM or the Printer Driver.

When you write a file by means of the "PRINT #channel" statement, each type of variable is stored in the file using a pre-defined format. When the program reading the file is another BASIC program, there are no incom- patibilities and the two programs can share data.

If the other program is not written in BASIC, you must investigate the format of the file required so that the information can be shared. This is easy in Z88 BASIC as it provides tools for writing data to files and reading the contents of files at a lower level than using PRINT #channel and INPUT #channel statements, so that you can alter the format to suit the other program.

Remember that, as when using INPUT and PRINT, files are always accessed by referring to a channel number which is returned after you have OPENed them with an OPENIN or OPENOUT statement. Don't forget to CLOSE all files when you have finished with them.

## BGET

The greatest degree of control is obtained by ensuring that all the data is transferred one character at a time. BASIC provides the BGET#(channel) function which does just this. You could, for example, examine each character of a file like this:

```
10 REM Reading a file
20 Channel = OPENIN "test1"
30 REM Repeat for each character in file
40 REPEAT
50 REM Get ASCII code of the next character
60 Char=BGET#(Channel)
70 REM Display the code
80 PRINT Char
90 REM do until end-of-file encountered
100 UNTIL EOF#(Channel)=-1
110 CLOSE #Channel
```

## BPUT

Similarly, it's possible to write a file one character at a time using the BPUT # channel statement. For example, we could copy the data to another file by substituting a BPUT statement for the PRINT statement.

```
10 REM Copying a file
20 InChannel = OPENIN "test1"
30 OutChannel = OPENOUT "test2"
40 REM Repeat for each character in file
```

```
50 REPEAT
60 REM Get ASCII code of the next character
70 Char=BGET#(InChannel)
80 REM copy the code
90 BPUT #OutChannel,Char
100 REM do until end-of-file encountered
110 UNTIL EOF#(InChannel)=-1
120 REM Close both files
120 CLOSE #InChannel : CLOSE #OutChannel
```

Notice how both lines 70 and line 90 refer to the ordinary variable "Char" - this variable will hold the ASCII code of each character in the input file. Frequently, you'll need the characters as a string and so you'll call the CHR$ function to convert from an ASCII code to a single-character string.

## Where is the End of the Line?

If you wish to process lines in a text file and you cannot use the INPUT statement, you should note that your program will be responsible for detecting the end of lines and that different programs may separate lines in different ways. PIPEDREAM uses a Carriage Return code (which is 13 in ASCII) but some programs may include a Line Feed character (the ASCII code for this is 10).

## STR$ and EVAL

For interpretation of numeric data, Z88 Basic programs can use the STR$ and EVAL functions. The short demonstration program below illustrates their use:

```
10 REM Demonstration of STR$ and EVAL
20 string$=STR$(127.75)
30 PRINT string$
40 Number=EVAL(string$)
50 PRINT Number
```

Line 20 shows how the STR$ function converts a ordinary variable to a String and Line 40 shows how EVAL performs the reverse operation - converting a String to a number..

257

## Summary

Where you cannot share files because of format incompatibilities, you can write your program to access the files one character at a time with BGET and BPUT.

You will need to examine the format of the input file to determine how the data is stored and how lines are separated.

Always use EVAL and STR$ to process numeric data.

## OZ and BASIC

To obtain a printout of a listing, use the Print command. Type □ + P before LISTing the program and then type □-P to return to normal mode.

The "Talking to Weirdos" section includes instructions for driving the printer from a Basic program. Other devices, such as the serial port, can also be worked with like files. Star commands (*DELETE and *RENAME) provide access to some of the facilities of the Filer from within Basic programs to delete and rename files.

The OSCLI statement sends CLI commands from within a BASIC program. However, the CLI only gains control when the keyboard is being scanned for a keypress. To force this to happen, you must include a call to the INKEY function. For example:

```
10 OSCLI("CLI .*test.cli"):dummy=INKEY(0)
```

## What you have Learnt

By reading this chapter, and working through the examples, you'll have gained an insight into programming in BASIC.

You should know what a BASIC program is, how to go about writing one and you should be able to read most BASIC programs.

We hope that you are already writing short programs or modifying some of the examples - Programming is a practical skill and you can only learn by experience.

This page intentionally left blank.

# Pipedream Mailmerge and Report Generator

## Concept

The method of mailmerge described below allows the text of a letter to be written once and then discreetly addressed to many recipients. In addition the letter may contain within the text references which are once off for that recipient only. Once a set of letters has been prepared the report generator can be used to produce a printed report of all the particulars with eight or ten records on one page. Also a one line report can be prepared with 55 records to the page. The report generator can be used in its own right for reporting and printing from a database.

This mailmerge uses a marked block when printing and hence it does not make any material difference whether the letter is at the top of the file or the bottom. A pre-existing address database can become the basis of the mailmerge. The database can be updated and used for further letters as required.

Printing is called in the normal way ( ◇PO) or can easily be controlled by a CLI file executed once all the preparatory work is complete. The method described has been used to print a mailing of nearly 100 letters. A one page letter will print on a laser (page) printer at the rate of one every 30 seconds, a line printer can be used just as well, if not so quickly, and is preferable for the report generator.

The system requires that the letter, the expressions (used to run the system) and the address database are all present in one PIPEDREAM file. The CLI file is kept separate and indeed several CLI files can be saved and the particular one required for the job in hand executed.

# Getting Started, the database

The names and addresses as well as any text to be embodied in the letter need to be kept in a normal Pipedream database, i.e. one line, one record. The left hand column is reserved for a line number. This starts at 1 and is incremented consecutively. This number may be used as a customer number but plan to have another column to hold customer numbers if required. The line number must be entered as an expression, or altered to an expression once entered as text. However, begin by leaving column A empty.

The database needs as many columns as name lines, address lines, telephone number line and other discreet items as you wish to use plus column A. Add columns to the right of column F with ◇EAC or insert columns with ◇EIC. A normal name and address may require 4 to 6 lines and unused slots should have an exact space ( ◇spacebar) entered into them, otherwise 0.00 will be printed out in each blank line of the address.

The standard column width of twelve spaces is more than enough for the database. Reduce the width ( ◇W) of each column in turn to 8 and thus increase the number of columns visible without scrolling across. The amount of text to be entered into each slot will often be more than 8 digits wide so it is essential to turn off word wrap by going to the options page O and moving down to Wrap and typing N. Narrow columns give more flexibility in planning the layout of the report generator. Whilst in the options page set Calc: Auto/Man to M. As the database becomes larger this will allow data to be entered more quickly.

A row of titles is very useful so start by tabbing to B1 and type NAME. Tab to C1 and type ADD1, continue across the row and after say six columns for the address type PHONE or whatever other details you want to file in the database. Before moving the cursor off this row use the Fix Row command ( ◇LFR) to fix it at the top of the screen.

| ........A..........B..........C..........D..........E..........F..........G..........H..........I.......... | | | | | | | | |
|---|---|---|---|---|---|---|---|---|
| NAME | ADD1 | ADD2 | ADD3 | ADD4 | 1st NAME | PRIZE | FOR | |
| J. Smith Esq., | | | | | | | | |
| J. Smith14, | Hanover Street, | | | | | | | |
| J. Smith14, | HanoPETERBOROUGH | | | | | | | |
| J. Smith14, | HanoPETERBORPE2 3AG | | | | | | | |
| J. Smith14, | HanoPETERBORPE2 3AG | | | | | | | |
| J. Smith14, | HanoPETERBORPE2 3AG | | | | John | | | |
| J. Smith14, | HanoPETERBORPE2 3AG | | | | John | First prize | | |
| J. Smith14, | HanoPETERBORPE2 3AG | | | | John | First prize | Dahlias | |

The example above shows how a one line entry is built up. At the time of
entry each slot will spill over those on the right but as soon as the slot is
complete and you press TAB the cursor will move to the start of the next
slot and the excess text will be hidden. Note that it is still in place and at
any time you can return to the slot by using the TAB key or the back arrow
key. Once in the desired slot all the normal text commands can be used
to delete or correct it as required. The arrow keys work as normal but the
text will scroll past the narrow window as you move around the entry.
Completed entries will look like this:

| A | B | C | D | E | F | G | H | I |
|---|---|---|---|---|---|---|---|---|
| NAME | ADD1 | ADD2 | ADD3 | ADD4 | 1st NAME | PRIZE | FOR | |
| J. Smith | 14, Hano | PETERBORPE2 3AG | | | John | First prize | Dahlias | |
| Mrs L. | 14, Highcrowland | PETERBORPE14 8QT | | | Lucy | Highly com. | Sweet peas | |

Once the list is complete enter the control numbers into column A. For
a shortish list this is most easily done by typing 1 in slot A1 and ENTER,
type 2 in slot A2 and repeat to the bottom of the list. Mark the bottom
slot ( ◊Z) and then ◊UP-ARROW, now you will be in slot A1 and mark
that slot, the whole block will be highlighted. Type ◊ENT to enter the
numbers as expressions, type ◊LAL to left align the numbers and ◊LDP
to alter the decimal places, type 0 at the prompt, then ENTER. Now the
control numbers are neatly in place and the block can be removed with
◊Q.

# Getting Started, control expressions

At this stage plan ahead and decide how many lines need to be left clear
between the bottom of the database and the top of the letter. Allow for
possible growth in the number of database entries. If the database has 40
entries then enter the control expressions on line 50.

If the database has 40 lines, and allowing 5 lines for extra entries, range
one will be slots A1 to A45. Range 2 will be B1 to B45 for column B and
C1 to C45 for column C etc. The key slot (in this case A50) uses an 'If,
then, else' expression which acts in one of two ways. The 'else' part is used
to give a particular line number when starting the mailmerge. Normally

this would be set to 1 but can be changed to any other number in range 1, the mailmerge will then start at that line. The 'then' part is used to incre-ment the line number one at a time to allow you to run the mailmerge, and the 'if' part allows switching between the two different modes.

The expression for slot A50 is If(A49 = 1,A50 + 1,1)

The expression for slot B50 is LOOKUP($A50,$A$1$A$45,B$1B$45)

The $ sign makes the reference absolute, when used before the letter freezing the column and when used before the number freezing the row.

Now use ◇BRE to replicate B50 to C50 and across the rest of the row to the end column. At the first prompt type B50 and ENTER and at the second prompt type C50I50 and ENTER, the expression will be repli-cated all the way across to column I.

Now enter as an expression 0 in slot A49. Type ◇A to recalculate the spreadsheet and the entry in row 1 of the database will be represented in row 50.

The expression line will now look very similar to line 1 of the database. If the word Lookup is printed across the line then slot A50 is probably not an expression, go to A50, Type ◇X and ENTER and recalculate again, all should now be well. Alternatively, the number in the slot is not within the range of numbers in range 1.

# Getting Started, the letter

Firstly return to the options page and reset Wrap to Y. The letter can be written, or amended, and a series of @Fields used to pull the information out of the expression line and into the text of the letter. @Fields allow normal justification of the text within the letter by using a string of @@'s after the slot reference. However, the extra @@'s are not needed in the address because there is no text following the @Field. Start the letter about 10 lines below the control expressions.

The name for the letter is in slot B50 so the @Field is @B50@, the first line of the address is in slot C50 so the @Field is @C50@, and so on for all the remaining fields.

Whilst typing each line the entry will be:

@B50@
@C50@
@D50@
@E50@
@F50@

Dear @G50@,

I am pleased to write that your @@I50@@@@@@@@@@ won @@H50@@@@@@@@@ in the show yesterday.

This will print out normally. Now enter 1 into cell A49, recalculate (êA and the next line of the database will be put into the @Fields of the letter. The letters prepared as above will look like this:

J. Smith Esq.,
14, Hanover Street,
PETERBOROUGH
PE2 3AG

Dear John,

I am pleased to write that your dahlias won first prize in the show yesterday.

---

Mrs. L. Jones,
18, High Street,
Crowland,
PETERBOROUGH
PE14 8QT

Dear Lucy,

I am pleased to write that your sweet peas won highly commended in the
show yesterday.

---

# Getting started, the report generator

This is simply another set of @Fields set out so as to make a neat report
within the area of the Z88's display and positioned between the control
expressions and the letter. An example is shown below but your own display should be tailored to your needs.

| | |
|---|---|
| Mrs. L. Jones, | 1stname Lucy |
| 18, High Street, | |
| Crowland, | prize: highly commended |
| PETERBOROUGH | for: sweet peas |
| PE14 8QT | |

The words 1stname, prize: and for: are typed into the desired slots and
the other slots contain the necessary @Fields.

# Printing, the letters

Prior to printing check that the key slot is set to 1 as described above, the printer is ready and with paper in place.

As stated in the introduction printing is controlled by the use of a marked block. Mark the top and bottom of the letter with ◇Z in the normal way, call the printer menu with ◇PO and press ENTER.

Before printing the next letter recalculate the database with ◇A and then print again when you are ready. All the letters can be printed in this way.

# Printing, the report generator

This is printed in a similar fashion but the normal default setting in the options page will need altering to make a more sensible use of space, i.e.

    Margins: Top 0
           Header 0
           Footer 0
           Bottom 1

Headers and footers will still print so they will also need deleting. Mark the block of the report and print it, recalculate the database and print the next report. Carry on until all the reports are printed. Eight display sized reports will fit on one A4 page and 55 or more one line reports with no spaces between the lines. For this the options page will need altering again so that the bottom space is also 0.

# Automatic Printing and Recalculation

Printing can be controlled by a CLI file so that after each letter has been printed the database will be recalculated and printing will then continue. The following CLI will print and recalculate twice and then stop. The file is best saved in the same directory as the PIPEDREAM database.

Start in a new PIPEDREAM file and enter the top line in slot A1, enter line 2 in slot A2 and so on, but do not press ENTER after the last line.

```
  ~ I
  :[
  :PO ~ E
  .D200
  :A | PO ~ E
  .D200
  :A
```

Save the file as 2print.CLI and alter the Save plain text option to Yes.

Lines 1 and 2 start off the CLI, lines 3 and 4 order the first printing and then instructs a delay of 2 seconds to allow the print buffer to clear (this may not be needed at all, or may need to be increased). Lines 5 and 6 order a recalculation, the next printing and a delay. Line 7 orders a recalculation to prepare the database for the next use of the CLI.

To test the CLI file return to the database and check that all is ready to start printing, i.e. the key slot is set to 1 by entering 0 in slot A49, calculate the file and then enter 1 in A49, mark the block you want to print and finally check that the printer is all set.

Now go directly from the database to the FILER with ☐ F, locate the CLI file and (with the cursor on the title) mark it by pressing the TAB key, cursor down the COMMANDS to EXECUTE and press ENTER. Sit back and watch the CLI get back to your database and then printing will commence!

Once you are satisfied that the CLI is working correctly lines 5 and 6 can be duplicated as lines 7 & 8, 9 & 10 etc. one less time than the total items that you wish to print. Lines 3 & 4 look after the first printing. Put line 7 in as the last line and save the file as 8print.CLI (or whatever) as detailed above.

This system of printing is fine for letters on a Laser printer or line printer using continuous stationery. It is also fine for printing say 8 reports on one page using a line printer. However, to print more than one report per page with a laser printer the methods detailed above would need altering so that there were (say) 8 expression lines and 8 reports. Each report would have to pick up its own expression line and upon recalculation the expressions would have to advance 8 lines. For printing mark all 8 reports as a block.

Using such a method would allow the use of headers and footers which cannot be achieved automatically with the single report system. If headers and footers are required then this is probably the best way even when using a line printer. Note that the CLI will only need to contain one print and recalculate instruction for each page.

# Final Tips

If required an 'If, then, else' expression can be used to test the 1st name for "sir" or "madame" and if found put "faithfully" after "Yours". If not found put "sincerely". This expression could be used in a slot on the expression line or in the report, and pulled from either location into the letter. The expression for this example would be:

IF(G50 = "sir" | G50 = "madam","faithfully","sincerely")

The maximum number of lines that the lookup expression can handle has been found to be 256. This is probably quite enough for most purposes and in any case a database with 256 lines will be getting quite big and using up a lot of memory.

The use of a spelling checker to check a PIPEDREAM database file will use excessive memory as both files will be suspended activities. If a spelling checker is available do not use it to check names and addresses, it will report almost every word for checking.

However, the letter could easily be written in another file, checked for spelling and saved. Then, having loaded the database, the letter file is loaded to the main file by altering the Insert at slot option to Yes and giving the top left slot reference where you wish to start the letter. This should be at the bottom of the file, otherwise all sorts of layout problems will result.

A final tip is that the database should be filed to backup files (EPROM or tape) on a frequent basis. There is nothing worse than to loose a lot of work to a battery failure or fail message.

In conclusion the above method is powerful and is capable of development to suit individual needs. Many users of much larger computers would not be able to create a mailmerge without obtaining special software and even so might be unable to develop it to suit their own needs.

# Working with the Wizard

In this chapter, we're going to be looking at OZ - the wizard in the Z88. We'll begin by looking at what OZ does and then we'll see how you can ask the wizard for help. Some of the information in this chapter will be found elsewhere in the book as well - we've repeated it here so that we can tell the complete story.

## OZ - the All Powerful Wizard

OZ is the "operating system" of the Z88. He controls what the computer is doing, records the passing of time and, most importantly, allocates resources to the various application programs and popdowns.

On the Z88, memory is the most important resource, so it's hardly surprising that a considerable part of OZ's effort is devoted to ensuring that the memory is allocated properly. This is particularly significant on the Z88 since the machine is never actually off - it just goes to sleep and when woken up, you expect to be able to carry on where you left off. OZ never has the chance to start again with a clean slate unlike other computers.

OZ must decide which part of the working memory (that is, the internal 32K RAM and any RAM cartridges) is used for programs and which is used to hold files. OZ seems to use free memory in any cartridge to hold informationk for programs to use.

OZ regards each cartridge (and the internal memory, :RAM.0) as a separate device and will not allow a file to be split between them. The ":RAM.-" device is like memory used for programs as OZ can use whatever free memory it chooses. Remember, though, that there's a bug in Version 2.2 which means that :RAM.- must be cleared before a reset.

The wizard is also responsible for control of the input/output devices. This is where most users meet OZ.

On the Z88, the input/output devices include not only the keyboard and display screen, the cartridge slots and a printer (connected via the serial port) but also the clock, the power monitoring circuitry and even the reset switch.

## Help from the Wizard

The wizard provides lots of information about what's happening in the Z88. For example, the INDEX page shows which programs are available as well as what activities are suspended. In addition, you can persuade the wizard to tell you more by giving him the appropriate spell.

From the index page, typing ◇CARD reveals which cartridges are in the machine. Hitting the HELP key and then the left arrow key displays a page which includes the version number of your Z88's software.

Even more information can be prised from OZ by more complex incantations, like all magic spells, some of the results may be unpredictable! The BASIC program below will produce a short report showing some parameters which OZ maintains about your Z88:

```
10 REM
20 REM Display a report showing attributes of
your Z88
30 REM
40 REM See whether it's expanded
50 PRINT "OZ reports that this Z88 is ";
60 IF EOF#-1 THEN PRINT "expanded" ELSE PRINT
"un-expanded"
70 REM Find out how much free memory you have
80 PRINT "You have approximately ";EXT#-1;"
bytes of free memory"
90 REM Get the number of file handles and the
ROM version
100 handles=PTR#-1 DIV &10000
110 version=PTR#-1 AND &FFFF
120 PRINT "Currently, there are ";handles;" free
file handles"
130 PRINT "Your machine has Version ";version;"
ROMs"
140 END
```

Remember that BASIC itself uses memory - so the amount of value displayed for available memory is only approximate and may differ from that displayed in the options page of PIPEDREAM.

The "free file handles" is an indication of how many files you can use in application programs at one time. Don't assume that it's equal to the number of suspended copies of PIPEDREAM you could have as, on our machine, each copy of PIPEDREAM needs three file handles - presumably, PIPEDREAM creates some temporary files.

The "ROM version" is retrieved from :ROM.0 - the internal ROM. It is displayed as a code number - versions 2.2 and 3 are both reported as "3".

To run this program, enter BASIC by ☐B, type "NEW" (to clear any program which may have been left there), enter the program exactly as it is written and then type RUN.

## The Wizard as Director

We will explain how you can use OZ to replace the standard input/output devices with other devices or even files. There are some restrictions: for example, it would make no sense to try using a printer as a keyboard!

To show the permitted combinations of files and devices, let's divide the devices and files into two groups; "inputs" (that is, things which supply information) and "outputs" (that is, things which can receive information). We'll use the diagram shown below:

INPUT     keyboard           file

                        OZ

OUTPUT    screen     printer       file

We'll repeat this diagram as we develop the ideas. For now, notice how "files" can be used for both input and output. That's not to say that you can use the same file for both input and output at the same time - you'd have to use different names.

The normal situation is illustrated below:

INPUT     KEYBOARD         file

                        OZ

OUTPUT    SCREEN     printer       file

That is, input is taken from the keyboard (when you press a key) and the result of the Z88's processing of each key press is immediately displayed on the screen.

Now, let's look at another combination:

INPUT     KEYBOARD         file

                        OZ

OUTPUT    screen     PRINTER       file

This diagram shows that while input is still taken from the keyboard, output is "re-directed" to the printer. Why should you want to do this?

If you have a printer, we can show you...

Enter the FILER with ☐ F, select "Catalogue Files" type ☐ + P and the press ENTER.

No doubt you're very surprised to see a listing of the files appear on your printer!

If you have a lot of files, you may notice that "Page Waits" (that is, the need to hit the space key to view the next page) no longer occur while this is happening. Also, it's worth pointing out that not all applications and pop-downs give useful information when their output is sent to the printer.

As soon as the listing is complete, type "☐-P" to tell OZ that you've finished using the printer.

If OZ goes into a trance (as will happen if you don't have a printer or it isn't powered and on-line) you'll have to give OZ the magic spell SHIFT-ESC (that is, hold the SHIFT key down while you press the ESC key). This will revive OZ immediately.

To repeat what we've achieved: output that was directed to the screen, in our case, the file catalogue, was sent to the printer as well. Our diagram should really have been:

INPUT     |KEYBOARD|                         |file|
                              |OZ|

OUTPUT    |SCREEN|          |PRINTER|        |file|

This shows that output was sent to both the screen and the printer. In technical terms, this is called "Tee Re-direction" by analogy with a Tee-piece in pipework where water flows down both arms of the T.

You could have re-directed the output of the file catalogue to a file by using "☐ + S" before the listing and "☐ -S" afterwards. This would have been represented in the diagram shown below:

INPUT KEYBOARD file
OZ

OUTPUT SCREEN printer FILE

There's no opportunity to name the file which holds the listing - OZ always uses the name ":RAM.-/S.sgn". Each time you do a "☐ +S", OZ reuses the same file - any listing already stored in this file is lost.

You should remember that Version 2.2 of the Z88 contains a serious bug in its handling of files in :RAM.-. Always copy any files in :RAM.- to another cartridge and then delete the original - otherwise you won't be able to do a soft reset.

Having copied the file, you may then look at it in PIPEDREAM - it's plain text so don't forget to set "Load as plain text" to Yes before loading it.

To show re-direction of the input using files is a little more complicated as it involves the dreaded "CLI", so we'll leave that until the next section.

## Summary

You can ask OZ to send output to the printer as well as the screen by using the "☐ +P" command. To turn the printer off, use "☐-P".

Output can be sent both to the screen and a file called ":RAM.-/S.sgn" if you type "☐ +S". To close the file, type "☐-S". You can not change the name of this file. Remember that you must use the FILER to copy the file from :RAM.- and then delete the original.

In both these cases, output is directed to the screen as well as re-directed to the printer or file - it is "Tee Re-directed".

## The Wizard's Tape Recorder

In this section, we're going to look at CLI. "What is CLI and what does it do?" We will look at the background to CLI and then explains the relationship between CLI and re-direction of the input.

CLI stands for "Command Line Interpreter" which, even if you're a computer freak, is not a very helpful description of what it does because there's no "command line" in the Z88. We suggest that you just remember the initials and forget the original meaning!

OK, why is this section called "The wizard's tape recorder?" As we've done before, let's type some commands into the Z88 and let it help explain itself... Even if you haven't a clue what's happening, do it - all will be revealed shortly!

Go into the INDEX and type the following commands without hitting ENTER between each one - please press the ☐ key seperately before pressing the next key in the sequence:

☐ + k
☐ t
☐ r
c
12
+
34
=
☐ i
☐ -k

Remembering the bug in Version 2.2 of the Z88, you'd better copy the file that this has created, which is called ":RAM.-/K.sgn" to another cartridge and then delete the original. Let's call it "first.cli" and store it in the Default Device.

Now, enter the FILER with ☐ F and find the "Execute" command. It's off the bottom of the commands displayed initially but you can scroll down to it or type ◇EX to select it. When your Z88 displays "Name:" type "first.cli" - that is, the name of the file we've just created.

You'll be amazed to see your Z88 behave as if the keyboard is under the control of a robot who is replaying exactly the commands you gave it...

We have used "☐ + K" and "☐ -K" to record a sequence of keystrokes which are then replayed by the Filer execute command. Hence, the wizard has a tape recorder!

Let's explore what's happening in a little more detail using the diagrams we used in the last section. Actually, to explain the "record" process, we need a slightly modified diagram to show how the file is created.

INPUT  |KEYBOARD|                           |file|

       |FILE|
                        |OZ|

OUTPUT  |screen|        |printer|          |file|

This shows that during a recording, it's the keystrokes which are being recorded, not the output from the Z88.

The diagram below explains what happening during a FILER execute command:

INPUT   |keyboard|                          |FILE|
                        |OZ|

OUTPUT  |SCREEN|        |printer|          |file|

You can see that doing a FILER execute command has achieved the re-direction of the input of the Z88 from a file. In passing, CLI files can be executed from two other places; in an ALARM (if the alarm type is set to "Execute") and in BASIC programs.

## What's in a CLI file?

We have created a CLI file, we've even executed one. What is inside it?

Load "first.cli" into PIPEDREAM as a plain text file - you should see:

~ At ~ Arc12 + 34 = ~ Ai ~ A-k

This may look like a meaningless mess of characters but look what we get if this is laid out underneath the original commands entered and spaces are inserted between each command:

Commands:☐ + k ☐ t ☐ r c 12 + 34 = ☐ i ☐ -k
CLI File: ˜ At ˜ Ar c 12 + 34 = ˜ Ai˜ A-k

We hope that you can see a pattern emerge... In fact, what we are looking at is a "CLI file". In the next section, we'll give a description of all the
special characters and commands that can appear in one of these files.

## Summary

CLI files allow sequences of commands to be given to the Z88, just as if
they were typed in.

OZ's recording mode is started by "☐ + K" and terminated by "☐ -K".

The file that holds the record of keystrokes is always called :RAM. -/K.sgn

To replay a CLI file, use the FILER's execute command.

# Talking to the Wizard

In the last section, you saw how a CLI file is merely an "coded" representation of key presses that you might make while recording with the
☐ + K command.

We saw that we can look at this file by loading it as a plain text file in
PIPEDREAM. We hope that you're asking "Can I create my own CLI
files?"

Yes, you sure can! This section includes a full list of the commands that
you can use. All the keys that can be recorded are included, but there are
additional commands which are only available if you create the CLI file
yourself.

## Down to details...

The following characters have special meanings within CLI files:

\#                          Equivalent to holding down ☐ while press-
                            ing another key.

279

| | Equivalent to holding down ◊ while pressing another key. |
| . | As the first character of a line, introduces a "File Control Command". |
| ~ | Used in conjunction with a letter to represent most of the special characters available from the Z88 keyboard. |

The following commands can appear within CLI files to represent the specified keys:

| ~A | Single press of the □ key; ~A ~A has no effect. |
| ~C | Single press of the ◊ key; ~C ~C has no effect. |
| \| | The ESC key. |
| ~E | The ENTER key. |
| ~S | The SHIFT key. This only has any effect if pressing the SHIFT key (on its own) has any meaning. |
| ~I | The INDEX key. |
| ~M | The MENU key. |
| ~H | The HELP key. |
| ~X | The DEL key. |
| ~U | The up arrow key. |
| ~D | The down arrow key. |
| ~L | The left arrow key. |

| | |
|---|---|
| ~R | The right arrow key. |
| ## | Used to represent a single "#". |
| \|\| | Used to represent a single "\|". |
| ~ ~ | Used to represent a single "~". |
| ~. | Represents a single "." at the beginning of a line. Unfortunately, the sequence you would have expected - ".." - doesn't work as any number of "."s at the beginning of a line are treated as a single full-stop. |

The User Guide calls the commands in the following group the "File Control" commands. We prefer the term "Re-direction Control" commands:

| | |
|---|---|
| . < file | Takes the input from the named file. |
| . > file | Re-directs the output to the named file. |
| .T < file | Sends a copy of the input to the named file (similar to ☐ + K). |
| .T > file | Sends a copy of the screen output to the named file. |
| . = file | Sends the printer output to the named file. |
| .T = file | Sends a copy of the printer output to the named file. |

It's worth noting that these commands can refer to devices as well as files. So, to re-direct the screen output to the printer as well as to the screen, we could include:

.T > :prt.0

If you wish to turn off re-direction of an output in the middle of a CLI file, you can re-direct the output to a special device called ":NUL.0".

Finally, there's a group of "Control" commands:

.;                              Introduces a comment - the rest of line is ig-
                                nored by OZ.

.Dn                             This command delays for 'n' centiseconds. A
                                delay of two seconds (say) would be ac-
                                complished by the command ".D200". This
                                command can be useful when you wish to see
                                the contents of the Z88 display during the ex-
                                ecution of a CLI file.

.J                              Inhibits the interpretation of any special
                                characters (such as "#" or " ~ ") for the rest of
                                the current CLI file. In Z88 terminology, it
                                "jams" the CLI file.

.*file                          Starts the named CLI file and, when that file
                                has been executed, return control to the cur-
                                rent file. You should note that the asterisk in
                                this command has nothing to do with
                                wildcards - it's just part of the command
                                name.

                                For example, to run a file named "test.cli", you
                                would record this in your CLI file as:
                                ".*test.cli".

.S                              Suspends the current CLI file. An detailed
                                explanation of the effect of suspension is
                                given below.

Line breaks in CLI files are ignored - it doesn't matter whether you put
them after each command or use them to indicate groups of related commands. You must use the " ~ E" command when you want to playback the
ENTER key in a CLI file.

Since you begin a CLI file from the FILER, all the commands will be in-
terpreted as if they were typed when the FILER was running. When you
wish to change to another application or popdown, you must explicitly do
by using a "#" command, immediately followed by the name of the application; actually, you use the single letter code given in the Index page
so, for example, to direct commands at the Diary, you'd use "#D".

When you're using applications (such as PIPEDREAM) which permit multiple copies to be suspended, and you popdown the FILER from inside the copy that you wish to run the CLI file from, you would expect that you could use the "|[" command to generate an ESC key press to return you from the Filer to the current copy. Unfortunately, the Z88 software contains a bug which means that you must go via the INDEX page and then escape from there back to the application. The correct commands are "~ I|[".

You should note that it is not possible to ensure that a particular copy of an application is started where multiple copies are suspended. Even selecting the INDEX page and using the cursor control command ~ D wouldn't work as OZ re-orders the list of suspended activities so that the most frequently used activity is at the top of the list.

## Putting CLI on hold

To explain the meaning of "CLI suspension" let's begin with it's formal definition:

"A suspended CLI file leaves all the effects of the file intact. However, input characters are fetched from the keyboard, not the CLI file."

What are the effects of a CLI file other than reading input from a file rather than the keyboard? A CLI file can have set up some re-directions (if it includes the various Re-direction Control commands) and it always turns on the "CLI" flag just below the OZ symbol on the extreme right of the Z88 display.

The practical effects of a suspended CLI file are that:

|  | 1) The CLI flag will be showing. |
|  | 2) Any re-directions will still be in force. |
| AND | 3) The Z88 will accept keyboard input. |

## Built in CLI files

This situation should be familiar to you - do you remember what happened when you tried the "☐ + P" command?

Well, perhaps you didn't notice, but while you were marvelling at the wizard's ability to print the catalogue, the CLI flag was on... Yes, the "□ + K", "□ + P" and "□ + S" commands are just quick ways to access built-in CLI files which suspend themselves! For example, □ + P is the same as .T > :PRT.0 .S.

You've already heard of the magic spell called "SHIFT-ESC" - which exits a single CLI file. There's a more powerful one, ◊ESC, which exits all CLI files which are currently executing or suspended. You can use it to ensure that all the re-directions set up by any CLI files are removed.

## Summary

You can create CLI files as plain text files in PIPEDREAM.

Use the commands listed in this section to represent control keys.

Use CLI files to set up re-directions as, unlike □ + K and □ + S, the files which are created can be given individual names. It also permits multiple re-directions.

Re-directions set up by CLI files remain in effect if the file is "suspended" but input can then be accepted from the keyboard.

SHIFT-ESC terminates a single CLI file and ◊ESC terminates them all.

Be aware that the "context" of CLI files is initially the application which starts them and that you must change applications yourself. Use "~ I | [" to ESC back to the current application having popped-down the FILER in order to start the CLI file.

# Applying the Wizard's Power

In this section, we're going to give three examples of CLI files. They all perform useful functions, doing the sorts of things that most Z88 users will need occasionally. They've been chosen to illustrate different aspects of applying CLI files.

The examples are:

a) Reformatting an entire document within PIPEDREAM.
b) Ensuring that your diary is always showing today's appointments.
c) Automatic recovery of all the files in an EPROM.

## Reformatting a PIPEDREAM file

One facility which PIPEDREAM lacks is any means of applying one command to an entire file. In this example, we show a CLI file which can be used to apply sequences of PIPEDREAM commands:

```
.; this CLI file reformats an entire document
.; it should be called "rf.cli"
~I|[
|~L|R
.*rf.cli
```

Let's look at each line in turn:

~i|[            This is equivalent to typing □I (INDEX), ESC. This forces OZ to re-enter the copy of PIPEDREAM which was running when we started the CLI file.

|~l|r            This is equivalent to typing: ◇ left arrow, ◇R. This moves the cursor to the left of the line and then reformats the paragraph. After this command, the cursor will be at the beginning of the next paragraph.

You can put any sequence of PIPEDREAM commands here but they must cause the cursor to move through the text after the commands have finished.

.*rf.cli            This is the clever one!

                                Recall that the ".*" command causes the named file to be executed as a CLI file. There's no reason (apart from the limitations explained below) why this file shouldn't be the same file as we're currently executing.

Let's see what happens after this command has been executed. Well, the first line of the new CLI file is " ~ I | [" which enters the INDEX page and immediately returns to the current copy of PIPEDREAM.

The next line in the new CLI file is " | ~ L | R" which, as we already know, reformats the current paragraph and moves on the the next one.

So, we've now formatted two successive paragraphs.

We couldn't include a " | ~ U"( ◊ ⇑) command to go to the top of the file as we want to process one paragraph after another - the user must remember to move to the beginning of the file before running this CLI file.

The next line in the new CLI file is ".*rf.cli" which merely repeats the process, gradually formatting each paragraph in the document...

Starting the identical file again by putting it in a ".*" command as the last line of a CLI file (the technical term is "Tail Recursion") is the only way to create loops in CLI files.

It is a bit of a "kludge" and, as such, has some limitations.

There's no means of controlling when the loop will stop. In theory, it should continue forever but each time a CLI file is started, a record is kept of its name. The size of this list grows as more copies of the CLI file are executing until, eventually, the space available becomes exhausted and the looping stops.

On our Z88, we are able to process about three pages of text at a time by this method. That means to process longer documents, you have to start this CLI file first from the beginning of the file and then, when that one's finished, start it again from the FILER to cause the entire process to be repeated.

As the reformatting takes place, you can see its effects on the Z88 screen. When the end-of-text is reached, this CLI file doesn't immediately exit. This is because the process of reformatting is still being performed even though nothing is happening. This is one of the occasions for a little magic; use ◊ESC to escape from all the copies of the CLI file.

## Keeping your diary open at today's date

As we've mentioned, CLI files can be started as a result of an alarm. Let's see how we can use this to turn the pages of your Z88's diary so that the page for today's date is always showing.

Briefly, you set an alarm at one minute past midnight every day which clears the alarm and then selects the CT function in the diary.

The CLI commands to clear the alarm and select "Today" in the diary are:

#A~R~R~E|[#D|CT

Let's explain these commands:

| | |
|---|---|
| #A | This ensures that the ALARM popdown, (☐A)is selected for the commands that follow. |
| ~R~R~E | This clears the ALARM. Sequences like these are common in CLI files as they simulate selecting items from the Z88 menus. |
| \|[ | The ESC key exits from the ALARM popdown. |
| #D | Move to the DIARY application. |
| \|CT | Equivalent to presing ◊CT to tell the DIARY (☐D) to display today's appointments. |

To actually run this every day, you set an alarm at one minute past midnight (0:01:00) on tomorrow's date, put these CLI commands in the "Reason/Command" field and set the other fields to:

| Bell | Alarm Type | Repeat Every | No. of Times |
|---|---|---|---|
| Off | Execute | 1 day | Forever |

Notice how the CLI commands themselves, not the name of a CLI file, is used in the ALARM. If a number of commands are needed, it may be better to put a ".*file" command in the ALARM and then list the commands (together with comments which explain them) in a file.

## Automatic EPROM file recovery

As an example of a complex CLI file, we've included this one. Rather than go through each line, we'll explain the major steps and then highlight a number of interesting features.

This CLI file, which we've called "restore.cli", reads all the files contained in an EPROM and stores them on the Default Device. It does not cope with files in directories.

Part of this CLI file contains the keystrokes to write a BASIC program, it actually uses CLI commands like ˜ E. They will be translated when the CLI file is executed to load and run the BASIC program. This program then writes another CLI file which contains the names of all the files in EPROM. When this second CLI file is executed, it fetches each file from EPROM.

To do this, four steps are necessary:

STEP 1:                The names of the files in the EPROM must
                       be determined.

                       We've used the Filer "Catalogue EPROM"
                       command and re- directed the output to a file
                       called "eprom.tmp".

STEP 2:                A CLI file is built which copies the files from
                       EPROM.

                       We've written a short BASIC program which
                       reads the "eprom.tmp" file and creates a file
                       called "restore.tmp".

                       Each line of the file being written is a Filer
                       "Fetch from EPROM" command for one of
                       the files listed in the Catalogue.

Each line of the file being read contains the name of a file in the EPROM.

STEP 3: The CLI file containing the fetch commands is executed.
The files are recovered from the EPROM one at a time and stored in the default device.

STEP 4: The temporary files should be deleted.

This "hybrid" approach - using both CLI files and BASIC programs - works well on the Z88. You'll normally find that they have features which complement one another.

The source code of "restore.cli" was created as a PIPEDREAM plain text file and is shown below:

```
.; This CLI file restores all the files from
.; an EPROM.  It uses two temporary files
.; which are deleted at the end of the run.

.; STEP 1: get the EPROM catalogue
#F
.T>eprom.tmp
|CE
.T>:nul.0

.; STEP 2: run basic program to create CLI file
#B
NEW~E
10 REM Basic Program to analyse the catalogue
of~E
20 REM the EPROM and build the CLI file to
recover~E
30 REM the data~E
40 Catalogue = OPENIN "eprom.tmp"~E
50 CLIfile = OPENOUT "restore.tmp"~E
60 REPEAT~E
70 INPUT ##Catalogue,EpromName$~E
80 LineFeed=BGET ##Catalogue~E
90 IF EpromName$="*END*" THEN GOTO 130~E
```

```
100 FileName$=RIGHT$(EpromName$,LEN(EpromName$)
-1)~E
110 CLIline$="||EF"+FileName$+"~~E~~E"~E
120 PRINT ##CLIfile,CLIline$~E
130 UNTIL EOF##(Catalogue) = -1~E
140 CLOSE ##Catalogue~E
150 CLOSE ##CLIfile~E
RUN~E
```

```
.; STEP 3: Run the CLI file just created to
recover
 .; the files from EPROM
#F
.*restore.tmp
```

```
.; STEP 4: Delete the temporary files
|EReprom.tmp~E~E
|ERestore.tmp~E~E
```

Don't worry if you cannot understand the CLI keystrokes that make up the BASIC program. We've included the source of the program in the file rather than store it as a separate file so as to show you what's possible with CLI files.

Notice that we re-direct the output to ":NUL.0" to close the file after we've stored the EPROM catalogue.

Since BASIC needs line breaks, we've had to use " ~ E"'s at the end of each line of the program and after the "NEW" and "RUN" commands.

The program itself reads each line and then reads the Linefeed character which will follow each line. It then checks for the terminating string "*END*".

If not found, the file name (that is, all the characters after the "/") is extracted and a line representing a FILER "fetch from EPROM" command is formed and added to the "restore.tmp" file.

When all lines have been processed, the input and output files are closed.

## Summary

Tail Recursion, that is, calling the same file at the end of a CLI file, can be used to provide a limited looping capability.

Often, you will find that you must simulate selection of items from menus by using the CLI codes for the cursor commands.

Always ensure that commands in CLI files are directed to the correct application or popdown by preceding each group of commands by the appropriate "#" code.

When writing more complex CLI files, remember that the files can be generated by BASIC programs.

This page intentionally left blank

# Z88 Tutorial

## Wordprocessing  Exercise 1

### Witches

Witches are very nice,
So don't feed them mice,
If you do, they might sue,
Before you can roll the dice

By Chris aged 9

Switches'[£]£ = -'£[/0-- =
Switches are very nine,
Sp dpn't feed xyym dine,
If ypu dp, xyyy might sue,
Befpre ypu can rpll xyy mine

By Chris aged 9

These two poems started life as two copies which were as like as two peas
in a pod! We have had some fun mucking the second one up for you!
Copy the second version into your Z88 and see if you can get it back into
it's pod!

To do this you will have to use:

◊G and then insert other characters
◊LAC
◊ESL
◊N
◊EJL
◊Y
◊D
◊BRP with or without ⌃? and/or ⌃#

and a bit of ingenuity Although not necessarily in that order!! Remember you can always refer back to the PIPEDREAM section if you need
to.

HAVE FUN!

# Wordprocessing Exercise 2

## WORKING WITH BLOCKS AND COLUMNS

Type these blocks into your Z88 after splitting your file into 3 columns each 24 characters wide. Don't forget BLOCK COPY, it will help you a great deal here. To put the blocks in order you will then need to move them around. BLOCK MARK. CLEAR and MOVE will be essential. Also the column editing commands will help you line everything up at the end. This exercise may look easy but you should learn something about the way PIPEDREAM moves things around.

```
.................................A.................................B.............................................
         24                          24                          24
aaaaaaaaaaaaaaaaaaaaaaaa bbbbbbbbbbbbbbbbbbbbbbbb cccccccccccccccccccccccc
aaaaaaaaaaaaaaaaaaaaaaaa bbbbbbbbbbbbbbbbbbbbbbbb cccccccccccccccccccccccc
aaaaaaaaaaaaaaaaaaaaaaaa bbbbbbbbbbbbbbbbbbbbbbbb cccccccccccccccccccccccc
          3                           2                           3
aaaaaaaaaaaaaaaaaaaaaaaa bbbbbbbbbbbbbbbbbbbbbbbb cccccccccccccccccccccccc
aaaaaaaaaaaaaaaaaaaaaaaa bbbbbbbbbbbbbbbbbbbbbbbb cccccccccccccccccccccccc
aaaaaaaaaaaaaaaaaaaaaaaa bbbbbbbbbbbbbbbbbbbbbbbb cccccccccccccccccccccccc

bbbbbbbbbbbbbbbbbbbbbbbb cccccccccccccccccccccccc aaaaaaaaaaaaaaaaaaaaaaaa
bbbbbbbbbbbbbbbbbbbbbbbb cccccccccccccccccccccccc aaaaaaaaaaaaaaaaaaaaaaaa
bbbbbbbbbbbbbbbbbbbbbbbb cccccccccccccccccccccccc aaaaaaaaaaaaaaaaaaaaaaaa
          3                           1                           1
bbbbbbbbbbbbbbbbbbbbbbbb cccccccccccccccccccccccc aaaaaaaaaaaaaaaaaaaaaaaa
bbbbbbbbbbbbbbbbbbbbbbbb cccccccccccccccccccccccc aaaaaaaaaaaaaaaaaaaaaaaa
bbbbbbbbbbbbbbbbbbbbbbbb cccccccccccccccccccccccc aaaaaaaaaaaaaaaaaaaaaaaa

cccccccccccccccccccccccc aaaaaaaaaaaaaaaaaaaaaaaa bbbbbbbbbbbbbbbbbbbbbbbb
cccccccccccccccccccccccc aaaaaaaaaaaaaaaaaaaaaaaa bbbbbbbbbbbbbbbbbbbbbbbb
cccccccccccccccccccccccc aaaaaaaaaaaaaaaaaaaaaaaa bbbbbbbbbbbbbbbbbbbbbbbb
          2                           2                           1
cccccccccccccccccccccccc aaaaaaaaaaaaaaaaaaaaaaaa bbbbbbbbbbbbbbbbbbbbbbbb
cccccccccccccccccccccccc aaaaaaaaaaaaaaaaaaaaaaaa bbbbbbbbbbbbbbbbbbbbbbbb
cccccccccccccccccccccccc aaaaaaaaaaaaaaaaaaaaaaaa bbbbbbbbbbbbbbbbbbbbbbbb
```

# PUTTING DATABASE THEORY INTO PRACTICE

**B**elow is some "raw data" that needs to be organised before it can be useful. For MAGICADATE - our dating agency - to be successful the information needs to be easy and quick to access. You are the new database expert! It is your job to design a database, process the information and see whether there are any likely couples in our first mailbag. Below the raw data are two sample layouts to give you some ideas. If you want to create more raw data yourself you can add as many entries as you like once your database is set up. DON'T FORGET TO TURN WRAP OFF

MAGICADATE Questionnaire - STRICTLY CONFIDENTIAL First Name Winnie       Surname Warbler    Age 89  status WITCH Address 5 Lovage lane, Lew Wood, LANCS. Personal Attributes 1 GOOD TOOTH.
2 HEALER                3 LOVES ANIMALS Details of person you would like to meet;- Age96-9 status WARLOCK personal attributes 1 ANIMAL LOVER
2 FLYING TEACHER - I NEVER LEARNT    3 GOOD CONVERSATIONALIST

MAGICADATE Questionnaire - STRICTLY CONFIDENTIAL First NameZDARF          Surname ZONTE      Age76  statusWLOCK Address FLYING BROOM,WEST WIND c/o BROMSGROVE POST OFFICE personal Attributes 1 ENJOY MAKING LIGHTENING STRIKE TWICE
2 TURNING HORSESHOES THE WRONG WAY UP 3 GOOD MISCHIEF MAKER Details of person you would like to meet;- Age-50 status WITCH personal attributes 1 GOOD SENSE OF HUMOUR
2 NOT TOO GOODY GOODY         3 LIKES A GOOD TIME

MAGICADATE Questionnaire - STRICTLY CONFIDENTIAL First Name WANDA        Surname WANDA      Age45  statusWITCH Address 7 WITCHERY LANE, WINCHESTER personal Attributes 1 LIKE A GOOD TIME
2 GOOD DANCER             3 MAKE BEST HEMLOCK WINE EVER Details of person you would like to meet;-  Age80 + status WIZARD personal attributes 1 DANCER
2 LIKES HEMLOCK WINE        3 CAN TEACH SPELLS

MAGICADATE  Questionnaire - STRICTLY  CONFIDENTIAL
SOMETHING LIKE First Name HILARITY          Surname HICKS
Age90 / status WITCH Address 77 HILL ROAD, HENLY personal Attributes 1 GOOD WARDROBE AND CLOTHES SENSE
2 LIKE MAKING MISCHIEF            3 GOOD LAUGH Details of
person you would like to meet;- Age70 + status WIZARD personal attributes 1 TALL DARK AND HANDSOME
2  GOOD SPELLCASTER            3 HUMOROUS

MAGICADATE  Questionnaire - STRICTLY CONFIDENTIAL First
Name I.M.          Surname DEAD      Age169 status WLOCK Address
THE END OF THE ROAD, GRAVESEND. personal Attributes 1 I
NEVER GET IN THE WAY (NEVER THERE!)
2 LIKE SCARING PEOPLE            3 SABOTAGING OTHER
SPELLS Details of person you would like to meet;-  Age 150 +
statusWITCH  personal attributes 1 GOOD COOK
2 LIKES HELPING TO SABOTAGE SPELLS      3 TIME
TRAVELLER

MAGICADATE  Questionnaire - STRICTLY CONFIDENTIAL First
Name MERLIN          Surname    ?      Age OLD! status WIZARD
Address THE CAVES,UNDER CASTLE,TINTAGEL personal Attributes 1 FLY'S (AEROPLANES!)
2 ROCK KILLER            3 VERY GOOD MAGICIAN Details
of person you would like to meet;- Age OLDISH status WITCH personal
attributes 1 KIND
2 GOOD WITH LITTLE BOYS        3 GOOD HOMEMAKER

Possible Database Layout

Note, The numbers underneath the Column Names are the Column
Widths. It is a good idea to make a note of these because it is easier to
change like that. Otherwise you'll get dizzy trying to count the number of
spaces in each column if you need to change the widths!

## Sample 1

| A | B | C | D | E | F |
|---|---|---|---|---|---|
| REF NO | NAME | ROAD | TOWN | COUNTY | AGE | STATUS |
| 3 | 20 | 20 | 12 | 5 | 4 | 8 |
| 1 | WINNIE WARBLER | 5, LOVAGE LANE | LEW WOOD | LANCS | 89 | WTCH |

| G | H | I | J | K |
|---|---|---|---|---|
| Personal Attribs(PA)1 | PA2 | PA3 | AGE TO MEET | STATUS TO MEET |
| 20 | 20 | 20 | 7 | 8 |
| GOOD TEETH | HEALER | ANIMAL LOVER | 96-9 | WLCK |

| L | M | N | O |
|---|---|---|---|
| Desirable PA1 to meet | Desirable PA2 to meet | Desirable PA3 to meet | |
| 20 | 20 | 20 | |
| ANIMAL LOVER | FLYING INSTRUCTOR | CONVERSATIONALIST | |

## Sample 2

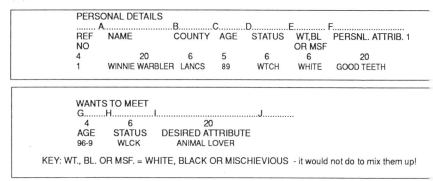

### (A) MATCHING FILE

PERSONAL DETAILS

| A | B | C | D | E | F |
|---|---|---|---|---|---|
| REF NO | NAME | COUNTY | AGE | STATUS | WT,BL OR MSF | PERSNL. ATTRIB. 1 |
| 4 | 20 | 6 | 5 | 6 | 6 | 20 |
| 1 | WINNIE WARBLER | LANCS | 89 | WTCH | WHITE | GOOD TEETH |

WANTS TO MEET

| G | H | I | J |
|---|---|---|---|
| 4 | 6 | 20 | |
| AGE | STATUS | DESIRED ATTRIBUTE | |
| 96-9 | WLCK | ANIMAL LOVER | |

KEY: WT., BL. OR MSF. = WHITE, BLACK OR MISCHIEVIOUS - it would not do to mix them up!

### (B) NAME AND ADDRESS FILE

| A | B | C | D | E | F |
|---|---|---|---|---|---|
| REF NO | NAME | ROAD | VILLAGE | TOWN | COUNTY | PST C |
| 4 | 20 | 20 | 12 | 12 | 6 | 9 |
| 1 | WINNIE WARBLER | 5, LOVAGE LANE | LEW WOOD | | LANCS | |

NB. Splitting the info. into smaller databases in different files saves time and memory when you do not need to see everything at the same time. PIPEDREAM cannot cross reference between databases but you can!

Neither sample is perfect! See if you can do better. Then you can use the SORT command on various columns to see the effect. To find compatible couples you could try the CONDITIONAL SAVE or PRINT commands. Remember to tell PIPEDREAM that the reference numbers are numbers if you want to sort the file back into numerical order at any time

# Exercise 1a

This exercise is a straightforward "invoice type" form.

The commands used are:-

* (Multiply)
Replicate
SUM
Leading Characters

| | A | B | C | D | E | |
|---|---|---|---|---|---|---|
| Product | Qty | | Description | | Investment Value | |
| | | | | | Each | Total |
| Candlestick | | 230.00 | Beeswax Candlesticks | | 0.43 | £   98.90 |
| Broomsticks | | 600.00 | Broomsticks | | 1.00 | £ 600.00 |
| Hats | | 367.00 | Conical Hats | | 4.00 | £1468.00 |
| Toads | | 5.00 | Toads | | 2.47 | £   12.35 |
| Mushrm | | 42.00 | Mushrooms | | 0.46 | £   19.32 |
| CatFood | | 34.00 | Tins of Cat Food | | 1.24 | £   42.16 |
| CatWhisk | | 4.00 | The Cat's Whiskers | | 26.00 | £ 104.00 |
| | | | TOTAL | | | £2344.73 |

Answers Row 7 (Candlestick)

Column A  Candlestick
Column B  230
Column C  Beeswax Candlesticks
Column D  (Not Used)
Column E  .43
Column F  B7★E7
Cell F15    sum (F7F13)

Replicate F7 to F7F13
Leading Characters F7-F15

,

# Exercise 1b

This is an extension of the previous example with an additional Discount Table. This table is used to see how much discount to give depending on the total. This is achieved by comparing the total with the figures given in the discount table, if it is valid the percentage discount is carried across to another column. Finally MAX is used to pick out the maximum discount that is valid for this transaction. The commands used are:-

Trailing Characters
MAX
* Multiply
/ Divide
- Subtract
IF
$ To fix the cell numbers and letters
= relationals
Replicate

| Product | Qty | Description | Investment Value Each | Total |
|---|---|---|---|---|
| Candlestick | 230.00 | Beeswax Candlesticks | 0.43 | £ 98.90 |
| Broomsticks | 600.00 | Broomsticks | 1.00 | £ 600.00 |
| Hats | 367.00 | Conical Hats | 4.00 | £1468.00 |
| Toads | 5.00 | Toads | 2.47 | £ 12.35 |
| Mushrm | 42.00 | Mushrooms | 0.46 | £ 19.32 |
| CatFood | 34.00 | Tins of Cat Food | 1.24 | £ 42.16 |
| CatWhisk | 4.00 | The Cat's Whiskers | 26.00 | £ 104.00 |
| | | TOTAL | | £2344.73 |
| | | Discount | 7.50% | £ 175.85 |
| | | Sub TOTAL | | £2168.88 |

Discount table

| Amount | Discount | |
|---|---|---|
| 0.00 | 0.00% | 0.00 |
| £ 100.00 | 2.00% | 2.00 |
| £ 400.00 | 5.00% | 5.00 |
| £1000.00 | 7.50% | 7.50 |
| £2500.00 | 10.00% | 0.00 |

Answers

Cell E17 Trailing Characters (%)
Cell E17 max (C23C27)
Cell F17 F15*E17/100
Cell F18 F15-F17
Cell C23 if ($F$15>=A23,B23,0)
Replicate C23 to C23C27

# Exercise 1c

This is the final extension of the last two previous examples showing the VAT calculations.

The commands used are:-

Trailing Characters (%)
INT
* Multiply
+ Add
/ Divide

```
                        A...................B...................C...................D...................E...................↓F
          Product       Qty          Description              Investment Value
                                                              Each            Total
          Candlestick   230.00  Beeswax Candlesticks          0.43      £    98.90
          Broomsticks   600.00  Broomsticks                   1.00      £  600.00
          Hats          367.00  Conical Hats                  4.00      £1468.00
          Toads           5.00  Toads                         2.47      £   12.35
          Mushrm         42.00  Mushrooms                     0.46      £   19.32
          CatFood        34.00  Tins of Cat Food              1.24      £   42.16
          CatWhisk        4.00  The Cat's Whiskers           26.00      £  104.00
                                ─────────────────────────────────────────────────
                                  TOTAL                                 £2344.73

                                  Discount            7.50%      £  175.85
                                  Sub TOTAL                      £2168.88

          Discount table

          Amount          Discount
              0.00         0.00%      0.00
          £  100.00        2.00%      2.00
          £  400.00        5.00%      5.00
          £1000.00         7.50%      7.50
          £2500.00        10.00%      0.00

                                  VAT @              15.00%      £  325.33

                                  MAIN TOTAL                     £2494.21
          Answers

          E30   15 Trailing Characters (%)
          F30   INT((F18★E30)+0.5)/100
          F32   F18+F30
```

# Bank Example

## Bank Statement

This exercise uses a 'hidden' column to calculate the actual balance. The hidden column (E) is then used to give the appropriate information to the Balance (column F using ABS) and the O/D (column G using the IF and SGN to show "O/D" if the balance is negative).

You need to know about the following:-

Dates
+
-
if
Changing the widths of Columns (including Column E to 0)
ABS
SGN

| | A | B | C | D | E | F | VG |
|---|---|---|---|---|---|---|---|
| Date | Details | Withdrawals | Deposits | Balance (£) | | O/D | |
| 30.6.89 | Balance from Sheet | | | | 500.00 | | |
| 1.7.89 | Cheque 1 | 600.00 | | | 100.00 | O/D | |
| 2.7.89 | Winnings | | 800.00 | | 700.00 | | |
| 3.7.89 | Mortgage | 1000.00 | | | 300.00 | O/D | |
| 4.7.89 | Gas | 131.00 | | | 431.00 | O/D | |
| | | | | | 431.00 | O/D | |
| | | | | | 431.00 | O/D | |

Answers for line 4

Cell E    E3 - C4 + D4
Cell F    abs (E4)
Cell G    if (sgn (E4) = -1,"O/D","")

# TECHNICAL APPENDIX

## Z88 Cable Pin-outs

| Z88 Computer | | | to PC Computer | | or Printer | |
|---|---|---|---|---|---|---|
| 9 way plug | Name | Direction | 2 5 way plug | Name | 2 5 way SKT | Name |

1. DO NOT USE for RS232 signals carries +5v at 10uA even when the Z88 is turned OFF!

| | | | | | | |
|---|---|---|---|---|---|---|
| 2. | TxD | --> | 3 | RxD | 3 | RxD |
| 3. | RxD | <-- | 2 | TxD | 2 | TxD |
| 4. | RTS | --> | 5 | CTS | 5 | CTS |
| 5. | CTS | <-- | *4 | RTS | 20 | DTR |
| 6. | DO NOT USE PIN 6 ON THE Z88 CONNECTOR | | | | | |
| 7. | GND | | 7 | GND | 7 | GND |
| 8. | DCD | <-- | *20 | DTR | 20 | DTR |
| 9. | DTR | --> | *8 | DCD | "6,8" | (DSR,DCD) |

Pin 9 is the DTR signal. It provides +5v at 1mA while the Z88 is switched on for powering the circuitry in the Parallel Printer Cable.

CTS must be HIGH on the Z88 for the Z88 to transmit.
DCD must be HIGH for the Z88 to receive.

For simple operation just link the "*" connections together and use the three wire connection to the other computer. Be sure to use Xon/Xoff in this mode!

# Batteries

## Inserting new batteries

The Z88 was four alkaline AA MN1500 or LR6 batteries. They fit into the battery compartment on the bottom of the Z88 adjacent to where the stand folds away.

When the battery low indicator appears in the bottom right hand corner of the screen, and you are running on batteries, this is your first warning that you are low on power. You can continue using it for a while because the power level does not become critical until the display goes out. You must then insert new batteries before you can use the Z88 again. Even if you are not going to use it the batteries must be changed if you want the information that is being held in memory to be retained. The Z88 still needs power to keep its memory alive and the clock ticking over even when it is turned off.

If the battery low symbol appears when you are running on mains adapter there must be something wrong with the connections. Turn the Z88 off, check that all the plugs are in correctly and then turn it on again. If the battery low symbol doesn't return fairly quickly you have solved the problem. You must make a mental note to put in some new batteries. Your Z88 has been running off its batteries and drained them while the mains had not been getting through. If the battery low symbol comes back repeatedly you may have a problem with your mains adapter.

When changing your batteries you must be aware of the time constraints placed on you. Your Z88's memory has a very short life without batteries. If you do not have a mains adapter. You have:- three minutes (with no external RAM), one minute (with one RAM pack) and thirty seconds (if you have 2 RAMs fitted), to effect the change. EPROMs do not take any power unless they are being accessed so they don't make any difference but if you have fitted a third RAM in Slot 3 the power consumption is considerably higher. For this reason the manufacturers do not recommend that you use slot 3 for RAM.

To change your batteries. Turn the Z88 off, turn it over and take the battery compartment's cover off. Get the new batteries ready and polish the ends. Take the old ones out - you may have to tilt the Z88 sideways to slide the end ones out - and throw them away, or at least put them some-where where you are not going to confuse them with the new ones. Put two new batteries at either end of the compartment making sure they are the right way round - the diagram at the bottom of the compartment will show you the "right" way. Then put the remaining two in so that they wedge themselves in to form a pointed arch which is sticking up towards you. Again make sure they will be the right way round when they are pushed down into place. You do that by placing pressure on the point of the arch until the batteries click into place. Make one final check to see that they are all the right way round and then you can relax. That pitstop has been successfully completed! Now all you have to do is put the battery compartment's cover back on, turn the Z88 over, and turn it on by pressing both SHIFT keys together.

# Rechargeable batteries

## HEALTH WARNING

Rechargeable batteries fitted internally into the Z88 can damage its health - and yours.

Although we are aware that rechargeable batteries are sometimes supplied with the Z88. we strongly recommend that you do not use them in place of ordinary batteries..

We say that for two reasons.

1 Rechargeable batteries have a lower voltage than disposable batteries, Four rechargeable the same size as the ones you should use in your Z88, will only supply 4.8 volts as opposed to 6 volts from the disposable ones. Your Z88 needs to run on 6 volts.

2 The discharge rate on rechargeables is much steeper than on disposables. That means that the gap between the time when your battery low symbol appears and the point where the Z88 can no

longer keep its memory alive is much shorter - sometimes almost instantaneous.

# Using rechargeable batteries externally

There is nothing to stop you using rechargeable batteries externally, i.e. in a pack, outside the computer which plugs in through the power socket. That way when they have run down your Z88 can still switch over to its internal batteries. The 7.2v battery pack for model racing cars is ideal. You need one which tells you when it is low before the Z88 switches over to, and drains, the internal batteries.

# Accessories

## Installing RAM ROM and EPROMs

When putting in or taking out any cards to or from the CARD SLOTS you must:-

Leave the Z88 switched on

Put the Z88 into the INDEX

## Inserting

Push the card in straight - if you don't you might short the pins which will result in a soft reset.

IF installing an EPROM - Initialise by selecting the FILER with ☐ F and then catalogue it with ◇CE

Check to see that the Z88 knows about the new card - after closing the flap - by selecting ◇CARD. If not, reopen the flap and make sure the card is in as far as it will go then close the flap and try again.

Removing ROM - Make sure the program is not running as part of a suspended activity. If it is, ◇KILL that activity before removing the card.

Removing RAM - You have to do a SOFT RESET

ALWAYS CLOSE THE FLAP WHEN YOU HAVE FINISHED IN-STALLING OR REMOVING A CARD.

# RESETS

## SOFT RESET

If you have taken out a RAM or if the Z88 is not responding to the keyboard you will have to do a soft reset. Press the reset button twice on the side of your Z88 with a blunt instrument, BUT LEAVE THE FLAP SHUT. This will have a similar effect to ◇PURGE. It will KILL all your suspended activities but leave your files intact

If your Z88 still refuses to answer to the keyboard you will have to do a HARD RESET

## HARD RESET

The HARD RESET is the same as an INITIAL RESET. To do that OPEN THE SLOT COMPARTMENT and press the reset button twice with a blunt instrument.

This will KILL all your suspended activities, erase all your files in RAM and put the CLOCK back to the day it was born. All the other setting will have returned to their original values

You will then - apart from crawling into a corner with a bottle of Whis-key asking yourself why you had never done any back ups! - have to set up the CLOCK and the PANEL again. You can then load back onto the system any backed up Files you have saved.

# ASCII

The "keyboard" column shows which key, or combination of keys, you must press to cause your Z88 to process that code. The "screen" column shows the effect of the code on the Z88 screen. The "ASCII" column shows the standard description of the code in ASCII.

| Dec | Hex | Symbol | Keyboard | Screen | ASCII |
|-----|-----|--------|----------|--------|-------|
| 0 | &00 | NUL | ◇= | Ignored | Null |
| 1 | &01 | SOH | ◇A | Escape character for special functions | Start of Header |
| 2 | &02 | STX | ◇B | | Start of Text |
| 3 | &03 | ETX | ◇C | | End of Text |
| 4 | &04 | EOT | ◇D | | End of Transmission |
| 5 | &05 | ENQ | ◇E | Escape character for printer filter and screen driver | Enquiry |
| 6 | &06 | ACK | ◇F | | Acknowledge |
| 7 | &07 | BEL | ◇G | Make a beep | BEL Bell |
| 8 | &08 | BS | ◇H | Left BS | Backspace |
| 9 | &09 | HT | ◇I | Right HT | Horizontal tab |
| 10 | &OA | LF | ◇J | Down LF | Line feed |
| 11 | &OB | VT | ◇K | Up VT | Vertical tab |
| 12 | &OC | FF | ◇L | Clear screen | Form feed |
| 13 | &OD | CR | ◇M | CR | Carriage return |
| 14 | &OE | SO | ◇N | | Shift out |
| 15 | &OF | SI | ◇O | | Shift in |

| Dec | Hex | Symbol | Keyboard | Screen | ASCII |
|---|---|---|---|---|---|
| 16 | &10 | DLE | ◇P | | Data link es-cape |
| 17 | &11 | DC1 | ◇Q | | Device control 1 (XON) |
| 18 | &12 | DC2 | ◇R | | Device control 2 |
| 19 | &13 | DC3 | ◇S | | Device control 3 (XOFF) |
| 20 | &14 | DC4 | ◇T | | Device control 4 |
| 21 | &15 | NAK | ◇U | | Negative ac-knowledge |
| 22 | &16 | SYN | ◇V | | Synchronous idle |
| 23 | &17 | ETB | ◇W | | End of trans-mitted block |
| 24 | &18 | CAN | ◇X | | Cancel line |
| 25 | &19 | EM | ◇Y | | End of medium |
| 26 | &1A | SUB | ◇Z | | Substitute |
| 27 | &1B | ESC | ◇[ | | Escape |
| 28 | &1C | FS | ◇] | | Group separator |
| 30 | &1E | RS | ◇£ | | Record separator |
| 31 | &1F | US | ◇- | | Unit separator |
| 32 | &20 | | | | Space |
| 33 | &21 | | ! | | Exclamation mark |
| 34 | &22 | | " | | Double quote |
| 35 | &23 | | # | | Currency sign |
| 36 | &24 | | $ | | Dollar sign |
| 37 | &25 | | % | | Percent |
| 38 | &26 | | & | | Ampersand |
| 39 | &27 | | ' | | Apostrophe |
| 40 | &28 | | ( | | Open paren-thesis |
| 41 | &28 | | ) | | Close paren-thesis |
| 42 | &2A | | * | | Asterisk |
| 43 | &2B | | + | | Plus |

| Dec | Hex | Symbol | Keyboard | Screen | ASCII |
|---|---|---|---|---|---|
| 44 | &2C | , | | | Comma |
| 45 | &2D | - | | | Minus |
| 46 | &2E | . | | | Full stop |
| 47 | &2F | / | | | Slash |
| 48 | &30 | 0 | | | Zero |
| 49 | &31 | 1 | | | One |
| 50 | &32 | 2 | | | Two |
| 51 | &33 | 3 | | | Three |
| 52 | &34 | 4 | | | Four |
| 53 | &35 | 5 | | | Five |
| 54 | &36 | 6 | | | Six |
| 55 | &37 | 7 | | | Seven |
| 56 | &38 | 8 | | | Eight |
| 57 | &39 | 9 | | | Nine |
| 58 | &3A | : | | | Colon |
| 59 | &3B | ; | | | Semicolon |
| 60 | &3C | < | | | Less than sign |
| 61 | &3D | = | | | Equals sign |
| 62 | &3E | | | | Greater than sign |
| 63 | &3F | ? | | | Question mark |
| 64 | &40 | @ | | | At |
| 65 | &41 | A | | | Upper case A |
| 66 | &42 | B | | | Upper case B |
| 67 | &43 | C | | | Upper case C |
| 68 | &44 | D | | | Upper case D |
| 69 | &45 | E | | | Upper case E |
| 70 | &46 | F | | | Upper case F |
| 71 | &47 | G | | | Upper case G |
| 72 | &48 | H | | | Upper case H |
| 73 | &49 | I | | | Upper case I |
| 74 | &4A | J | | | Upper case J |
| 75 | &4B | K | | | Upper case K |
| 76 | &4C | L | | | Upper case L |
| 77 | &4D | M | | | Upper case M |
| 78 | &4E | N | | | Upper case N |
| 79 | &4F | O | | | Upper case O |
| 80 | &50 | P | | | Upper case P |
| 81 | &51 | Q | | | Upper case Q |
| 82 | &52 | R | | | Upper case R |

| Dec | Hex | Symbol | Keyboard | Screen | ASCII |
|---|---|---|---|---|---|
| 83 | &53 | | S | | Upper case S |
| 84 | &54 | | T | | Upper case T |
| 85 | &55 | | U | | Upper case U |
| 86 | &56 | | V | | Upper case V |
| 87 | &57 | | W | | Upper case W |
| 88 | &58 | | X | | Upper case X |
| 89 | &59 | | Y | | Upper case Y |
| 90 | &5A | | Z | | Upper case Z |
| 91 | &5B | | [ | | Open square bracket |
| 92 | &5C | | / | | Backslash |
| 93 | &5D | | ] | | Close square bracket |
| 94 | &5E | | ^ | | Caret |
| 95 | &5F | | _ | | Underline |
| 96 | &60 | | | | |
| 97 | &61 | | a | | Lower case A |
| 98 | &62 | | b | | Lower case B |
| 99 | &63 | | c | | Lower case C |
| 100 | &64 | | d | | Lower case D |
| 101 | &65 | | e | | Lower case E |
| 102 | &66 | | f | | Lower case F |
| 103 | &67 | | g | | Lower case G |
| 104 | &68 | | h | | Lower case H |
| 105 | &69 | | i | | Lower case I |
| 106 | &6A | | j | | Lower case J |
| 107 | &6B | | k | | Lower case K |
| 108 | &6C | | l | | Lower case L |
| 109 | &6D | | m | | Lower case M |
| 110 | &6E | | n | | Lower case N |
| 111 | &6F | | o | | Lower case O |
| 112 | &70 | | p | | Lower case P |
| 113 | &71 | | q | | Lower case Q |
| 114 | &72 | | r | | Lower case R |
| 115 | &73 | | s | | Lower case S |
| 116 | &74 | | t | | Lower case T |
| 117 | &75 | | u | | Lower case U |
| 118 | &76 | | v | | Lower case V |
| 119 | &77 | | w | | Lower case W |
| 120 | &78 | | x | | Lower case X |

| Dec | Hex | Symbol | Keyboard | Screen | ASCII |
|-----|-----|--------|----------|--------|-------|
| 121 | &79 | | y | | Lower case Y |
| 122 | &7A | | z | | Lower case Z |
| 123 | &7B | | { | | Open curly bracket |
| 124 | &7C | | \| | | Vertical bar |
| 125 | &7D | | } | | Close curly bracket |
| 126 | &7E | | ~ | | Tilde |
| 127 | &7F | | DEL | Draw black box | |
| 163 | &A3 | | £ | | Pound sign |

# INDEX